THE
EVOLUTION
OF
DEMOCRACY

THE EVOLUTION OF DEMOCRACY

THE EMERGENCE OF SYNERGISTIC DEMOCRACY

TOWARDS A PLANETARY AWAKENING OF UNIQUE SELF SYMPHONIES OF EROSVALUE

. . .

From Conscious Evolution 1.0 to Conscious Evolution 2.0

One Mountain, Many Paths: Oral Essays
Volume Thirty-Five

DR. MARC GAFNI AND
BARBARA MARX HUBBARD

Author: Marc Gafni and Barbara Marx Hubbard
Title: The Evolution of Democracy
From Conscious Evolution 1.0 to Conscious Evolution 2.0

Identifiers: ISBN 979-99934-088-2 (electronic)
ISBN 979-99934-087-5 (paperback)

Edited by Elena Maslova-Levin, Talya Bloom, and Rachel Keune

World Philosophy and Religion Press, St. Johnsbury, VT
in conjunction with

IP Integral Publishers

https://worldphilosophyandreligion.org

JOIN THE REVOLUTION!

CONTENTS

CHAPTER 3   **RESTORING PUBLIC CULTURE AND
THE INTEGRITY OF DIGITAL INTIMACY**

CHAPTER 4   **EVOLUTION OF PUBLIC CULTURE
AND DIGITAL INTEGRITY**

EDITORIAL NOTE ABOUT AUTHORSHIP, EDITING, AND THE RADICAL CONTEXT FOR THIS SERIES

ORAL ESSAYS FROM THE ONE MOUNTAIN, MANY PATHS WEEKLY BROADCAST

This volume is part of the Oral Essays library, a series of lightly edited, compiled transcripts of oral teachings given by Dr. Marc Gafni and the late Barbara Marx Hubbard in their weekly online broadcast, *One Mountain, Many Paths,* which they co-founded in 2017. Originally called an "Evolutionary Church," *One Mountain, Many Paths* became a key venue for the articulation of an inspired and deeply grounded new Story of Value in response to the meta-crisis. Marc and Barbara—together with Zak Stein,[1] Kristina Kincaid, Ken Wilber, Sally Kempton, Lori Galperin, Aubrey Marcus and dozens of other thought-leaders over the years—began to articulate what they call a World Philosophy and World Religion[2] as a context for our diversity.

---

1   Zak, together with Ken Wilber, has been Marc's primary intellectual partner and an initiate lineage holder in CosmoErotic Humanism.

2   This project is grounded in four core organizational frameworks: 1) The Center for World Philosophy and Religion, co-founded by Marc Gafni, Zachary Stein, Sally Kempton, and Ken Wilber, and chaired over the years by John P. Mackey, Barbara Marx Hubbard, Aubrey Marcus, Gabrielle Anwar and Shareef Malnik, Carrie Kish and Adam Bellow, and Kathleen J. Brownback. 2) The Office for the Future, chaired by Stephanie Valcke and Ivan Bossyut. 3) The World Philosophy and Religion Press, founded and chaired by Aubrey Marcus, together with Marc Gafni and Zachary Stein. 4) The Foundation for Conscious Evolution, founded by Barbara Marx Hubbard and currently chaired by Peter Fiekowsky. For a complete list of key leadership, see the Office for the Future website, www.officeforthefuture.com.

Until Barbara's passing in 2019, she and Marc transmitted teachings together as evolutionary partners and "whole mates," weaving together insights and transmissions from their decades of practice, study, teaching, and activism into a synergy of wisdom, a grounded vision for future policy across all sectors of society.

Much of the *dharma* material below comes directly from Marc, so it was originally all in quotation marks—but that looked a little odd. So per his suggestion we removed them, and the reader should consider the paragraphs on the next several pages as one extended quote from him. We are joyfully grateful to Marc for the clarity of his *dharma*, the elegance and "second simplicity" of this language, and the mad, Outrageous Love with which he transmits his teachings.

Barbara and Marc called the mission of *One Mountain* "a Planetary Awakening in Evolutionary Love Through Unique Self Symphonies." We are an evolutionary community with a deeply grounded, radically alive, and "post-tragic" revolutionary spirit. We are activating a new humanity and awakening as a new species: *Homo amor*, the fulfillment of *Homo sapiens*.

One Mountain is committed to articulating a Story of Value that can become the ground for the new society that must be birthed in response to the meta-crisis. We recognize that we are living at a pivotal moment in history. In this "time between stories," the great moral imperative is to tell the new Story of Value. It is ours to do, personally and collectively, with great trembling and ecstatic joy.

FROM DOGMA TO DHARMA: ETERNAL AND EVOLVING FIRST PRINCIPLES AND FIRST VALUES

The teachings are grounded in decades of deep study across many wisdom traditions. Over the years, week by week, these teachings were incrementally developed within the framework of the *One Mountain, Many Paths* broadcast. We often refer to these teachings as *dharma*.

This word was originally used in lineage traditions to refer to something like universal law. This is a crucial realization: just as there is universal law in mathematical value, there is also a sense of universal law in ethics and value.

Historically, *dharma* often devolved into unchanging dogma. Evolution was ignored, and the natural process of *dharma* evolution became disconnected from its deep, eternal context. The weakness of the word *dharma* is that too often it did not include the evolving insights of the sciences, it confused local cultural truths with universal truths, and it used words like "eternal," as in "eternal Tao," as opposed to words like "evolution."

Eternal came to mean unchanging, and that kind of thinking often led to overly ethnocentric readings of *dharma*. Local systems would claim their religious and cultural insights as immutable, which stood in the way of the emergence of a genuine world Story of Value that is real, inherent to Cosmos, and backed by the Universe—even as it is also always evolving.

Or, as we often say, "eternal value is evolving value. The eternal Tao is the evolving Tao."

We have shown that, emergent from profound insights in the "interior sciences," eternal does not mean unchanging in time; it means what we call the deeper Field of ErosValue that is beneath culture, geography, and history, which lives beneath all individual and collective values, and beneath time and space itself.

As such, we have gradually transitioned from the term *dharma* to the term *Value*, in the sense of the Field of Value that lives beneath all values. This Field of Value discloses as First Principles and First Values embedded in a Story of Value.

Indeed, as the interior sciences knew and the exterior sciences imply, Reality arises in a Field of ErosValue in which an entire set of mathematical, musical, molecular, moral, and mystical values are the very ground of all being. That Field of Value is eternal—the true ground of the Good, True and Beautiful—even as it is evolving.

But of course, it is equally critical not just to talk about evolving value, but to ground the evolving value in its true nature, the eternal Field of First Principles and First Values, always reaching for ever-more life, ever-more love, ever-more care, ever-more depth, ever-more uniqueness, ever-more intimate communion, and ever-more transformation.

As such, when we refer to the word *dharma*, which still appears in these texts together with the word value, we refer to an evolving *dharma* grounded in an *eternal and evolving* Field of Value. Indeed, eternity and evolution are two faces of the whole, opposites joined at the hip, that characterize the nature of our Cosmos in virtually all of its expressions.

It's in these terms that we ground a robust world philosophy that integrates the validated, leading-edge insights of premodern traditional wisdom, modern wisdom, and more recent postmodern insights, weaving them together into a new whole greater than the sum of its parts.

This new whole is a shared Story of Value rooted in First Principles and First Values that are both eternal and evolving.

These First Principles and First Values of Cosmos are woven together into a new Story of Value as a context for our diversity, a new Universe Story. This new Story gives us the best possible responses we have to the mystery, and to the great questions:

- Who am I? Who are we?
- Where am I? Where are we?
- What should I do? What should we do?

It is only through such a shared Universe Story—a narrative of identity and ethos as a context for our blessed diversity—that we can realize how what unites is so much greater than what divides us.

Only a new Story of Value will allow us to both respond to the meta-crisis and participate together in birthing the most true, good, and beautiful world that we already know is possible.

THIS ORAL ESSAYS SERIES IS AN ENTRYWAY TO THE GREAT LIBRARY OF COSMOEROTIC HUMANISM

This Oral Essays series is part of the overarching project of the Great Library at the Center for World Philosophy and Religion, led by Dr. Marc Gafni, together with Dr. Zak Stein. The aim of the Great Library project is to articulate a robust and comprehensive new Story of Value, CosmoErotic Humanism, in the form of dozens of well-researched and extensively footnoted academic works.

Our vision is to provide the philosophical framework that will be vital for navigating humanity through this time of immense crisis and transformation.

To begin your journey into CosmoErotic Humanism, we tenderly refer you to the book *First Principles and First Values*, co-authored by Marc Gafni, Zak Stein, and Ken Wilber, under the name David J. Temple. David J. Temple is a pseudonym created for enabling ongoing collaborative authorship at the Center for World Philosophy and Religion. The two primary authors behind David J. Temple are Marc Gafni and Zak Stein, and for different projects, specific writers will be named as part of the collaboration, such as Ken Wilber and others.

Three other volumes complete this introduction: *A Return to Eros*, by Marc Gafni and Kristina Kincaid; *Your Unique Self*, by Marc Gafni; and *Education in a Time between Worlds*, by Zak Stein.

We hope that the Oral Essays in this volume, with their informal style of transmission, will serve as an allurement and entryway for you into the more formal books of the Great Library that provide the robust intellectual underpinnings of the new Story of Value.

A NOTE ABOUT THE EDITORS

This Oral Essays collection has been edited by students of the new Story of CosmoErotic Humanism. Each of us has actively participated in *One Mountain, Many Paths*, and most of us have been in deep "Holy of Holies" study with Dr. Marc Gafni for many years.

We have been privileged to find ourselves well-versed in the teachings, and even emerging as lineage-holders of CosmoErotic Humanism.[3]

We view this editing project as a privilege and a deep practice of study and clarification. We experience ourselves as a *mystical editing society*, frequently meeting and conversing together about the content—the depth of knowledge and wisdom offered here—as well as the technical intricacies involved with publishing a beautiful and coherent series of books. In so doing, we function as a "Unique Self Symphony," which itself is a Dharmic

---

3   CosmoErotic Humanism is a world philosophical movement aimed at reconstructing the collapse of value at the core of global culture. Much like Romanticism or Existentialism, CosmoErotic Humanism is not merely a theory but a movement that changes the very mood of Reality. It is an invitation to participate in evolving the source code of consciousness and culture towards a cosmocentric *ethos* for a planetary civilization.

The term CosmoErotic Humanism, initially coined by Dr. Gafni and colleagues, points to a complex, multi-faceted, layered, and nuanced evolutionary set of insights that has evolved over decades of intensive research, teaching, and spiritual practice from deep within a wide range of wisdom traditions (including the Wisdom of Solomon lineage tradition, Bodhisattva Buddhism, and Kashmir Shaivism), as well as multiple disciplines including complexity theory, chaos theory, emergence theory, molecular biology, and the more classical disciplines of the humanities.

The seeds of CosmoErotic Humanism were planted with Dr. Marc Gafni's work on a two-volume, 1,000-page opus called *Radical Kabbalah* (Integral Publishers, 2012). This scholarly work, sourced from deep study within the esoteric lineage texts of the Wisdom of Solomon, points to a non-dual, or acosmic, realization which—unlike the prevailing conceptualization of non-duality—does not efface the human being; rather, it is highly humanistic in its nature. The next step in the evolution of CosmoErotic Humanism was the insight that all of Reality is evolving Eros, which lives in, as, and through the human being.

A failure of Eros leads inexorably to the creation of narratives of "pseudo-eros." CosmoErotic Humanism is a response to the modern mental and social breakdown sourced in the proliferation of multiple forms of pseudo-eros and its broken narratives, such as rivalrous conflict governed by win/lose metrics and the dogmatic denial of intrinsic value in Cosmos, which together generate our current "global intimacy disorder."

term that connotes an omni-considerate collaboration between realized Unique Selves synergizing our unique gifts into a new emergence greater than the sum of the parts. Even as we worked diligently to standardize our editing styles, meeting on a weekly basis to debate the nuances of phrasing, we also operated from within a deep appreciation of the unique style that each editor brought to his or her work. As such, the reader might notice some variation in editing style among the books.

Please note that Dr. Marc Gafni has not reviewed these edited Oral Essays, as he is deeply engaged in writing the formal books of the Great Library. But he has been generous in responding to questions and providing overall guidance in the project. Overall, as Marc's students and students of the *dharma*, we have made it a key project at the Center to publish these pieces of work relatively independently.

OUR UNIQUE ORAL-ESSAY EDITING STYLE PRESERVES THE ENERGY OF THE ORIGINAL TRANSMISSION

Dr. Marc Gafni is a uniquely gifted teacher whose oral transmission is imbued with a quality that has proven transformative for his students. Many of us feel mystically transformed by both the content and the underlying energy of the transmission style. Therefore, as we like to say, *trust the magic ways the dharma comes through your unique understanding!*

As Marc's empowered students, colleagues, and beloved friends, we have a deep knowing that these teachings are vital for the survival and thriving of humanity as we know it, and we recognize the importance of publishing his teachings in a written format that will be accessible by future generations. At the same time, we sought to preserve the Eros of the original oral transmission with all of its nuance, power, and depth. Our intention in the editing process, to the greatest extent possible, has been to keep these spoken artifacts intact in order to maintain the flow of the original transmission. We have therefore chosen not to engage in intensive formal editing, as we found that doing so resulted in the loss of the energetic transmission that is so key to fully receiving the *dharma*.

After experimenting with many ways to present these texts, we developed a specific way of laying out the text on the page. Marc, in collaboration with Zak Stein and Russian intellectual/artist Elena Maslova-Levin—and ultimately all of the editors, through many conversations—developed a unique, artistic presentation of the text, using bolding, italics, bullet points, and other stylistic features which together serve to accentuate the immediacy of the oral transmission.

As part of this editing style, intended to preserve the integrity of the original transmission, we have refrained from removing the frequent recapitulations of key themes. We found that each recapitulation contributes something vital to the rhythm and music beneath the words, like the beating drum of our hearts. These recapitulations not only review previous material but also add important new emphases, perspectives, and elements of the new Story of Value. We ask for your patience as a reader to trust the rhythm of these texts, and we trust you as a reader to have the depth and steadiness to find your way through.

KEY COMPONENTS: LINK TO THE ORIGINAL BROADCAST, EVOLUTIONARY LOVE CODES AND PRAYER

To supplement the written word, each episode includes a QR code linking to the original broadcast on YouTube, as well as occasional links to featured songs and video clips.

Each episode also centers around an "Evolutionary Love Code," formulated by Marc. These codes are part of the ongoing articulation and distillation of the *dharma* as it unfolds and emerges, week by week, over the course of many years, through the mystical process we call Outrageous Love or Evolutionary Love.

Another core component of the *One Mountain, Many Paths* episodes is what Marc and Barbara called "Evolutionary Prayer." Prayer is experienced in *One Mountain* not in the old fundamentalist sense of a "cosmic vending-machine god" who is alienated from Cosmos. Marc refers to this as the "god you do not and should not believe in"—and he often adds, "the god you don't believe in does not exist."

GOD IS THE INFINITE INTIMATE

In fact, in the *dharma* of CosmoErotic Humanism, a new name for God has emerged: the "Infinite Intimate," who appears in first-, second-, and third-person expressions. Marc first shared this name as he heard it whispered in 2023, although earlier intimations and formulations of the name appeared as early as 2010.

In first person, God is infinitely alive and as intimate as our own first-person experience.

In second person, God is the infinitely intimate Personhood of Cosmos that knows our name and holds us—the God about whom we say, *whenever we fall, we fall into Her hands.* This is the God who is our Beloved, Father, Mother, Lover, and Evolutionary Partner.

Finally, in third person, God inheres in all of the First Principles and First Values of Cosmos, and in the laws of science (both interior and exterior) that govern manifest Reality.

Therefore, we have a realization of God as not only the Infinity of Power but also the Infinity of Intimacy.

In *One Mountain, Many Paths*, we are reclaiming prayer at a higher level of consciousness. And we are reclaiming prayer as deep, alive, loving, and intimate conversations with God as the Infinite Intimate who knows our name.

REFLECTING ON THE CO-CREATION BETWEEN
DR. MARC GAFNI AND BARBARA MARX HUBBARD

Barbara and Marc met five years before Barbara passed. As Barbara said so often, "before I met Marc, I was sure that I was done." Barbara had taught so beautifully for decades, focusing particularly on a powerful articulation of "conscious evolution." Indeed, it would not be inaccurate to say that Barbara was the greatest storyteller of conscious evolution of her time.

Conscious evolution was also a premise in Marc's thinking, but drawn from an entirely different set of sources and experiences. Barbara drew from the classical sources of evolutionary spirituality, such as Teilhard de Chardin, Buckminster Fuller, and many others. Indeed, she was closely associated with Fuller, and was perhaps de Chardin's most ardent intellectual devotee.

Marc drew a somewhat different vision of conscious evolution from the interior sciences of the great wisdom traditions, with a primary emphasis on what he refers to as the "Solomon lineages," merged together with careful readings of the leading edges of the sciences.

In the old version of conscious evolution, the movement from unconscious to conscious was a movement of evolution by chance to evolution by choice.

Together Marc and Barbara evolved the old version of Conscious Evolution, pointing out that evolution itself was always in some sense conscious, but as Marc formulated it, the awakening to conscious evolution refers to the awakening of evolution as human consciousness, coupled with the human realization of being conscious evolution in person, and the human capacity to locate oneself within the context of the larger evolutionary story.

Marc focused his attention on an entirely different dimension of Reality, which he and his colleagues began to call CosmoErotic Humanism. The Intimate Universe, Homo amor, Unique Self and Unique Self Symphonies, God as the Infinity of Intimacy, Eros and the CosmoErotic Universe, distinctions like Role Mate, Soul Mate and Whole Mate, the Four Selves,

Evolutionary Love, Outrageous Love, Evolution: the Love Story of the Universe, First Principles and First Values, Evolving Perennialism, the Evolution of Love, and many more are terms articulated by Gafni and shared with Barbara in their conversation, study, and creative engagement.

Some terms they coined together, for example "a Planetary Awakening in Love through Unique Self Symphonies," where Gafni described Unique Self Symphonies, and Barbara aligned her vision of a planetary Pentecost to Marc's vision of Unique Self Symphonies.

Other key terms were unique and articulated by Barbara, for example: conscious evolution, teleros, telerotic, from joining genes to joining genius, regenopause, vocational arousal, birthing of humanity, synergy engine, and of course her work around what she called the Wheel of Co-creation.

Ultimately, Marc and Barbara attempted to synergize their work in what they called the Wheel of Co-creation 2.0. Barbara and Marc experienced themselves as merging their respective *dharma* into what they began to refer to as Conscious Evolution 2.0, or later, CosmoErotic Humanism.

The first 129 episodes of One Mountain, Many Paths took place in the last period of Barbara's life and reflect the depth and texture of the stunning evolutionary whole-mate meeting between her and Marc.

As Barbara was deep in study with Marc, a lot of what she shared in Evolutionary Church was the *dharma* of their deep study and collaboration.

Although sometimes it may be clear who is speaking, we generally publish these early episodes in what we are calling "one voice." The first 129 episodes, with Marc and Barbara together, have been grouped chronologically. Episodes 130 to 400 and onwards, which were transmitted by Marc, have been grouped by topic.

THE INVITATION

We invite you to find your way into this revolution. Each one of our Unique Selves and unique gifts are desperately needed as we co-create this new Story of Value together, as part of the covenant between generations, for the sake of the whole.

Let's *play a larger game* and evolve the very source code of consciousness and culture together.

With mad love,

The Editors

LOVE OR DIE

LOCATING OURSELVES: ARTICULATING THE ESSENTIAL CONTEXT FOR THE ONE MOUNTAIN, MANY PATHS ORAL ESSAYS

SETTING OUR INTENTION

Intention setting is everything.

We're here—as da Vinci was with his cohort in the Renaissance—**to play a larger game, to participate in the evolution of love, which is to tell the new Story of Value rooted in First Principles and First Values.**

- Our intention is to recognize the critical historical juncture in which we find ourselves.
- Our intention is to take our seat at the table of history and to say, *we take responsibility for this.*
- Our intention is to participate as revolutionaries for the sake of the whole.

What we're here to do is revolution; revolution for the sake of the evolution of love.

It's a revolution for the sake of the trillions of unborn lives that will not manifest:

- The unborn loves
- The unborn creativity
- The unborn goodness
- The unborn truth
- The unborn beauty

All of it looks to us.

Not because we're engaged in grandiosity. Not at all!

- We're trembling before She.
- We're trembling with joy at the privilege.
- We're trembling with joy at the responsibility.
- We're trembling with joy at the Possibility of Possibility.
- We have to enact a new Story in this moment of time. Because it is only a new Story that can change the vector of history.

The most revolutionary act that we can do—the greatest moral imperative of this time—**is to articulate a new Story at this time between worlds and this time between stories.**

Story is not made up, as postmodernity suggests. **We all live in inescapable frameworks; our framework is the story we live in.** Right now, Reality lives according to win/lose metrics, a story that is generating existential risk. **We need to change that story.**

When we change that story, when we tell a new Story—not a made-up story, but a new Story of Value, rooted in First Principles and First Values—**then it all changes.**

We need to participate in the evolution of the source code of consciousness and culture, which is the evolution of love.

It's the most important, exciting, evolutionary, revolutionary act that we can do to alleviate suffering: to be lovers.

Like Rumi, the great poet of Sufism, we have to be "mad lovers," because it's the only sanity.

To be mad lovers is to see around the corner, to not be so obsessed with the details of the contractions of my life.

Let me see bigger.

Let me take complete care of myself in every possible way, let me completely attend to those in my circle of intimacy and influence, and then—*let me expand my circle.*

That's what we're here for.

- Our intention is to participate in the *LoveForce*, the *LoveIntelligence*, the *LoveBeauty*, the *LoveDesire* that literally animates Cosmos all the way up and all the way down.
- Our intention is to participate in the evolution of love.

[In the next few pages we will cover some key concepts which are essential to locating ourselves and setting the context for all the One Mountain, Many Paths Oral Essays. —Eds.]

OVERVIEW: EROS IS NO LONGER A LUXURY—IT'S LOVE OR DIE

Eros is life.

The failure of Eros destroys life.

Our lack of Eros is poised to destroy the world.

All civilizations have fallen because the stories that they lived in were, in some sense, stories based on rivalrous conflict governed by win/lose metrics. Every civilization was weakened by interior polarization caused by the lack of a shared Story of Value.

We now have a global civilization, but we haven't created a shared Story of Value.

We haven't solved the generator functions that caused all civilizations to fall. Our global civilization has exponential technologies and extraction models depleting the Earth of resources that took billions of years to create, which is going to lead to a civilizational collapse.

Existential risk is risk to our very existence.

The choice is clear: love or die.

It's that simple.

Eros is no longer a luxury. It is an absolute necessity for the survival of the individual and the planet.

In the last half a century, modern psychology has documented an age-old truth: a fully nourished baby who is not held in loving arms will die.

So too, our world, both personal and global—even with all the resources of intelligence and technology at our disposal—will die without being held in love, in the embrace of Eros.

We must embrace a personal path of love and a global politics of love.

Not ordinary love. Not love which is "mere human sentiment," but Eros, or what we sometimes call Outrageous Love, which is the heart of existence itself.

We live in a world of outrageous pain.

The only response is Outrageous Love.

WHAT IS EROS?

Eros is the experience of radical aliveness, moving towards, seeking, desiring ever-deeper contact and ever-greater wholeness.[4] Eros is the core fabric of Reality's being and the motivational architecture of Reality's becoming.

Eros is what animates the evolutionary impulse itself, from the very inception of Cosmos all the way to our very selves, who awaken to the realization that the evolutionary impulse throbs uniquely in each of us.

The realization of human awakening and transformation that lies at the core of the interior sciences is the invitation—or even the urgent and desperate demand—of a madly loving Cosmos animated by infinities of power and infinities of intimacy.

The demand—the desperate invitation, the plea, the tender and fierce command of Cosmos that lives inside every human being—is to awaken: to awaken to our true nature as unique incarnations of Eros and Ethos that are needed and desperately desired by All-That-Is. Said slightly differently: Reality is Eros. Or: God is Eros.

The failure of Eros destroys life. The collapse of Eros is always the hidden (or not so hidden) root cause for the collapse of ethics.

This is true both personally and collectively. We live in a moment of a worldwide and personal collapse of Eros. Our lack of Eros is poised to destroy

---

4 We define Eros through what we refer to as the Eros equation (one of a series of what we call interior science equations):

> *Eros = Radical Aliveness* x *Desiring (Growing + Seeking)* x *Deeper Contact* x *Greater Wholeness* x *Self Actualization/Self Transcendence (Creation [Destruction])*

There are good reasons for the formal language of the interior science equations in these writings, and the reader is invited to explore them on their own, in particular, in our work, David J. Temple, *First Principles and First Values: Forty-Two Propositions on CosmoErotic Humanism, the Meta-Crisis, and the World to Come* (World Philosophy and Religion, 2024).

the world. Humanity is currently experiencing what has come to be known as existential risk, a risk to our very existence, or what I will refer to as the Second Shock of Existence.

EXISTENTIAL RISK: THE SECOND SHOCK OF EXISTENCE

The first shock of existence is the death of the human being—the realization that we will die, which dawns in human consciousness at the beginning of history. We are not talking about the biological fact of death but the *existential* realization of death. Although the interior sciences disclose that death is a portal between two days (there is vast empirical,[5] philosophical,[6] and anthro-ontological evidence[7] for the continuity of consciousness[8]), death is also, in our own direct surface experience, a stark end. And that is obviously not a bug but a feature in the system.

---

5   We refer to evidence gathered by the most serious of researchers, beginning with Henry and Edith Sedgwick at Cambridge University and William James at Harvard University, and continuing in highly rigorous form for the last 150 years, as recapitulated by Whiteheadian scholar David Ray Griffin in multiple volumes. See also, for example, Dean Radin, *Real Magic: Unlocking Your Natural Psychic Abilities to Create Everyday Miracles* (Potter/TenSpeed/Harmony, 2018), *The Conscious Universe: The Scientific Truth of Psychic Phenomena* (HarperCollins, 2010), and other books. Or see the earlier classic by Frederic William Henry Myers, *Human Personality and Its Survival of Bodily Death* (Longmans, Green, 1907).

6   This requires a cogent analysis of materialism and dualism, and the introduction of the far more cogent third possibility which we have called "pan-interiority."

7   We discuss Anthro-Ontology in some depth in *First Principles and First Values*, and see also the fuller conversation in David J. Temple, *First Principles and First Values: Towards an Evolving Perennialism: Introducing the Anthro-Ontological Method*—both published by World Philosophy and Religion Press, in Conjunction with Integral Publishers. For now, we will simply define it as an "innate and clear interior gnosis directly available to the human being."

8 See Dr. Marc Gafni and Dr. Zachary Stein's essay in preparation, "Beyond Death: Anthro-Ontology, Philosophy, and Empiricism." This essay is slated to appear in the book *Towards a World Religion: Homo Amor Essays*. The essay is also the ground for a larger book by the same authors, *Twelve Portals to Life Beyond Death: Responding to the Second Shock of Existence,* in which we discuss three forms of material: the empirical, the philosophical, and the anthro-ontological, and show how each form discredits the notion of death as the end.

Our first-person experience is that death ends this life. It is not the *totality* of our experience if we go deeper inside, but it is obviously intended to be the central, potent, and painful dimension of every human life. Indeed, as Ernest Becker potently reminded us, the denial of death is at our peril.

All the stories and all the plotlines and all the threads of living end at that moment. Whatever happens beyond, we have an actual experience of ending. **Paradoxically, that ending, the experience of the finality of mortality, is what presses us into life.** From the implicit demand of the first shock of existence, human beings were activated and pressed into creative emergence, and what emerged was all of human culture, both interior and exterior.

The second shock of existence is the realization of the potential death of all humanity. After all the stages of human history—matter, life, and mind in all of their stages of evolutionary unfolding—we have come to this place in the evolution of humanity, in which the gap between our exponentially expanding exterior technologies and our stalled (or even regressing) interior technologies of value has created dire catastrophic and existential risks.

This gap generates extraction models and exponential growth curves, rivalrous conflicts based on win/lose metrics, tragedies of the commons, and multipolar traps, in which everyone has to keep producing to the *n*th degree, including weaponized exponential threats to our very existence because we are afraid that the other parties are going to do it and not be transparent—hide it from us and then dominate us.

GENERATOR FUNCTIONS FOR EXISTENTIAL RISK

Let's outline clearly the main *generator functions for existential risk.*

Rivalrous conflicts governed by zero-sum, win/lose metrics. Rivalrous conflicts generate extraction models at the core of the economic system and exponential growth curves. Both of these drive and are driven by a contrived system of artificially manufactured desires and needs, delivered into culture by ever more precise forms of micro-targeting to individuals and groups through the ever more immersive environment of the internet.

Next, rivalrous conflicts and exponential growth curves animated by win/lose metrics generate **complicated, fragile world systems** highly vulnerable to myriad forms of collapse. Fragile local systems are made exponentially more fragile on a global level by our inability to meet global challenges with social, legal, political, economic, and ethical infrastructures that remain largely local.

All of this is a direct result of the failure to develop more adequate interior technologies that would be sufficiently compelling to displace "rivalrous conflict governed by win/lose metrics" as the motivational architecture for the human life world.

This failure has led to the conditions that will cause the implosion of systems that are already and quite literally on the brink of collapsing themselves. That's what we mean by the *second shock of existence*.

To recapitulate: the second shock of existence is not the death of the human being, but the potential death of humanity.

It is the *Death Star* moment of our species.

THE DECONSTRUCTION OF INTRINSIC VALUE

We stand in this moment poised between utopia and dystopia, at a time between worlds and a time between stories. We need a new Story of Value, eternal yet evolving, rooted in First Principles and First Values, which would become a universal grammar of value and a context for our diversity.

This is exactly what the Renaissance was. It was a time between worlds and a time between stories. In the Renaissance, we had recently been challenged by the Black Death, a pandemic that swept across Europe. The

Black Death destroyed between a third to half of Europe and a huge part of Asia. People died horrifically, brutally, in the streets. They had no idea how to meet this challenge, and so, in response to the Black Death, da Vinci and Ficino and their cohorts understood that they had to tell a new Story of Value.

That story was the story of modernity. Did they get it right?

- They got part of it right, which birthed, to use Jürgen Habermas' phrase, "the dignities of modernity," such as new ways of gathering information and universal human rights.
- But they also deconstructed the source of Value. They lost the basis for the Good, the True, and the Beautiful.

The basis used to be divine revelation: *God told us*. But this claim was owned by religion, and every religion began to overreach and over-claim. The revelation was thus often mediated through cultural categories and wasn't fully accurate.

Modernity threw out revelation, but was unable to establish a new basis for value.

Value was just assumed to be real. As it says in the founding document of the American Revolution: *We hold these truths to be self-evident*—that is, *we don't really have a basis for value; we just take it as a given.*

In other words, modernity took out a loan of social capital from the traditional world. The source of value was never worked out.

And then, gradually, value began to collapse.

- The Universe Story began to collapse.
- The belief that the Good, the True, and the Beautiful are real began to collapse.
- The belief that Love is real began to collapse.

As Bertrand Russell is reported to have said, "I cannot see how to refute the arguments for the subjectivity of ethical values, but I find myself incapable of believing that all that is wrong with wanton cruelty is that I do not like it."

What do you do if you grew up in a world in which value is not real? A world without a source of value, without a Universe Story, without a story of human identity, without a story of desire, without a narrative of power?

In the words of W.B. Yeats, *the center does not hold.*

- You have a collapse at the very center of society, because you no longer have Eros.
- You no longer have a Reality in which value is real, and so you have this lingering sense of emptiness.
- You have a complete collapse at the very center.
- We become *the hollow men and the stuffed men*, gesture without form.

And that's the source of our current existential risk.

THE DEEPER ROOT CAUSE OF THE META-CRISIS: A GLOBAL INTIMACY DISORDER

Above, I have outlined the major generator functions of existential risk. But there is a deeper cause for the existential risk that lurks underneath the rivalrous conflict governed by win/lose metrics and the fragile systems they engender.

And we cannot take the Death Star down without discerning and addressing this. We have already alluded to this root cause above, but at this point we need to make it more explicit so that, from this context, the adequate root response will become clear.

Modernity threw out the revelation, but was unable to establish a new basis for value.

This ostensibly surprising statement can be understood in a few simple steps:

1. All of the catastrophic and existential risk challenges we face are global: from climate change to artificial intelligence, pandemics, systems collapse, and exponential arms races.
2. Every global challenge self-evidently requires a global solution.
3. Global solutions can only be implemented with global co-ordination.
4. Global co-ordination is impossible without global coherence.
5. Global coherence is only possible if there is a global resonance between the parts.
6. Global resonance is only possible if we have global intimacy.

ONLY A SHARED STORY OF VALUE CAN GENERATE GLOBAL INTIMACY

Global intimacy—just like intimacy in a couple—is only possible when there is a shared story.

Not just a shared history, but a shared Story of Value.

- It is only a shared global story that can generate a new emergent quality of intimacy: global intimacy.
- A shared Story of Value must be rooted in shared ordinating values, or what we have called evolving First Values and First Principles.
- Intimacy requires a shared grammar of value as a matrix for a shared Story of Value.

The global intimacy disorder is the root cause for existential risk. The global intimacy disorder underlies the core generator functions for existential risk.

The global intimacy disorder is rooted in the failure to experience ourselves in a field of shared intrinsic value. This failure derives from the deconstruction of value.

Indeed, it is wholly accurate to say that **the root cause of the two generator functions of existential risk is the failed story of intrinsic value, or what we might also call the breakdown of Eros.**

1. The first generator function is **the success story**. Our modern success story is rivalrous conflict governed by win/lose metrics, which violates all the terms of the Intimacy Equation: there is no shared identity and no mutuality of recognition, feeling, value or purpose, and instead of *relative* otherness, there is *alienated* otherness. Such a story generates complicated fragile systems with no allurement or intimacy between the parts, systems which optimize for efficiency (as an expression of win/lose metrics) and not for resiliency and life.

2. The second generator function is **the deconstruction of intrinsic value** itself. The deconstruction of value is the sense that human value does not participate in the intrinsic value of the Real, for the Real is dogmatically declared to have no intrinsic value. Thus, there is no shared identity between the interior of the human being and Reality. There is no common participation in a field of shared intrinsic value. Instead of being intimate with value, we are alienated from value. And only intrinsic value can arouse will: political, moral, and social will.

To sum up, without a shared grammar of value there is no global intimacy, and therefore no global coherence, and no global coordination in response to catastrophic and existential risk, which means, put simply, there will be, quite literally, no future.

HEALING THE GLOBAL INTIMACY DISORDER
REQUIRES THE EVOLUTION OF INTIMACY

But we are not hopeless. On the contrary, we are filled with great hope. Hope is a memory of the future. That memory of the future *is* the direct hit that takes down the Death Star, the culture of death. **The direct hit must be**—as it has always been in history—**the emergence of a new stage of evolution**.

Crisis is an evolutionary driver, and every crisis is, at its core, a crisis of intimacy: from the oxygen crisis of the single cells dying which generated multicellular life at the dawn of existence, to the existential risk in this very moment.[9]

The direct hit is therefore structurally self-evident: the evolution of intimacy itself.

What is intimacy, as a structure of Cosmos all the way down and all the way up the evolutionary chain? We engage this inquiry in depth in other writings, but for now we will simply adduce what we have called the "Intimacy Equation":

Intimacy = shared identity in the context of [relative] otherness x mutuality of recognition x mutuality of pathos x mutuality of value x mutuality of purpose

Intimacy is about the capacity of parts to generate a *shared identity* while retaining their otherness, or distinct identity. This requires multiple mutualities, including recognition, pathos (or feeling), value, and purpose. The parts must recognize and feel each other, even as they share value and purpose. But all of this must lead to intimate union—and not pathological

---

9 We demonstrate this principle in some depth in the multi-volume series, *The Universe: A Love Story* (forthcoming) (https://worldphilosophyandreligion.org/early-ontologies), *The Intimate Universe: Global Intimacy Disorder as Cause for Global Action Paralysis* (forthcoming), and in other writings of CosmoErotic Humanism.

fusion, where the distinct identity of the parts disappears—like subatomic particles that successfully become an atom, or two people who successfully become a couple.

THE DECONSTRUCTION OF VALUE IS THE DECONSTRUCTION OF INTIMACY

We have identified the global intimacy disorder as the root cause of existential risk. But the underlying ultimate failure of intimacy is the deconstruction of value itself.

The deconstruction of value means that human value does not participate in any sense of intrinsic value of the Real. This is not about individual *values,* but about *the Field of Value* that underlies all of them. **When the human being**—moved, often sincerely or even nobly, by myriad cultural, historical, and psychological confusions—**claims to have stepped out of the Field of Value, then intimacy itself is deconstructed.**

The deconstruction of value is the deconstruction of intimacy.

In the absence of a shared Story of Value, a story that is an authentic expression of Reality's Eros, a story rooted in *pseudo-Eros* takes center stage and becomes the generator function for existential risk. Our modern pseudo-Eros story is *rivalrous conflict governed by win/lose metrics.* Such a story catalyzes in its wake the second generator function of existential risk: *complicated fragile systems with no allurement or intimacy between the parts.* It is in that sense that we have argued that the first generator function for existential risk is the success story.

- The failure of intimacy is precisely the impotent experience that there is no shared identity between the interior of the human being and Reality. **There is no shared identity in the sense of any kind of common participation in a field of shared intrinsic value.**
- **But only a shared Story of Value can arouse the global will**

required to engage catastrophic and existential risk. For it is only global political, moral, and social will—and we can even say *erotic* will—that can generate the most Good, True and Beautiful world that we have always known is possible.

THE EVOLUTION OF LOVE IS THE TELLING OF A NEW STORY

Coupled with the Intimacy Equation is the scientifically grounded realization, in both the exterior and interior sciences, that Reality is a progressive deepening of intimacies, or, said slightly differently:

Reality is Evolution. Evolution is the evolution of intimacy.

- ◆ The evolution of intimacy requires—both personally and collectively—a deeper, more accurate discernment of the nature of our universe, ourselves, and our beloveds.
- ◆ This new discernment generates a new global Story of Value.
- ◆ The new global Story of Value generates an emergent, heretofore unseen global intimacy and heals the global intimacy disorder.

The new Story of Value is the direct hit that takes down the Death Star and replaces it with the hope that invokes the memory of our best future.

Global intimacy facilitates global coherence, which facilitates global coordination, which activates the possibility of our creative and effectively coordinated global responses to the global meta-crisis in its entirety and its specific expressions.

To solve Bertrand Russell's challenge—the apparent argument for the subjectivity of ethical values—**we have to reground value theory in eternal yet evolving First Principles and First Values, and articulate a new Story of Value.**

This is what we call CosmoErotic Humanism.

CosmoErotic Humanism—together with other emergent strands—**needs to become the ground of a world religion as a context for our diversity.** We need religion, even as we need science, to articulate a shared global grammar of value.

As we said at the beginning, our choice is simple: love or die.

- To love means to participate in the evolution of love, which is the evolution of the human Story of Value.
- To love means to evolve and activate a new cultural enlightenment—rooted in a new narrative of identity, a new narrative of value, a new narrative of intimate communion, a new narrative of desire, a new narrative of power—all of which will birth new narratives of economics and politics.
- The evolution of love is the telling of a new Story.

The new Story that must be told is a love story, for in fact that is the deepest truth of Reality, rooted in the best exterior and interior sciences, that we have at this moment in time:

- Reality is not merely a fact. Reality is a story.
- Reality is not an ordinary story. Reality is a love story.
- Reality is not an ordinary love story. Reality is an Outrageous Love Story.

Story doesn't mean it's *made-up*.

It means doing the hard work of integrating the validated insights of the traditional world, the modern world, and the postmodern world.

This is the intention at the heart of telling the new Story of CosmoErotic Humanism.

ABOUT THIS VOLUME

Democracy is a monumental achievement in the evolution of consciousness.

It is in this time between worlds and time between stories that evolutionary achievement is challenged to evolve once more.

For today democracy is fundamentally broken.

To focus on some of the fractures for a moment:

1. Many of the key issues of the day are not being voted on.
2. When we do vote on key issues, they are often too complex for anyone other than the most proficient experts to understand and form a position.
3. Moreover, we are voting within the context of nation states, but the real issues are global.
4. To make matters worse, it is simply true that elections can be and are statistically swung via manipulation by social media.
5. More fundamentally even, the current win-lose structure of democracy undermines democracy itself.
6. Finally, democracy disenfranchises all those who supported the loser in an election, even if that loser wins just a fraction less of the vote than the winner.

The next stage of democracy is what we are calling *synergistic democracy*. Synergistic democracy is rooted in a politics of Evolutionary Love, which generates a planetary awakening in love through Unique Self Symphonies.

Synergistic democracy is about how we create a shared field of value, based on a universal grammar of evolving value. To have a real democracy, we need a shared sense of sense-making, which in turn requires a shared grammar of value that allows for shared evaluation. For the next stage of democracy, we need a shared Story of Value, rooted in First Principles and First Values.

The win/lose democracy is built on the parliamentary procedure. In contrast, synergistic democracy is built on rules of synergistic order.

Synergistic order is grounded in the field of value, populated by first principles and first value that are in relationships of intimate coherence within the context of a larger, ever evolving, Story of Value.

We cultivate vocational arousal in the synergistic democracy of people choosing what they want to create, saying what they need to create it, and having others join them to create it. We cultivate social synergy, coming together to co-create.

Social synergy at its very core is the synergy of value.

Vocational arousal is the arousal to value.

Everyone has a seat at the table. No one is left out of the circle. Conversations take place in which no one is excluded from the circle.

The insights of the various factions are traced to their deep root in a shared field of value. Synergy between competing perspectives of value becomes the order of the polis, instead of domination through narrowly won elections.

Volume 35

These oral essays are edited talks delivered by Marc Gafni and Barbara Marx Hubbard between January 2017 and March 2023, as well as presentations from the 2021 Center for Integral Wisdom board meeting, and a 2021 conversation between Marc and Layman Pascal.

CHAPTER ONE

FROM POWERLESSNESS
TO SACRED ACTIVISM

Episode 13 — January 20, 2017

TUNING INTO THE IMPULSE OF CREATION

I am coming to you with gratitude for the healing and the potentiality of the evolving species that is here now on Earth, **where the sacred story of evolution has an expression through each of our hearts,** that sacred story of evolution that carries billions of years of genius in it.

Wherever we are, whoever we are, whenever it is, it is always *on.*

We, in that sense, are always *on.*

Tune into the impulse of creation within us, in our resonance, in preparing for this planetary birth, this planetary awakening, this inaugural of the next stage of human evolution.

Tune in now. Breathe deep into the impulse. Allow it to speak within you, as to what is being inaugurated now, in you, as you, and into the politics of Evolutionary Love.

Carrying the astonishing frequency of creativity into the field of love, awakening through the irresistible force of

creation, guiding us to fulfill the potential in each of us, for the sake of the good of the whole.

We are taking the great traditions of our culture and **deepening it to be the emergence of the new human and the new world**.

PRAYERS TO THE POWER OF DEMOCRACY

We must have gotten sixty or seventy emails this week from people who said they would be at the march in Washington, where the president was inaugurated and people were protesting the president. Both of those are beautiful. Let's hold that beauty as we enter into prayer.

Let's understand, where are we?

We are in an epic, historic undertaking.

We are in Bethlehem.

We are at a crossroads in history.

We are delighted that people were protesting yesterday, and we are delighted that people are at the inauguration because that is democracy. That is how democracy works.

I'm with Barack Obama—and Barbara is with Barack Obama—in wishing President-elect Trump the very best term, even as we are offering our prayers to those who are protesting.

Yes! Yes! We are in this place where we are offering prayers on all sides. **Because there are no sides, there's a greater evolutionary impulse.**

- ◆ We are standing against those who demonize the protesters and make them *the crazy liberals*.
- ◆ We are against those who demonize the people who are with Trump and make them *the crazy, alt-right conservatives*.

Because actually, we're all Outrageous Lovers; we have the evolutionary impulse of love awake and alive in us.

There's no question in my mind that Barack Obama is right, that president Trump in his deepest place wants to be the greatest president that he can be and not only because of distortions of ego. President Trump may have distortions of ego and so may President Obama, but actually, deep down, the highest President Trump that wants to emerge, wants to create prosperity for the whole world, wants to be a president for the entire country, wants America to be a force for the good. We are going to protest, *and* we're going to stand *with* him because that is the American way; that is the greatness of democracy.

I want to offer our prayers now to President Al Gore who became president but didn't quite get elected. I remember being at the airport, at Kennedy in New York, and Al Gore was giving his concession speech. I was in tears, tears were flowing down my face because that was democracy in action. He had won the presidency, he thought that the Bush team had rigged the Supreme Court vote, but democracy was greater than anything else. Democracy!

We are offering our prayers to the power of democracy.

> *We are going to offer a new vision of democracy because democracy is not a static, eternal, platonic form.*

Democracy needs to evolve.

What would synergistic democracy look like? What would democracy based on a Unique Self Symphony look like?

We're going to talk about principles of the politics of a personal Evolutionary Love and how we are personally implicated in these politics. How does our actual life— our move from loneliness to loving and awakening—shape and change democracy?

We're about to enter into prayer, friends. What is prayer? We're evolving prayer. One of the reasons President Trump won this election is because the liberal world forgot about prayer. What I mean is, the liberal world got so lost in talking about Spirit as the force moving through Reality. But the liberal world forgot the teaching of the great traditions, which is a beautiful, gorgeous teaching that has nothing to do with fundamentalism.

It's the teaching of Rumi. Remember Rumi?

Rumi is *the arms of the Beloved.*

Rumi is *the arms of the Beloved.*

Rumi is the LoveIntelligence of Reality that manifested the most sophisticated forms of mathematics, before there was a neocortex.

It's the LoveIntelligence that manifested mitosis and meiosis, before there was a human being, that manifested photosynthesis before there was any supercomputer.

It's the wild, infinitely gorgeous LoveIntelligence of Cosmos that is personal. The quality of personalness that exists between us, that quality of personal intimacy, that is not just us.

That is the *us* participating in the Infinity of Intimacy, which is the divine Reality that knows our name.

Physics, chemistry, the laws of science, and the billions of light years are all the third person of Reality. That is God in the third person: the infinite power, supernovas, and all of the greatest mathematical formulas that guided the Apollo spaceships to the moon, working within the principles of Reality with infinite power, infinite time—and multiverses mediated inside.

We shut our eyes. All of that Infinite Power is sitting in a chair in front of us right now and saying, *I want to know you.*

REALITY YEARNS FOR US

Reality yearns for us. Reality has a personal face that's more personal than any one of us. Imagine your most personal moment with your most intimate beloved and exponentialize that moment billions of billions of times, and you will have the sense of personal, infinite love that Reality has for you.

When fundamentalists talk about it and say, *Christ knows you*, they're actually right. They might be wrong about saying it only using the name called *Christ*.

Rumi has a different name. Rumi said, *The Friend loves you.*

Kashmir Shaivism has a different name. It talked about the personal face of Shiva and Shakti embracing you, and Rama and Sita.

Kabbalah in Judaism has its own words.

Meister Eckhart in Christianity has his own words.

The native traditions have their words.

It is the infinite personal face of Reality that knows us, that holds us, that desires us.

Every place we fall, we fall into God's hands. That's why we sing *Hallelujah*. Because what *Hallelujah* means is *hallel*—pristine praise.

Holelut, is part of our ritual, is the drunken intoxication. *Holelut* is the drunken intoxication of our lives in their broken moments. And then the Holy moments, the pristine moments, the gorgeous moments, but all of those moments are Hallelujah.

All of those moments are held by the Divine. All of those moments are happening within the Divine who cares about the infinite details. Who cares about the infinite detail of our lives. God's there with us every moment. God knows our name.

So we sing before God.

Hallelujah

Well I heard there was a secret chord

That David played, and it pleased the Lord

But you don't really care for music, do ya?

Well, it goes like this, the fourth, the fifth

The minor fall and the major lift

The baffled king composing Hallelujah

[Chorus]

Hallelujah, Hallelujah

Hallelujah, Hallelujah

Well, your faith was strong but you needed proof.

You saw her bathing on the roof.

Her beauty and the moonlight overthrew you.

And she tied you to her kitchen chair

and she broke your throne and she cut your hair

and from your lips she drew the Hallelujah

[Chorus]

Well, baby, I've been here before,

I've seen this room, and I've walked this floor.

You know, I used to live alone before I knew ya.

And I've seen your flag on the marble arch,

and love is not a victory march,

it's a cold and it's a broken Hallelujah.

[Chorus]

Well, there was a time when you let me know

what's really going on below,

but now you never show that to me, do ya?

But remember when I moved in you

And the holy dove was moving, too,

and every breath we drew was Hallelujah

[Chorus]

Maybe there's a God above,

but all I've ever learned from love

was how to shoot somebody who outdrew ya,

It's not a cry that you hear at night,

it's not somebody who's seen the light,

it's a cold and it's a broken Hallelujah.

[Chorus]

It's a cold and it's a broken Hallelujah. There is no one who doesn't know moments of *cold and a broken Hallelujah*, as well as moments of ecstasy. We offer it all up to the Mother, Ramakrishna. Ramakrishna, whose student Vivekananda started the parliament of world religions, Ramakrishna would walk into the ashram and say, *MOTHER! MOTHER!*

What do you think? That he was premodern, that he was a fundamentalist? He wasn't a fundamentalist. He just said, *Oh my God, I offer it all up to the Mother.* The Mother is the creative LoveIntelligence that holds us. He would scream, *MOTHER! MOTHER! MOTHER! MOTHER!*

Mother carry me

A child I will always be

Mother carry me

Back to the sea.

The river is flowing

Growing and flowing

The river is flowing

Back to the sea.

The sea, the ocean, is always the Goddess, the *Shekinah*.

Because we look at the ocean for the same reason that we look at a beautiful man or a beautiful woman, just *because*.

We're all beautiful. You can look at anyone's face and fall in love.

- *Fall in love* doesn't mean I'm going to sleep with you or I'm going to marry you.
- *Fall in love* means I see your infinite beauty, you're gorgeous, I'm delighted.

We turn toward the Divine, the creative LoveIntelligence—which in evolutionary science Stuart Kauffman the great physicist called the incessant, ceaseless creativity of cosmos—which has a personal face, which is *MOTHER!*

Let's offer our prayers to Mother. The gates are all open. The gates are open, my friends.

We get to be excited. We are not politically correct. We are spiritually incorrect. We are evangelists. We are evolutionary evangelists. We are bringing the good news that the evolutionary impulse is alive. And there's a politics of personal Evolutionary Love that's about to be ushered in.

Everybody wants to express their creativity, but most people close their hearts because the pain is too overwhelming

Mine eyes have seen the glory of the coming of the Lord.

He is trampling out the vintage

where the grapes of wrath are stored.

We want to celebrate two people, and then celebrate that very same impulse in us.

Think about Gandhi and Martin Luther King.

Think about how Gandhi, in India, was able to sit and sew and think. He was able to gain the awareness that by doing that Salt March, guiding people to go across India, to be hit, to be destroyed, to be hurt, that he would liberate India from the British.

Let's get inside of Gandhi for a moment.

What did it take for that small man to stand up, walk across India, have people follow him, have them put in jail, have so much destruction, and win liberation of India?

We are tuning into the spirit of Gandhi and *truth force*.

It is so much stronger than anything in the world.

Now tune into Martin Luther King, standing at the mall in Washington DC, with hundreds of thousands of people in front of him. He was going to make a speech he prepared. He wasn't sure exactly what to say when somebody pulled the speech away from him. Some friend, who was standing behind him, said, *Just talk, Martin.*

What did Martin say? He said, *I have a dream.* He had a dream of equality. He had a dream of blacks and whites living together.

He had that dream, and look what happened. From that dream—that power, and that presence holding that dream—came a black president of the United States.

We have enormous empowerment of people of color as well as people who are white.

We remember from Gandhi and Martin Luther King—*I am going to liberate India,* and *I have a dream.*

We have Gandhi, we have Martin Luther King, now we have thousands, and hundreds of thousands. Let each of us experience that unique expression of our gift to the planetary birth, of our unique sound and note, going within, to state it internally first.

9

Take the lid off the top of your potential. Literally take the roof off the top of your head. You're literally going to allow the impulse of evolution, for the billions of years that it took to get to be in you, by your *Yes*—by your triumph—to actually be heard all the way up.

Let's feel into the same organizing capability that organized the entire universe, the invisible process of creation, that brought quark to quark, electron to electron, proton to proton, all the way up and all the way down the process of allurement.

Let's let everybody's unique gift to the planetary shift be given now as a symbol and an experience of how this can be a planetary awakening of humanity, as a living expression of Divine intent.

Take the lid off the top of your head, allow the impulse of evolution to go all the way through, up into the planetary connectivity through the Unique Self Symphony.

We are inviting everybody on Earth to express their gift to the planetary awakening, people in every culture around the world asking the Universe to allow them to give their gift all the way through.

The Unique Self Symphony moving toward a Planetary Awakening. We feel ecstatic when we are doing that!

A collective planetary birth of what's good, what's true, what's beautiful, then everyone on Earth, people in every culture, all around the world, asking the Universe to allow them to give their gifts, the whole way through, simultaneously.

We are the heralds of the planetary birth.

Who's conducting the symphony?

The same Conductor who originated the universe!

The incredible Conductor who did those first two seconds of the Big Bang. Now that Conductor is a great conductor, as you can imagine!

We are encoded with the Big Bang. We are encoded with fifty-two trillion cells that have been through the entire journey of evolution, that remember what happened.

That's how they do eyes, ears, and thumbs.

How do you suppose they know how to see, hear, and speak?

They are all—the entire body of cells and every one of us—conducted!

> *The organizing capability that's conducting you is actually also conducting the Unique Self Symphony.*

We want to declare a vision that is potentially completely as true as Gandhi and Martin Luther King, and in fact, even more obvious. Here it is:

Every single person on Earth wants to express their creativity.

Every single person on Earth wants, in some way, to be able to realize their potential self. However they name it, whatever description they give it, it is life force itself, in everyone.

In our Unique Self Symphony, let us all hold together, that this particular symphony is orchestrating what will be, potentially, a planetary awakening in love, in our lifetime, before we have to go into further dissolution and destruction on this planet.

This force is as strong as the Big Bang. This force is as strong as the life impulse of billions of years.

Let's call on it. Let people shout out, go the whole way with your voice.

Feel it the whole way. Let the lid off!

If we take the sense of what the Unique Self Symphony is, while simultaneously every single person is giving their gift, then what actually begins to happen?

11

Let's understand it:

What is our response? What is our dream? What is our vision? What is our response to where we are in the world today?

We are *spiritually incorrect*.

Imagine tens of millions of people in the world who all know: *I am a Unique Self; I am a unique expression of the Outrageous Love.* People wake up with a phrase in their minds, and they say, *We live in a world of outrageous pain. The only response to outrageous pain is Outrageous Love*— which is the sutra, the verse.

I am an Outrageous Lover, and I can commit Outrageous Acts of Love that no one that ever was, is, or will be, other than me, can commit, which are a function of my Unique Self, whether I'm eleven years old, in China, in Asia, in Bulgaria, in Idaho, in Canada, in New Zealand, a thirty-year-old, or a fourteen-year-old:

What is my unique contribution? What can I do? What is my Outrageous Act of Love?

When that happens, when that's in the source code of Reality, then all of a sudden, all of those Unique Selves join and become a Unique Self Symphony.

Our response to President Trump is: we love you, be a great president. But it doesn't depend just on you, President Trump. We are the Unique Self Symphony, the world of citizens, a bottom-up self-organizing universe.

This is the core realization of evolutionary science and complexity theory rooted in the English mathematician Alan Turing's classic essay, *Morphogenesis.* Turing tells us that there are fundamental notes of music— simple first principles of life—that generate Reality. I realized when I first came across Turing's *Morphogenesis* that **the simple first rules are not only rules of exteriors, they are also simple first principles of interiors.** These are the simple first principles and first values that animate and guide

Reality. These are the fundamental musical notes that generate the Unique Self Symphony.

It is not a top-down world dependent on a single separate self, an ego-driven leader, or President Trump. Rather the job of the leader is to be the maestro of the Unique Self Symphony.

So, if this is true, let's open our hearts and get really quiet; it's so deep, it's so beautiful, it's so gorgeous.

We're not disturbed, we're excited, we're awake, we're alive! Here's the question.

IT'S NOT OUR JOB TO HEAL THE WHOLE THING

If everyone has a unique gift, and everyone is a Unique Self, and everyone has a unique set of Outrageous Acts of Love to commit, then why isn't everyone out there doing it?

Why isn't everyone who believes in his vision at the inauguration cheering on Trump or at the protest?

Why did most people not vote?

Why are people disengaged?

Why are people not committing their Outrageous Acts of Love?

Why are people not stepping up to play their instrument in the Unique Self Symphony?

Why are people not addressing the unique need in their unique circle of intimacy and influence?

Open your hearts with me. It's so deep. Most of the enlightenment teachers tell us people are not out there changing the world because they are selfish, because they don't feel, because they are egocentric, or because they are narcissistic.

But we don't think that people stop giving their gift because they don't feel. We don't think that people don't show up to the Unique Self Symphony because they don't feel.

The opposite is true.

The reason people don't step up and play their instrument as sacred activists, expressions of Mother in the Unique Self Symphony, is because they feel too much.

They're overwhelmed.

They don't know what to do.

The suffering is so overwhelming.

The problems are so overwhelming.

The carnage is so overwhelming.

Yesterday, President Trump talked about the carnage in America. Carnage is a poor word for a president to choose. People are overwhelmed by the carnage all over the world. People say, *It's too much for me! I can't handle it.* People close their hearts. People are afraid to *feel* the pain because they don't know how to *heal* the pain.

In the gap between our ability to feel and our ability to heal, we close our hearts.

In the gap between our ability to feel the pain and our ability to heal the pain, we close our hearts. We close our hearts because we are paralyzed. There's a global action paralysis. There's a global action paralysis because Unique Selves all over the world are afraid to join the symphony. Because the carnage is so great.

President Trump's word, "carnage", is a bad choice because it evokes not our potency but our impotence. *Oh my God, I can't heal it*, is how we respond to carnage. *So, if I can't heal it, it's too painful to feel.* You've got to hear this; this is so important.

Here's where President Trump gets it wrong.

You see, when we close our hearts because we say *the gap between our ability to feel and our ability to heal is too great*, that's actually just the ego talking.

It is not our job to heal the whole thing.

It is our job to play our instrument, to address the unique need in our unique circle of intimacy and influence.

President Trump got it wrong when he said, *I'm the strong leader. I'm going to heal the carnage.* President Trump, we love you, and we wish you a great presidency. But we're not going to be healed by the strong leader.

We are past the age of the dictator or the strong president-leader, who is going to actually heal us. We're past the age, and this is where we disagree with the fundamentalists, where Jesus comes only from the outside.

Jesus Christ holds us, but Christ lives in us. We are Unique Selves. We can give our gifts.

Trump is not going to heal the carnage. The self-organizing universe that we talked about before, the maestro, the conductor, is the LoveIntelligence of Reality that knows our name and lives as us. **Each of us has the ability to heal some of the pain that no one else that ever was can heal.**

Every single person has a unique creativity.

Every single person has a unique voice.

Everyone has a unique gift.

WHEN WE CLAIM OUR POWER, WE CLOSE THE GAP BETWEEN OUR ABILITY TO HEAL AND OUR ABILITY TO FEEL

We claim our potency, our power.

We want to say something wildly unpopular for a second: Women and men, we have to claim our power in every arena of life.

Women, stop being victims.

Men, stop being victims.

We are powerful. We are potent. We are strong.

When we claim our power, we close the gap between our ability to feel and heal.

We do confessions of greatness. We hear each other and believe that the process of evolution itself is orchestrating through us. We begin to see that that process created a whole Universe.

We believe we discovered how to orchestrate the Unique Self Symphony. We have to do it together.

We're learning to orchestrate, each of us, such that the chorus that will be heard like Gandhi going on the Salt March and Martin Luther King's, *I Have a Dream* speech.

We're not just watching the movie *Selma*[1] about Martin Luther King; it is us! This is our turn.

CONFESSING OUR GREATNESS

We don't confess only our shortcoming and our vulnerability. Yes, we have to confess our vulnerability—but we confess our greatness.

---

1 *Selma*. Directed by Ava DuVernay. Los Angeles: Paramount Pictures, 2014.

We stand before the *Lord of song,* and we cry out *the holy and the broken Hallelujah.* By offering up not just the holy, but the broken *Hallelujah.* Love is not a victory march, *it's a cold and it's a broken Hallelujah.*

We offer up all our failure. And all our falling. And every moment that our heart broke open.

And from that place, when it's all offered up to the Mother:

- We find our strength.
- We feel our gift.
- We feel our goodness.
- We feel our power.

We close the gap between our ability to feel the pain and our ability to heal the pain.

We become great players in the Unique Self Symphony. Because **the great principle of a personal politics of Evolutionary Love is Unique Self Symphony.**

YOM KIPPUR STORY OF YANKEL

We end with a story and a chant together. But this story is everything.

Here is the story.

It's about a master. This master knows, he can see, and he understands everything. He's one of the great non-dual masters.

There is a student that comes in to him on the holiest day of the year. In this particular Hasidic tradition, it was Yom Kippur, the Jewish Day of Atonement—but it could be a Sufi story, a Confucius story, or a Christian story.

Here's what happens. A man comes before the Master, and the Master says, *Get out of here! You're going to die!*

The man said, *What do you mean, I'm going to die?*

The master said, *Get out of here, you're going to die! Leave me!*

The man was devastated. *That's not politically correct, telling me I'm going to die. You're throwing me out?*

The man was completely broken. He leaves the town, and he's trudging on the road. It's the eve of Yom Kippur, the holiest day in the Jewish calendar and a day of fasting. And he sees a wagon full of disciples of his master, who are on their way to visit the master for the holiday.

They say to him, *You look so dejected, Yankel. What are you doing?*

Yankel said, *The master saw me. He said I was going to die, and he threw me out!*

They said, *Wow, he told you were going to die, and he threw you out! Well, we've got to get a meal before the holiday because it's a fast day. Come and get a meal with us.*

So, what could Yankel do? He'd been thrown out by his master, he's about to die, his master told him. He has nothing better to do, so he gets on the wagon, he goes with the disciples, and they go to a local tavern.

The disciples said to him, *The master said you're going to die. We're right before the holiday, buy us all a drink. After all, you don't need your money, you're going to die.*

Yankel is so depressed and dejected that he says, *Okay.* He buys everyone a drink, and they raise their glass. In the Jewish tradition people say, *Le Chaim,* which means *To Life!*

So, the disciples raise their glasses on the eve of the holiday, even the dejected disciple who has been told he's going to die . They raise their glasses and say, *Le Chaim!* They drink it up.

Then the disciples say, *Pour us another round, after all you don't need your money, the master said you're going to die.*

18

They pour another round, they raise their glasses and go, *Le Chaim!* To Life!

And they drink up. They pour another round, they raise their glass, *Le Chaim!* To Life!

They drink up, they keep pouring rounds, and they keep screaming out, To life! *Le Chaim!* To Life! Until they're all together in a holy community, a band of Outrageous Lovers crying out, *Le Chaim!* To Life!

Then they're a little drunk, a holy and a broken Hallelujah, and they find their way again to the master. The holiday is about to begin. The master sees this disciple that he had just thrown out and told him *you are going to die.* He looks at him, and he says, *Oh my God, the angel of death has left. You're going to live!*

The disciple says, *Master, what happened? Why didn't you give me a blessing? You could have given me a blessing, you could have made me live.*

And the Master said, *No, there's no guru, there's no Master. No individual can do it. The only thing that can give us life is when we all come together as a Unique Self Symphony, and we raise our glasses, and we cry out, Hallelujah! Le Chaim! To Life!*

We offer it up, and we say that it does not depend on President Obama or former Secretary Clinton. Nor does it depend (as we offer him, as Obama did, our best wishes on his inauguration) on President Trump.

It depends on us!

We are the Unique Self Symphony.

We are the Outrageous Lovers.

We are the ones we've been waiting for.

So, we raise our glasses together, inaugurating a new period in human history in which the center of Reality is not a top-down Reality, but a bottom-up, self-organizing universe, a band of Outrageous Lovers.

We're excited. We're bringing the good news. The good news is us! Because we are alive, and we are awake!

CHAPTER TWO

EVOLUTION'S DESIRE FOR SYNERGISTIC DEMOCRACY

Episode 14 — January 28, 2017

AWAKENING A MEMORY OF THE FUTURE

We bring into our consciousness the sacred story of evolution. **The sacred story of evolution is the guide for understanding the next stage of our lives. Because there is no reason to assume that evolution stops here.**

Another way to say this is that you and I are called by a deep memory of the past—and a deep memory of the future.

The memory of the past in each of us, when we awaken it, goes back to the origins of creation. Even further, it goes to consciousness itself. The memory of the past in each of us goes to value itself.

Gaining our memory back to the origins of creation allows us to feel every molecule, every cell, every part of our brain, every expression of the trillions of cells that are making us up, that are alive to this memory.

We are bringing into actual form of consciousness that memory of the past as an intentional story of ever higher consciousness, freedom, and order.

Get in touch with the evolutionary impulse toward more life, toward more love, toward more creativity within you, and amplify it.

In this resonant Field, take a deep breath of remembrance that we are the story of creation come alive, consciously creating the next stage of self—social, scientific, and spiritual evolution.

We are welcoming the whole story of creation, as you and I—awake to the genius of the process of creation.

FINDING THE FIELD

The Lakshmi[2] chant is a great Hindu chant, and it enters into the interior faces of the Cosmos. It finds the vein of prosperity, the vein of abundance.

I wonder, how did those old-time Hindus, Kashmir Shaivites, come up with this sacred technology? There was no supercomputer. There was no artificial intelligence. They did not have access to all musical permutations and a Pythagorean array.

How did they do it?

They did it by getting deeply into the resonant Field, feeling the resonance of the Field.

There's noise around us. We can't find it. We are glancing over at a cell phone; we are glancing over here; we are glancing over there. We are disturbed.

If we are asking ourselves, *what's coming next?* or *what's coming up in the next hour?* We aren't able to find the Field. When we find our way in there, then we can drop in. That is what we have to do here.

---

2 The word *Lakshmi* is derived from the root word *laksha* which means goal or objective. To take a *laksha* means to take an aim. The *Lakshmi Mantra* is recited in order to know your goal and as a means to fructify that goal. *Lakshmi Mantra* is also called Money Mantra. But *Lakshmi Mantra* is a prayer not only to gain financial prosperity but also to give the intelligence to enlighten the minds with understanding. *Lakshmi* is the personification of all that brings good fortune, prosperity, and beauty.

The second we are out of the resonant Field, it becomes just a program we are doing. We are not building a program here.

We are in Bethlehem, friends.

We are in Jerusalem.

We are evangelists in the sense that we are bringing the good news.

We are not just evolutionaries, but we are evolutionary evangelists.

Our colleague, Michael Dowd, wrote a great book called *Thank God for Evolution*. What Michael meant was—and Michael and his wife, Connie Barlow, have been evangelizing for evolution—we stay in.

We are in, committed, committed all the way, committed all the way to bringing the good news.

We can bring the good news, my friends, only if we know the good news. We can feel the interior face of the Cosmos only by dropping so deeply into the silence, so deeply into the presence, that our own sense of presence and radical commitment is so apparent, deep, alive, committed, and true—that everyone can feel it.

The mystics tell us that the second our attention goes to something else, that we are not present, that we are not in; the heavens literally feel it. We focus our attention such that nothing else exists.

Eternity resides in that focus of a radical evolutionary moment.

Our good friend Richard Alpert changed his name to Ram Dass. The Jewish people, they do that. There's Ram Dass, there's Krishna Das, there's Surya Das, all these Jewish boys from the cities became the Das brothers. Amen, Hallelujah. So, the Das brothers, one of the things they were looking for was: Wow, man, let's drop in. Let's be love now. Let's be here now.

Do you see the paradox?

There's nothing else, just right here. We are here together in radical intimacy. In radical love.

THE EVOLUTIONARY GOD IS THE IMPULSE OF EVOLUTION AND THE BELOVED WHO HOLDS IT ALL

We are evolving God. We are reclaiming the possibility of possibilities.

Martin Luther King, together with his great colleagues, could not have started the civil rights movement without one institution—the deep presence of the Gospel church.

It was the animating Eros, presence and delight of the prayer of the Gospel church that carried the civil rights movement.

The deep presence of the African-American Gospel church was the source from which Martin Luther King went out from Selma, Alabama to Montgomery, Alabama, with the Student National Leadership Council[3].

We are now at the next great movement in history. This is as great as the Renaissance. We are redefining our worldview.

We are stepping up as evolutionaries, understanding that a new world spirituality is emergent, that we are evolution awakening as us, in person, that the evolutionary impulse, or what Aurobindo called *the evolutionary imperative*, is alive and awake in us.

We understand the great teaching of Abraham Kook.[4] Kook says, *What is more perfect, that which is perfect or that which is perfecting?*

Ahh, of course, someone who's born with a silver spoon, they've got everything, they were always refined and noble. That's lovely.

---

3 On 25 March 1965, Martin Luther King led thousands of nonviolent demonstrators to the steps of the capitol in Montgomery, Alabama, after a 5-day, 54-mile march. Source: *Selma to Montgomery March* in the King Encyclopedia of Stanford University.

4 The venerable Rabbi Abraham Isaac Ha-Cohen Kook (b. 1865–d. 1935) was the first Ashkenazi chief rabbi of Palestine and is one of the greatest philosopher-mystics of the twentieth century.

But do you remember that movie, *Slumdog Millionaire*, the Indian movie about a man who came from the deep darkness of Reality and managed to transform into nobility? That is perfecting—that is higher.

If perfecting is higher than perfect, and God is perfect, then God must be perfecting; God must be evolving.

So, we pray not to the old Santa Claus God pulling strings from the outside. We pray to the evolutionary God, and the evolutionary God is not only the Impulse of Evolution —

The evolutionary God is—what Rumi talks about—the Beloved that holds it all. It is the impulse that emerges out of the Beloved. It is the second face of God.

Let's weave it together.

When we do resonance, we are invoking what we might call the third face of God—the evolutionary impulse, the Field of evolution.

We always start with the Field. That is the resonance.

Then, we go to prayer.

Prayer is the second face of God.

Prayer is God as thou, said Martin Buber, *God that knows my name.*

Prayer is the arms of the Beloved into which Rumi falls, *knowing that wherever I fall, I fall into the arms of the Beloved.*

Blessed are you…You…YOU!

There is no place to go, there is no place to be, there is no place to get.

We are taking a stand as ourselves, committed and participating in the evolution of love.

We tell prayer stories. This story is about a master named Levi Isaac Berditchev. There's a formula for blessing in Hebrew, and the formula is

Baruch ata Adonai Eloheinu melech ha-olam: Blessed are you, God, King/ Queen of the World.

Levi Isaac Berditchev was the greatest non-dual mystic who ever lived, at least in the 19th century. He was wild, and he could never get through a blessing; he just couldn't do it. A little seven-year-old can make a blessing, but he could never make a blessing.

Why?

Because he would go *Baruch Ata... Blessed are You... You... YOU!* And he would start convulsing, and he would faint in ecstasy.

Because he felt you!

Any intimacy that we feel is participating in YOU, the personal face of the Divine. The Infinity of Intimacy knows our name and cares about every detail of our life.

And, Barbara, I (Marc Gafni) am going to tell you a little secret, love, just between us and please do not share. Yesterday morning, God was worried because you were a little dizzy in the morning. And you felt better, but literally—does everyone get this—the Infinity of Power was a little worried because Barbara woke up a little dizzy. And thank God, she's fine now, and of course we can all get a little dizzy. But God was like, *oh my God, what's up with My Barbara?*

Wow! That wasn't the Santa Claus God.

That was the **Infinity of Intimacy** that yearns for Barbara-ness, intended Barbara-ness, desires Barbara-ness, needs Barbara-ness.

That realization brings us to prayer. We turn to that Mother, to that YOU, and we pour out our prayers and say *Hallelujah.* We bring everything. We bring the holy, and we bring the broken *Hallelujah.*

We go into the hymn and prepare ourselves to open up for prayer that affirms the dignity of personal need. We open up with the dignity of our prayer, offering up *the holy and the broken Hallelujah*.

Hallelujah – Leonard Cohen[5]

♪ *Now, I've heard there was a secret chord*

that David played, and it pleased the Lord. ♪

But you don't really care for music, do you?

♪♪ *It goes like this, the fourth, the fifth,*

the minor fall, the major lift. ♪

The baffled king composing Hallelujah ♪♪

[Chorus]

Hallelujah, Hallelujah,

Hallelujah, Hallelujah. ♪

PRAYING FROM THE PLACE OF THE LONELY CHILD

We go from this place into prayer. We know that an evolutionary movement that bypasses *the holy and the broken Hallelujah* is not a kosher evolutionary movement.

Any theology, any spirituality, that ignores the lonely hearts, that ignores the broken hearts, that doesn't understand the shattered place is not a kosher theology or spirituality.

There is not one of us who doesn't know the pain of a broken heart. There is not one of us who doesn't know the pain of betrayal, whether we were betraying or being betrayed. There is not one of us who doesn't know that

---

5   Leonard Cohen, "Hallelujah", *Various Positions*, Columbia Records, 1984, LP. (https://youtu.be/oZJYab2BM3Q)

love is not only not a victory march, but it's sometimes a cold and a broken Hallelujah.

And the original word, *Hallelujah* in Hebrew is *hallel*, which means pristine praise, and it means *holelut*, which means drunken intoxication.

When we go to pray, we come not from the place of the brilliant evolutionary; we come from the lonely child. We come from the one who's throwing ourselves into the arms of the Mother. The Mother who is the LoveIntelligence of all.

Rama Krishna, the great non-dual mystic 150 years ago, when he would go into his temple, he would just cry out, *Mother, Mother, Mother!!!*

And The Beatles got it right when they got the power of *Mother Mary comes to me, speaking words of wisdom, let it be.*

We are praying to the personal face of the Beloved—the Infinity of Intimacy that knows our name. Prayer affirms the dignity of personal need.

ANNOUNCING SYNERGISTIC DEMOCRACY

Mine eyes have seen the glory

of the coming of the Lord.

He has trampled out the vintage

where the grapes of wrath are stored.

What does it mean to have a democracy of all?

In the United States of America, this win-lose structure has shown up to be the divided states of America, in order for one side to win over the other.

Think of what it was like before we had democracy. People lived like serfs, people had no names, and the monarchy could boil somebody in oil to see who was right and who was wrong. It wasn't even considered that every individual would have life, liberty, the pursuit of happiness, and the right to vote.

Let us make a deep prayer of thankfulness for the pioneers that liberated democracy to begin with—in the United States, in Europe, etc.—and how great that period has been in terms of liberating individual creativity and potential.

And we are recognizing that the structure of win-lose democracy through voting—great as it was for its time—cannot coordinate us for a planetary sense of connectivity, wholeness, oneness, and liberate the creativity of ourselves when we join.

We have hit a structural impasse because the win-lose structure in all existing liberal democracies is not working.

We are a seedbed for evolutionary democracy. That seedbed is a dharma that is growing in the consciousness of the people. If the black gospel church made it possible for Martin Luther King to speak *I have a dream*, and his dream was so great and so clear that it was realized to some extent, we are making it possible to state this dream.

Let us be the dream of the next stage of democracy, of the liberation of individual potential, to create a world equal to our divine destiny.

In the particular frequency that we have set, we announce the origin, fulfillment, and dedication to synergistic democracy.

I think we have to say, what is the synergistic democracy being announced here, whose text is the sacred Story of evolution?

In announcing this seedbed of synergistic democracy, we take in the sacred text of the Evolutionary Story as the Evolution of Love.

Feel the awesome generation of capacity that we have—the move from *I* have a dream, to *We* have a dream. The new structure of synergistic democracy is the Wheel of Co-Creation.

THE WHEEL OF CO-CREATION IN SYNERGISTIC DEMOCRACY

The essence of synergistic democracy is built on the win-lose voting structures that gave us the first ideas of individual freedom.

Synergistic democracy starts with the phrase *I want to create*. This is what I want to create.

This is what is my unique passion to express, to give, to become. I want to create.

The second thing that we say in synergistic democracy is: What do I need to create this better than I could do alone? The minute we ask each other this, we create our WeSpace, where we can create what w indeed together for the glory of the evolution of God.

So be it! Here we are in synergistic democracy, and every member of the evolutionary democracy will think:

- First: This is what I most want to create. Whatever it is, my Unique Self is yearning to create it.
- Second: What do I most need, to help me create it, vocationally?
- Third: What do I most want to give freely to everyone because I love to give it? Do I want to give my music? Do I want to give my healing? Do I want to give my humor? Do I want to give my love to caring for children? Whatever it is, I want to give it freely.

Imagine for a moment that the new structure of synergistic democracy is the Wheel of Co-Creation 2.0.

Democracy, as every other human endeavor, has a human structure upon which it was built. The parliamentary procedure is the structure upon which win-lose democracy is built. Synergistic democracy is built on something that we are all beginning to do, called rules of synergistic order.

What are those rules of synergistic order?

First, when I say, *I am yearning to create something, and this is what I need*, instead of somebody voting that they do not think what I want to create is any good, somebody in the evolutionary democracy is going to come to me and say, *I have a creative input to help you create what you want to create.*

Then, by me joining vocationally with you, within synergistic democracy, I am going to get to be more of *who I am*.

In other words, we cultivate vocational arousal in the synergistic democracy of people:

1. Choosing what they want to create.
2. Saying what they need to create it.
3. Having others join them to create it.

Let's say you have entered into the Wheel of Co-Creation 2.0 in the field of health, and you have a new healing process that you'd like to have known.

In order to do that, you might say, *I need media attention to what I have to offer*. Is there someone in the media section of the wheel who has what I need in order to help me create it? That person is going to say, *yes*, and you will have a vocational connection. You will experience the joining of genius to create because the person who is helping you will also need you to help them get what they want.

We start to cultivate social synergy, coming together to co-create.

It is a very natural tendency—win-lose voting is not as natural as joining together to co-create.

We had to go through win-lose democracy so that each individual could feel, *I am significant*.

We have come to the end of our ability to be significant as individuals winning or losing alone. In sponsoring the evolution of synergistic democracy, which is the destiny of the politics of Evolutionary Love and follows the great Story of evolution as a Love Story, there is an incredible coherence.

We are adding into the synergistic democracy the evolution of our network of communication, our noosphere, our planetary nervous system. We call for it within our communities. We hold small gatherings, we call them *Syncons* for synergistic convergence. We have wheel-like gatherings in the backs of churches and in small universities—anywhere we want to connect people to co-create.

Within this domain, we are now seeing the development of the next stage of democracy, a politics of love. We are going to be calling on the genius of the noosphere and all the young tech guys. And finally, we are going to be calling on the Office for the Future, which holds the Wheel of Co-creation within it and which carries us through, right to the United Nations of this world.

THE DEMOCRATIZATION OF ENLIGHTENMENT: EVERY UNIQUE SELF IS NEEDED BY ALL-THAT-IS

Synergistic democracy, social synergy, a Wheel of Co-Creation. We call this wheel, or what emerges from this wheel: Unique Self Symphony. We call this Wheel 2.0.

In Wheel 1.0, we have the leading innovators in their field. We connect the leading co-creators and innovators of what is working worldwide. We connect them, and that is the first wheel, and that is the elite, which is the leading edge.

But then there is a second wheel that we developed together. We realized that the leading edge is wherever you are.

We have realized that every Unique Self is, by definition, a leading edge with a particular gift to give, a poem to write, a song to sing, and a life to live that is needed by All-That-Is.

Because, once we get Chaos Theory, Complexity Theory, and Systems Theory, we get that it is not about elites.

- It's about the democratization of genius.
- It's about the democratization of superpowers.
- It's about what we like to call the democratization of greatness.
- It's about the democratization of enlightenment.

We say that in Wheel 2.0, you are the leading edge in precisely the right Story, at the right place, at the right time, with the specific and unique gifts to be given, that can be given only by you.

YOU'VE GOT TO TAKE A UNIQUE STAND

The transition happens when we awaken as a Unique Self.

We sat yesterday with John Hanley. John Hanley and Werner Erhard are really the fathers of the human potential movement. John Hanley started what was called Life Spring, a huge kind of Life Spring movement all over the world, all over the country. What he is really about is taking a stand.

He comes from a place that says something like, *Life is empty and meaningless, and the fact that life is empty and meaningless is empty and meaningless. So, therefore, take a stand.*

Your life is about taking a stand. It's so beautiful: it is the stand that you take.

That is half the story. He got exactly half the story. Meaning, **all the narratives we are telling, all the stories we are telling about our wounding, all the stories we are telling about our hurt, they're all true, and they're empty and meaningless**.

Let it all go. Deconstruct all the contractions of your separate self, and in that emptiness, take a stand. That's step one.

Step two is: You've got to take a *unique* stand. It's a stand that no one else but you can take.

For instance, the reason I (Marc Gafni) can be in devotion to my beloved whole mate, Barbara Marx Hubbard, is because I'm not supposed to be Barbara Marx Hubbard. It's not my job; it's not my Story. Therefore, I can delight in utter ecstasy and devotion as Reality is having a Barbara Marx Hubbard experience.

And, Barbara Marx Hubbard is not supposed to be Marc Gafni. It just wouldn't work. So, Barbara can say, *Oh, my God, we have these twin evolutionary impulses,* but we don't fuse, we join in union.

We are whole mates looking together at the future, at a shared vision, and that's where the Eros is, and we begin to say, *Oh, my God, I am not willing to be written in the book of life without you. I am not willing to go without you. I cannot do it myself.*

We come together in Unique Self Symphony.

That which unites us is so much greater than that which divides us. We live in one world. There is one love in one world.

> *We are all part of that one love; we are unique expressions of that one love, and we are here to take a stand. We are going to take a unique stand.*

We take that stand for that which is our unique gift, but we take it, not individually, not by ourselves, and not because we were at a foreign meeting and said, *Okay I'm going to take my stand.* We take it as part of the Unique Self Symphony, as our contribution to synergistic democracy. Then we have heaven on Earth.

We have heaven on Earth, oh, my god, and that is just the beginning.

MOVING BEYOND ORDINARY LOVE TO OUTRAGEOUS LOVE

We are going to pray for love. We are going to pray for love together, for what love is. We all want to know what love is.

We want to know what love is! We want to move beyond ordinary love, and we want to feel Evolutionary Love. We want to move beyond ordinary love, which is a strategy of the ego. We want to feel Outrageous Love as we live in a world of outrageous pain, and the only response to outrageous pain is Outrageous Love. We live in a world of outrageous beauty, and the only response to outrageous beauty is Outrageous Love.

I Want To Know What Love Is. This is also a chant that made its way into culture, and everyone thought it was this sweet, lovely, little moment that was purely personal.

But actually, it is the cry of evolution itself. It is the cry that says,

I want to know what love is.

I want to know what it means to awaken as an Outrageous Lover.

What it means to be an Evolutionary Lover.

I want you to show me.

I want to feel what love is.

I know you can show me.

That's the prayer, so let's hold it in this second, and let's open ourselves up to that space, which is Evolutionary Love. And, here it comes, take it away.

I Wanna Know What Love Is - Foreigner[6]

♪ I've gotta take a little time,

a little time to think things over.

I better read between the lines,

in case I need it when I'm older.

(Whoa, ooh-ooh, ooh-ooh) ♪

♪ And this mountain, I must climb

feels like the world upon my shoulders,

and through the clouds, I see love shine

it keeps me warm as life grows colder. ♪ ♪

[Pre-Chorus]

♪ In my life, there's been heartache and pain.

I don't know if I can face it again.

Can't stop now, I've travelled so far

to change this lonely life ♪ ♪

[Chorus]

♪ ♪ I wanna know what love is

---

6 Foreigner, *I Wanna Know What Love Is*, recorded November 1984, on *Agent Provocateur*, Atlantic Records, vinyl LP.

I want you to show me

I wanna feel what love is

I know you can show me

Oh, oh-oh, oh (ooh) ♪

♪ I'm gonna take a little time,

a little time to look around me.

I've got nowhere left to hide,

it looks like love has finally found me. ♪ ♪

[Pre-Chorus]

[Chorus]

[Outro]

♪ (And I wanna feel) I wanna feel what love is

(And I know) I know you can show me

Let's talk about love ♪ ♪

♪ ♪ (I wanna know what love is) The love that you feel inside

(I want you to show me) And I'm feelin' so much love

(I wanna feel what love is) No, you just cannot hide

(I know you can show me) Yeah ♪ ♪

♪ I wanna know what love is (Let's talk about love)

I want you to show me, I wanna feel

(I wanna feel what love is) And I know, and I know

I know you can show me (Yeah) ♪

♪ (I wanna know what love is) (I wanna know)

(I want you to show me) I wanna know, I wanna know, wanna know

(I wanna feel what love is) (I wanna feel)

(I know you can show me) ♪ ♪

Everywhere, we are feeling the deep yearning in the human heart for more love; it goes so deep into the heart. This is the yearning that when we can express it with each other in a field of synergy, it gives the possibility for the God-self to emerge the whole way.

In other words, we say the joining of genius creates the new world, the new humans.

The joining of genius creates the opportunity for God to express more fully through the joining of those in love.

YOUR UNIQUE RISK IS WHAT MAKES YOU ALIVE

Evolutionary Church is not Barbara Marx Hubbard, and it's not Marc Gafni.

Evolutionary Church is this *we-space*.

Evolutionary Church knows that the next Buddha is also a sangha.

Evolutionary Church knows that we are a band of Evolutionary Lovers.

Evolutionary Church knows that we are willing to take our Unique Risk.

And, Barbara, we've come together, you and I, to take a unique risk and—at the very edge of evolution—to grow newer, to stand for integrity, to stand for love, and to open our hearts again and again and again.

What we are inviting everyone to, and you are inviting us to, and we inspire each other, is to be your Unique Self—to actually be a Unique Self—and to take your unique risk.

Your unique risk isn't reckless, fearless, or easy. Your unique risk is what makes you alive.

I am going to tell you a little secret. Everyone's going to tell you not to do it, but there is a unique risk that is yours to take, where you stretch beyond your comfort zone and beyond being comfortably numb.

- For some people, it might be adopting a child.
- For another person, it might be taking a stand in public culture.
- For a third person, it might be giving up being right in your argument with your spouse. Even though we know you are right, but you are just going to give up being right and open your heart just because.
- For someone else, it might be to write the book that you've always wanted to write. For someone else, it might be not to write the next book.

Whatever it is, there is a place where you can wake up and be an Outrageous Lover. And you can give a gift of Outrageous Love that all of Reality needs, all of Reality yearns for, and when you wake up to your unique risk, you realize, oh my god, your deed is the evolutionary God's need.

Your deed is God's need.

We are delighted, and we are ecstatic, and the word is good, and we feel Evolutionary Love moving through us, and we feel the deep yearning of evolution. Allurement all the way up and all the way down—living, alive, and awake in us—yearns to create heaven on Earth.

Evolutionary Love yearns to invite Donald Trump to be—as our president—his highest and best self. We invite him, and we give him our radical love.

And we serve the greater good: we serve synergistic democracy.

Let us proclaim freedom throughout the land. And the word is good and all obstacles are melted away. And remember, there's nothing more whole than a broken heart.

The cosmic and the evolutionary merge with the intimate and the personal because they are one.

We bow to and praise the Evolutionary God.

CHAPTER THREE

RESTORING PUBLIC CULTURE AND THE INTEGRITY OF DIGITAL INTIMACY

Episode 33 — June 10, 2017

WE ARE INALIENABLY EQUAL AND INALIENABLY UNIQUE

In thinking about resonance in relationship to democracy, even in relationship to the evolution of democracy, what does it mean for us on the deepest spiritual aspect?

I have been thinking of the phrase: *We hold these truths to be self-evident that all people are created equal endowed by our Creator with the inalienable right to life, liberty, and the pursuit of happiness.* I realized we are endowed by the inalienable right. It started out with the right to know we are all equal in the eyes of God.

In our Church we declare we hold these truths to be self-evident. Each of us is given the inalienable right from the highest divine process of creation to realize that we are each unique.

We are not only *equal in the eyes of God.* Get in touch now with your *uniqueness in the eyes of God,* with

41

the magnificence of each individual, with the inalienable right and responsibility to express our uniqueness, to express our creativity, for the evolution of the self and the world.

We are focusing on where democracy is failing us through lack of truth, falsehood, falsehood through misuse of internet, cyberattacks of all kinds of false truth.

How can we as members of the first Evolutionary Church on earth set a new purpose for the evolution of the inalienable rights of every human being? As the United States once did with that one sentence and changed the world: *All people, all men are created equal.*

- All people are born creative.
- All people are born unique.

Each of us is endowed by our Creator with the inalienable right and response-ability (able to respond) through the expression of the divine process of creativity given to each of us.

WE PARTICIPATE IN THE EVOLUTION OF LOVE

We bring it all. We bring our tears, our joy, our frustration, our ecstasy— we bring everything. Barbara just spoke so beautifully about this phrase, which is so essential to our consciousness and to our republic and to our democracy: inalienable rights!

What is the unique message needing and wanting to happen in this period of time? Here in church, we view our mission, our delight, our joy because we *are* in joy, we *are* in delight to bring it down. We want to *bring it down.* We want to play together. We are playing together.

We are just at the beginning of the beginnings. We are in Bethlehem together, and there is always opposition. There is always complexity. We are seeking the support, like every liberation movement did in Bethlehem, to enact a new revolution of consciousness, to enact the next stage in the evolution of love. We have one great declaration: We are willing to step up and play a larger game.

We are willing to participate in the evolution of love.

To participate in the evolution of love we need to go back to the great truths of our republic. The inalienable rights, which began with all men, and ultimately all women. It took a while to get that written in, all men and all women got written in, but then it went beyond that—it is not just created equal. All men and all women, all human beings, *are creative*. It is not just that all human beings are creative. **It is that the creativity of every human being is intrinsically needed by All-That-Is.**

Let's go to the next sentence, emergent out of the resonance, as we set the tone for prayer.

All men and women are equal. All men and women are creative. All men and women are creative and their creativity is needed by All-That-Is. It is irreplaceable!

GOD IS THE INFINITY OF INTIMACY WHO NEEDS OUR GIFTS

We are about to head into prayer. *Who are we saying this for?* Is it to give people information? No. It is to invoke. It is *invocation* not information. We are invoking a new truth. What is the new truth we are invoking? The new truth we are invoking is evolutionary prayer.

God is not Santa Claus. God is not even the scientist's Stuart Kauffman's[7] *incessant, ceaseless creativity of cosmos.*

---

7   Stuart Kauffman is an American theoretical biologist and complex systems researcher known for his work in evolutionary biology, self-organization, and the origin of life. He has made significant contributions to understanding how biological complexity arises through natural processes.

God is the incessant, ceaseless creativity of Cosmos that lives in us, as us and through us and that is beyond us, that knows our name, in whom we can rest.

Rumi doesn't fall into himself; Rumi falls into the arms of God! We are held by God who is not only the Infinity of Power that expresses itself as us; God is the Infinity of Intimacy that holds us, in whom we can rest and who loves us madly. And here is the big sentence, holy dear friends, beloveds, brothers and sisters, oh my god:

God is the Infinity of Intimacy who needs us, who needs our intimate gifts.

Prayer affirms two things:

- Prayer affirms the dignity of our personal needs, so we ask for everything.
- Prayer also affirms the dignity of the Divine need who needs our unique creativity and who cannot complete the process of creation without us because we live in a co-creative, unfinished universe that awaits our gifts.

When we pray, we cannot bypass our personal needs—nothing split off; there is no broken *Hallelujah* that we can split off. There is nothing that can be ignored. We need to have our personal needs filled, exploding ecstatically in joy.

We bring everything and we put it on the altar of the Mother, the infinite, nurturing power of Divinity that awakens both as us, beyond us, and holds us.

We go now to our hymn to offer our holy and broken *Hallelujah,* then we turn to the infinite Divinity who is the Infinity of Power and the Infinity of Intimacy, who is also us at the same moment—the paradox of Rumi. We offer prayers asking for what we need, what we really need.

From there we are going to step into the message of our inalienable greatness, not just for ourselves. We are not just doing *church-tainment;* we are not just doing *wisdo-tainment.* We are going to do it for the sake of the evolution of love. Not just for the thousands of us who are gathered this morning but for the millions and millions who want to gather together under this banner of the planetary mission of the evolution of love.

And with our hymn we go into the holy and broken *Hallelujah*:

I pray for clear direction, the evolutionary impulse chooses to move through me, and courage to follow.

It is all *Hallelujah.*

Do not be a spectator like the Greeks saying *I am going to watch other people pray, not me.*

I pray to find the home that supports my evolutionary family's evolution. I pray for the courage to be myself.

Tell us exactly what you want. Clarity of new direction. This is the time to go personal. The holy and the broken *Hallelujah* is not abstract, it is not meta, but it is specific, and it is real, and this is the moment to get real. What do I really need? Make it specific. Make it real.

I pray for America to find her soul.

I pray for the courage to sing my eternal heart song of love to the world

I pray for understanding the source of my digestive distress.

Yes. What do you want. Tell us what you specifically you. We love you madly. What do you want? Press *your* lips on *God's* lips. No bypass. Friends, pray for the world, but do not bypass yourself. You can't go world centric if you bypass personal need. When you bypass your own personal needs, the next step is to bypass someone else's.

Love your neighbor as yourself. What we are modeling? It is not just us, we are bringing prayer back.

Let's not turn, *I am God*, into narcissism. I am God and God is beyond me and holds me. It is not just, *I am God*, it is the Divine that lives beyond me. It is the Divine that manifested mitosis and meiosis before there was a neocortex.

EVOLVING DEMOCRACY AS THE EVOLUTION OF PUBLIC CULTURE

The word is good, yes. It is coming through me, it is flowing through me about democracy and the lack of truth in our culture.

I am activating inside myself to be able to accept within myself, ourselves, all of us, the inalienable right not only to be equal but to be unique, to be evolutionary unique.

- It may well be that the reason democracy is faltering right now—facing this existential crisis to life on Earth—is in order to drive us forward as human beings.
- It may well be that the promise that our founding fathers were able to offer was for that phase of evolution.

In order for it to be realized and fulfilled, in you and me, we need the whole philosophy that we are coming forth from: **Every person is born unique. Every person is born needed.** And the need that each of us has is to be creative and to give that gift to the whole in such a way that we can see the vision of the awakening world through us.

Marc is bringing in these tremendous points on the attack on democracy and the need to evolve democracy, and I would like to add the evolution of the passion for what it means to evolve democracy. Because I think we have had enough of it—in American society of *the life, liberty, and the pursuit of happiness*, to recognize that there is something more needed to have life, liberty and the pursuit of happiness, for real.

Yes, we are blessed beyond most cultures on the face of this Earth to have it. But **life, liberty and the pursuit of happiness requires—now—something more from us, which is attunement to the inner impulse of creativity.**

When we become unique, we also become an evolutionary expression of uniqueness. We also become a new vocation that holds us. Every prayer that each of us is saying, in one way or another, is so that that uniqueness can be fulfilled in expression of our greatness, such that it is given, through us, to the world.

So, let's, in this moment celebrate democracy as the liberation of the evolutionary uniqueness of the human being on planet Earth. Let's declare that what we have called our goal—the planetary awakening through a Unique Self Symphony—is what we are doing when we are able to express that unique vocation, the whole way. Particularly when we can place it on the internet, which will allow the nervous system of the planetary body to begin to report as a nervous system of the whole who we are. In order to understand the importance of the actual source code of our culture here in the way that our smear campaigns work, the way in which democracy is being attacked by the lack of truth in our media, by the ability to say whatever we wish to say to destroy each other.

We cannot take the next step of democracy if that is what we allow.

I am beginning to see the very great importance of what Marc and I are particularly working on, which is public culture. **The evolution of public culture is not only restoring what we may have lost, but I think it is bringing in what we have not yet ever fully had,** which is the ability to express this uniqueness not only personally, not only in small groups, but in the planetary nervous system. I have seen this ever since I read Teilhard de Chardin being the next stage of human evolution.

I think we could see that what we are expressing in the Evolutionary Church—it would be interesting to think of it this way—**We are on the internet now, we are in the noosphere.**

We are communicating the words of the planetary awakening. What is needed in order for us to be able to do this with the truth and the clarity that we may have lost, and with the way it is being misused?

- What are the litmus tests for discerning the truth?
- What are the confirmation biases that can destroy us?

As we learn this, what is its purpose for us in Evolutionary Church? It is to unlock the genius of our communication, of our voice. This is the noosphere.

Evolutionary Church is the first to consciously activate the noosphere with the unique expressions for our greatness of each of us in the awakening of ourselves and the planetary awakening in love. I declare to the universe now to notice: *Universe, I want you to notice there are a few people who know what you are asking for.*

Ask and it is given. Knock and doors shall open. God has been asking for us to establish and declare our greatness and uniqueness in the noosphere, on the internet, which is our planetary nervous system, and invite millions of people to do the same.

What if Evolutionary Church is announcing the birth of the next stage of the noosphere? It is inviting all its members, starting with us, exactly us, when we confess our greatness. We are confessing it into the noosphere, and we are knowing it is our contribution to a planetary awakening because the universe forgets nothing, as Buckminster Fuller said, the universe remembers everything.

We are going to lay out the actual structures that have to be evolved in order for us to have truth in our nervous system accurately, to communicate where we are going with our practice in this church. We are going to practice in this church by our declarations and prayers of greatness. We are going to practice by every word that we say to each other, that we are consciously speaking, like the very early Christians who believed in the second coming of Christ.

The very early Christians could do anything because they believed that. We believe in the planetary awakening of humanity. We believe that absolutely everything we say and put on our internet which is our nervous system of the planet. **Not only are we going to be defending it from being corrupted, but we are going to liberate it to tell the truth of who we are as unique beings.**

I am very deeply excited about that as a purpose for every word that we say in this church. As the early church knew that they were there for an imminent possibility in the life of the church, imminent, any minute it could happen; it is the second coming of Christ in that particular religion.

How imminent is the planetary awakening for us? How imminent? Well, since the existential crisis is rapidly accelerating toward possible planetary extinction, the extinction of our species, the second shock of existence. I am adding to that: the first shock of amazement. *Hallelujah!* Radical amazement!

We are shocked by radical amazement that our input into the thinking layer of earth is shifting the intelligent system of the noosphere, not just privately, not just at home, not just in our own journals. As we clarify where we are corrupting it at the very same time, we are activating how we are going to dare to give our greatness. I have a lot of trouble giving my greatness, except to very few people because it is too great. It is too great to say what I really think, but I will say it right now here in church: I believe my greatness is to have a memory of the planetary awakening, almost a memory of the future that is encoded in me. As I get ever closer to it being a realizable goal, I become ever more awakened to this greatness. My deep desire is to be in a global association with others who know that their own uniqueness is part of that awakening. I believe we have this in this church.

This may be the first church that consciously gathered its folks, its people, to awaken the nervous system of humanity. Our prayers really are that for all of us. I am thrilled to actually think this is true.

Another thing about greatness: it comes true when you declare it.

- ◆ Let's hold this vision of our greatness gently.
- ◆ Let's hold this vision of our unique, gorgeous, creative contribution in the public realm.
- ◆ Let's hold this vision of this church, which is to evolve public culture.

EVOLUTION OF CULTURE IN THE SIXTIES: A VISION THAT DID NOT WORK

I want to go back to a vision of the evolution of public culture. I want to evoke it for three minutes by listening to that song "Age of Aquarius". It is a vision that exploded—and then didn't work. And then we are going to pick that vision up and resurrect it.

A song, you remember, from a long time ago: "The 5ᵗʰ Dimension Age of Aquarius", 1969. What was that about? What was that about? That was about evoking a moment in public culture.

> Love will drive the stars when the moon shines in the seventh house. Peace will guide the planet.

That was about a Unique Self Symphony! But they did not know what it was about. There was no Dharma, there was no articulation. *Let the sunshine in*: yes, but how is the sun going to shine in? How is it going to get in? It was this evocation of possibility without Dharma, without memetic structural way to enact the vision. It was without a sense of what an irreducible Unique Self meant. It was without a sense what it means to move from digital *abuse* to digital *intimacy*. **There was an explosion of love but there was no framework for our freedoms. There were no principles and structures that could actually guide a self-organizing universe.**

It was a moment in which all the old structures were undone as they needed to be undone, but the future vision was not articulated.

EVOLUTION OF PUBLIC CULTURE

What do we want to do? What are we here to do? What we are gathered here to do together is to "let love drive the stars." Dante wrote about the love that moves the sun and other stars. But what kind of love is it? It is not ordinary love. We are making distinctions here. It is Outrageous Love. Ordinary love is a strategy of the ego. **Outrageous Love is the love that moves the sun and other stars.** How do we get to it? How do we let the sunshine in? We do it by enacting a public culture. When the day is sunny and it is gorgeous outside, it is not a private moment, it is not a personal transformation moment. So, you walk into the public space and the sun is shining, you feel good, and it is awake, and it is alive! It is about public culture, my friends. We have abandoned our public culture.

Whether you are in favor of Donald Trump or against Donald Trump, is not the point. There are lots of people in this country, who are in favor of Donald Trump, they voted for him, so do not mock them. Mocking them is what caused this election to go the way it did.

The problem is not about opposition to Donald Trump's policies; the problem is he is not creating a public culture.

Leadership has to create public culture.

What is public culture about? What did we die for on the shores of Iwo Jima?[8] What did millions and millions of boys die for in Normandy and on beaches around Europe? What are American troops about, around the world today? They are about protecting democracy. Is someone talking about American troops protecting democracy considered a right wing, fascist thing to say. I do not think so. I pledge allegiance to the flag of the United States of America. I am a patriot because America stands for democracy.

---

8 Many soldiers died on the shores of Iwo Jima during the Battle of Iwo Jima (February 19 – March 26, 1945). The battle was one of the bloodiest in the Pacific Theater of World War II, with heavy casualties on both sides.

What is democracy? **Democracy is: the human being is being innocent until proven guilty.**

Democracy is that we don't live in a take-down culture where we try and figure out how to launch viral attacks on the web that bypass the mechanisms of fact checking, of evidence.

What is a public culture? A public culture is: *we are against the Salem witch trials* (in which people weaponized their personal story and accused a person of being a witch). The new form of being a witch is being accused of being a sociopath, and we bring our personal stories to prove it. But we *bypass* the mechanisms where proof would need to be offered. We weaponize personal story. We say that facts no longer matter; our feelings trump what is actually true.

President Barack Obama said in his closing speech to the United States put in two critical lines: *If facts stopped being the baseline of our culture, then our culture is destroyed.* Those aren't his exact words, but that is basically what he said. It is unbelievable. It is not just enough to say *someone is not conscious.*

What does consciousness mean?

- ◆ It means that facts matter.
- ◆ It means that fake news is not okay.
- ◆ It means that hiding our drive for power, under a kind of victim advocacy, does not work.

We do have to advocate for every victim. The way we do that is to affirm the rights of every individual. We protect anyone who has been abused, and we do not become abusers ourselves. Name rape, on the internet, is a form of abuse. False complaints are a form of abuse.

Using the internet as a forum—that wonderful Ted talk by Wael Ghonim,[9] who was one of the people who launched the Arab Spring. He has written

---

9 Wael Ghonim, an Egyptian activist who played a key role in the Arab Spring through his use of social media. In 2011, reflecting on the power of the internet in societal liberation,

about this in a number of articles he said, *when we launched the Arab Spring, this big uprising of hope in the Arab world, we thought as long as we have the internet, we could liberate reality.*

And now, five years later, after the uprising got utterly destroyed *on* the internet, he realized that *we don't need to liberate reality, we need to liberate the internet itself.*

We need to restore public culture, the integrity of digital intimacy.

We need to talk to each other, face to face. We need to be about truth and reconciliation, not about demonization. Does everyone get that? We cannot use Facebook comments as a way to release invective, bitterness, vile and venom. We have to actually love each other open on the internet. We need to adduce facts before we make claims.

FOUR LITMUS TESTS FOR DIGITAL INTEGRITY

How do we make the distinction between what is a legitimate uprising on the internet, standing for truth, justice, and integrity and a beautiful use of the internet to bypass structures of oppression to get to liberation which is what the internet should be about—and the internet being used for take-down culture with vile motives? Most of humanity exists dressed up under the fig leaf of noble motives.

Ghonim remarked, "If you want to liberate a society, all you need is the Internet." However, Ghonim's perspective evolved over time. He later acknowledged that while the internet can be a tool for liberation, it also has the potential to deepen societal divisions if not used responsibly. This evolution in his viewpoint underscores the complex role of digital platforms in modern activism and societal change.

For a deeper insight into Ghonim's reflections on social media's impact post-Arab Spring, you might find his talk *Wael Ghonim: Activism, a Balance Between Reason and Emotions* insightful.

How do we tell the difference? How do we tell the difference, friends? Let's feel into it. Let's make this real. Here are four different really simple litmus tests.

The first litmus test is: Is there a forum for checking facts?

Do facts matter? In an internet discourse if someone offers a new fact, does it get shut down, or do people say *thanks for the new fact?*

The second litmus test is: Do we check facts before we take action?

When there is an attack, do people take action before they check facts or afterwards? In other words, do they check facts, *before* we attack a person's character? *Before* we go to destroy an institution? *Before* we go to take something down?

Are we operating based on confirmation bias or have we checked facts and evidence?

The third litmus test: Am I willing to change my opinion?

I have to check inside.

When I receive new information do I change my opinion?

Am I willing to check out new information?

Do I read articles on both sides of the equation?

You are not going to like this, but I am going to make it clear: even on an issue like immigration, or building a wall . . . have I checked the facts on both sides? Trump's problem is that he is not providing leadership. Really smart people, like Charles Krauthammer[10] for example, have made a strong argument for building a wall.

---

10   Charles Krauthammer (1950–2018) was an American political columnist, physician, and commentator. He was known for his conservative viewpoints and intellectual rigor, contributing to The Washington Post, Fox News, and various other media outlets. He won the Pulitzer Prize for Commentary in 1987 for his work at The Washington Post.

Now, I am completely against building a wall, but I am not going to say that the people who are for it are idiots and attack them as being vicious, horrible, disgusting human beings, which is precisely what is happening today on the web.

I am going to listen to intelligent arguments on both sides, be moved by new evidence, engage in discourse based on facts and *then* champion my position.

I am dead set against building a wall, but I am not going to vilify and demonize people who have a different opinion and call them the worst of names because I am on the internet. This is what public culture has become.

Public culture has become name-calling and demonization.

The fourth litmus test: Are we demonizing or symphonizing?

This is the fourth litmus test. When you start demonizing and dehumanizing you know this is not *kosher*. It is not actually truth. We have to stand, we cannot just declare. We have to create mechanisms to make this happen, and to make this *real* in the most dramatic way. In order to participate in the evolution of love we need to create a public culture.

We have to start that by symphonizing which means we are listening to each other's instrument. From the discordant notes of different instruments, a symphony emerges.

We have lost the symphony.

We have to reclaim music.

We have to reclaim the different instruments.

We have to stop demonization.

We have to check facts.

We have to be open to change our opinion.

When was the last time we significantly changed our opinion? We *shifted?* When was the last time we shifted based on an internet conversation? We have to step into this space and evolve public culture.

We have to find a reason to dance.

The way we dance is we dance between different opinions, we hear their integrity, and we come to a higher synergistic truth—today, on the internet we just go to feeds that feed our position, and we engage in confirmation bias. We have lost that sense that *the other* is uniquely gorgeous. We have lost the sense of checking facts.

You are listening to me and you are thinking: Checking facts, that is not sexy, that is not hot. That does not evoke me. That does not move me.

My dear friends, what do you think the Age of Aquarius was about? We are talking about Evolutionary Unique Self and Unique Self Symphony.

We are talking about a memory of the future.

I am encoded with a memory of Unique Self Symphony.

I am encoded with a memory of the future.

I am encoded with a memory of the planetary mission. That is the way I was born.

It is why Barbara and I symphonize so well together.

If I just declare that and I bypass the structures of symphonizing, I bypass the structures of avoiding demonization, I bypass the structures of fact checking then I am just full of my own hot air. I am just filled with hot air, filled with my own declaration and not actually willing to be an evolutionary, to do the work of listening deeply, checking facts.

There is nothing hotter, nothing sexier, more erotic, more holy, more good, more true than checking facts and changing my opinion.

When you check facts you get new information, you change your view, and you are willing to bracket your ego. When I am willing to bracket my ego in the service of the larger truth then all those boys who died on the beaches of Normandy did not die in vain.

We have to get back to basics. The basics is that every human being is uniquely gorgeous. Because every human being is uniquely gorgeous and uniquely creative then every human being's rights matter uniquely.

To save one person is to save the whole world. We do not bypass justice. Justice—Lady Justice—is the Goddess. Every human story matters. Black lives matter. White lives matter. Chinese lives matter.

No one is extra and no one is sacrificed for the sake of the larger cause. No one is outside of the circle, and no one is left behind. We are going to do this together. Fact checking is not just important; fact checking is the Goddess.

Fact checking *is* the Unique Self Symphony. Fact checking *is* the evolution of love.

How could anyone ever tell you that you are anything less than beautiful?

CHAPTER FOUR

EVOLUTION OF PUBLIC CULTURE AND DIGITAL INTEGRITY

Episode 34 — June 17, 2017

THE EVOLUTION OF DEMOCRACY IS AN INDICATION OF HUMANS' RELATIONSHIP TO THE DIVINE

I would like to make an outrageous statement, based on Outrageous Love or Evolutionary Love, that I believe we could hold in this resonant field: **The evolution of democracy is an indication of the evolution of humans' relationship to the Divine.**

We started with *all men are created equal* and that changed the entire world. That one sentence. Wherever anyone was, in any part of the world, something new happened inside them, and they are the ones that had the courage to cross the seas and come to a new place then called America.

Through the huge success of America financially and by the numbers of people that have come here and created this fantastic new nation, we have hit a new impasse in democracy because the individual, as we are saying, is not only born unique, but born *creative*.

This means we are changing our relationship to the Divine, that **the Creator is designed through all these years of evolution to create co-creators.**

That means we were created in the image of God, to become awake as and in the image of the Creator or Creative Intelligence.

We are becoming co-creators with That. The evolution of democracy is so awesome in that it is calling every one of us to go within to that source of creativity and uniqueness and say *yes,*

Being called by That to an expression of unique creativity, vocation, love, action, is, in fact, the response to the existential risk and crisis we are facing.

The only way we are going to really respond to existential risk is through existential evolution of as many people as possible by evolving their own innate creativity and uniqueness.

I declare that the existential crisis, which is on a global scale, is activating existential expression, and that the United States of America is still the place where the most of this freedom can come forth more easily because we are cultivated toward that.

So, let's say a prayer of thanksgiving that we are created in the image of a Creative Intention, a universal process.

We are now radically evolving public culture to be able to respond to the existential risk with the existential creativity and evolutionary love that is in our souls.

THE THIRTY-SIX MEN AND WOMEN: THE LAST OF THE JUST

Now, *thirty-six,* you know, beloveds . . . remember Andrew Schwartzbart's great book, *The Last of the Just,* which is about thirty-six just men, you know, the thirty-six men and women who are the secret carriers, the wisdom keepers.[11] In Sufism, [12] they call it 'the pole', or the *axis mundi*, the people connecting heaven and earth.

It is thirty-six people who are the leading edge. It is the thirty-six people who are the band of Outrageous Lovers. But it is the thirty-six people who say that we are not just involved in the small self of our lives as important and beautiful as they are.

We are bringing the small self of our lives. We are bringing our holy and our broken *Hallelujah*.

We are evolving love itself by the way we live our lives.

We understand that every time we reach inside, and every time we expand, and every time we honor human dignity, and every time we smile when

---

11 In Hebrew mythology and Jewish mysticism, the Thirty-six Just Men are known as the *lamed vav tzadikim*—often simply called the *lamed-vavniks*. The *lamed vav tzadikim* are Thirty-six righteous individuals whose merit sustains the world. The belief is that, at any given time, there are exactly Thirty-six hidden *tzadikim* (righteous people) in the world. These individuals are unknown, even to themselves, and they live humble, modest lives. They do not seek recognition or reward; their righteousness is pure and selfless.

12 The **Abdāl** (or *Abdal*), sometimes also known as **Awtād, Nuqabā**, and **Qutb**—terms referring to a hidden hierarchy of spiritually enlightened saints who uphold the world. **Abdāl** (The Substitutes or Replacements): they are righteous individuals who maintain the spiritual balance of the world. Their number varies in different traditions, but 40 is a common number in many Sufi systems (similar to the 36 in Jewish lore). When one dies, another is immediately appointed by divine decree, hence the term *substitutes*. **Qutb** (The Pole or Axis Mundi): the supreme saint or spiritual leader of the time—the axis around which the spiritual world revolves. The Qutb is always alive, hidden from the public, and acts as the channel for divine grace (*baraka*) to flow into the world. 3. Awtād, **Nuqabā**, and **Nujabā**—various ranks in the spiritual hierarchy, according to some Sufi cosmologies: **Awtād** (Pillars)–usually four in number; Nuqabā (Leaders)–twelve in number; Nujabā (Nobles)–eight in number. Together with the **Abdāl** and **Qutb**, they form a spiritual hierarchy that maintains cosmic order.

Element	Jewish Mysticism (Kabbalah)	Sufism
Hidden righteous	36 Lamed-Vav Tzadikim	40 Abdāl
Spiritual function	Sustain the world	Sustain the world
Often unknown to self	Yes	Yes
Hierarchical structure	Implicit (no ranks)	Yes (Qutb, Abdāl, etc.)
Basis in mysticism	Kabbalah, Talmudic legend	Islamic mysticism (Tasawwuf)

we could have raged, and every time we are careful, and we feel the whole system when we could have gotten lost in our own narcissism. Every time we actually open up *in the actual reality of our lives,* not what we are declaring publicly, but what we are *living*—our sacred autobiographies, our actual lived lives **are the evolution of love**.

That is the great tradition in Hebrew mysticism of thirty-six. We are in the thirty-sixth week of Evolutionary Church. So, I would like to make a declaration. I would like to declare something.

We have got a declaration of independence. Let's have our declaration of inter-dependence.

Let's declare our interdependence, that we as creative human beings are interconnected and interdependent, and that if we in Evolutionary Church can say, *it is our turn*. It is our turn. **It is our turn to be that band of thirty-six**, although it might be thirty-six hundred, or thirty-six thousand, there's already 6,000 people involved in Evolutionary Church.

So, we are thirty-six hundred plus, but let's make it 360 thousand, or 3.6 million or 36 million . . . then 360 million. Let's exponentialize. Let's make that band of thirty-six all of us who are the Chosen People.

And who are the Chosen People? The people *who choose*, right?

We *choose* to offer up our lives and the *details* of our lives. It is easy to offer up my life in this kind of grand declaration, but our grand declaration is *let's give up grand declarations*. Let's live in the details of our lives and say *we are the evolution of love:*

- the way we look at other people
- the way we look at ourselves
- the way we let go of our limiting beliefs
- the way we stand and give our unique voice into the noosphere

- the way we stand for the unique creativity that we have to give to the world
- and we take a unique stand for love and for justice in the world.

We say, *this is our work*. And where is our work? Right in our lives. But we always think of our work as someplace else—I should be doing this; I should be doing that.

But actually, I should *be* right where I am.

My work is exactly right here in this place, in this time.

I have the perfect set of characters to do that work, and to give that gift, and to awaken as an Outrageous Lover, incarnating the evolutionary impulse, being uniquely creative in whatever way my life allows and taking a unique risk to *expand* my possibility for creativity.

I realize nothing is extra. I realize paradise is paradox. I realize I am great, divine, and beyond imagination. I was born trailing clouds of glory—and in my life are rumors of angels.

And I realize I am mortal, and animal-like. I am filled with pettiness, contraction, and grasping and I am willing to work with all of it to transform it. The fate of my life becomes my destiny, and *my life itself becomes a sacrament.*

My life becomes a sacred text and the details of my life, the sacred autobiography of my life, is offered up to the Divine. Nothing is left out. Nothing is split off. Nothing is covered over. The declaration of my life is the letter that I am writing in my Unique Self in the cosmic scroll.

That is the resonance, and we become the band of the thirty-six. Andre Schwartzberg: *Last of the Just*—The just men and women whose lives are offered up.

So, are we willing? Are we willing and I ask myself. Are we willing to play a larger game?

We are the thirty-six. Are we willing to play a larger game? Are we willing to participate in the evolution of love? **Are we willing to make the details of our lives declaration *with no bypass*, fearlessly facing everything, avoiding nothing, and becoming Evolutionary Love ourselves in the way, in the detail, in the nuance of the way we live.**

We are the thirty-six. As the thirty-six, we affirm the dignity of our lives together. We come and we offer before God our holy. Our broken *Hallelujah*. Nothing left out.

Not someone who has seen the Light, but rather, says Leonard Cohen, not someone who has seen the light, but *there's a blaze of light in every word, in the holy and in the broken Hallelujah*. And we are excited!

And we are going to pray. Don't be a spectator to all live and existence as the Greek said, don't watch it happen but be an activist. Right? Matthew Arnold, in his essay "Culture and Anarchy"[13] said, *the difference between Hebraism and Hellenism is the Hellenists were watching, and the Hebrews were getting involved.* Quick summation of intellectual history. So, get involved, my friends and let's offer up our prayer. Prayer affirms the dignity of personal need.

Our prayer is not to Santa Claus. Right? Not to the god who is outside, who demands our obedience and punishes us for masturbation. Not that god. But to God who is the Infinity of Intimacy. God who knows our name. God who every place we fall, we fall into Her hands. God who is the infinite personal place of the cosmos.

Let's offer up and ask for everything. Let's take these prayers and lift them up to the sky for us. With your message, right, I want to lift you, says Rumi, I want to lift you like a prayer to the sky. So, take our prayers into your message and lift us to the sky, beloved Barbara.

---

13 Matthew Arnold, Culture and Anarchy, ed. J., Dover Wilson (Cambridge: Cambridge University Press, 1932)

ASK AND IT IS GIVEN, KNOCK AND DOORS ARE OPENED

I love the phrase, *Ask and it is given; knock, and doors are open.* Jesus didn't say, ask and it *will be given*, or knock and doors *will be opened*. The *ask* is itself a declaration of power, of intention, of passion. And since the Universe is responsive to request, let's ask each person right now to take a moment to experience going into the intentionality of the process of evolution.

I would like to make a meta-context for all of this, as this church is the first church to be fully an expression of evolutionary spirituality. Here is the awesome truth of the billions of years of evolution, of which we are an immediate expression. It starts in consciousness itself in the Field.

The moment the Big Bang came, consciousness became *consciousness force.* This is Aurobindo's language.[14] Consciousness force began creating everything with the most awesome supra-mental genius from the simplest entity, whether it be a quark or an electron, a proton, a cell, a multi-cell. The DNA is awesomely intelligent all the way on up to the rock of Earth.

Now, if you saw that rock and you came from some other galaxy, it didn't look very promising. What came was a little DNA that connected with other DNAs and so on, and on, through the beginning of the biosphere, the fish, the animals, the humans, and now us.

Let's take that story and get in touch with the core of the spiral being consciousness force of divine intelligence. And let's take a moment of allowing the realization that that prayer that we just gave, that intention for what each of us need, want, and express has the power of the core of the spiral of supramental genius in it. Just let that sink in for a moment.

Ask and it is given; knock and doors are opened.

---

14 Often rendered as Chit-Shakti in Sanskrit.

GOD CREATES BY OUR INTENTION WITH US AS CO-CREATORS

I am asking at the level of the intention of creation that has, in this particular moment of history, on this planet, created co-creators.

We were created in the image of God. And creators we are becoming.

Let's take that seriously as an expression of the Evolutionary Church. The new thought movement has tried to say *God is indwelling in every one of us.*

That is the large new thought movement. But they don't bring in the billions of years of evolution, nor do they bring in that we are at the next stage of evolution and that *the internal impulse of creativity in each one of us is moving us to a new dimension of expression of creativity.*

Why is that? Because our species has gained powers of gods.

Our species has, not only developed spirituality, social evolution, and democracy, but we have developed powers of gods, nanotech, biotech, quantum computing, artificial intelligence, robotics, space travel. That is just the beginning.

I am reading a book called *Homo Deus*, Human God. This author, who is not a member of the Evolutionary Church, doesn't take it spiritually. He just points out that the new species that is emerging now has three goals: immortality, bliss, and divinity. When this core of the spiral goes into our generation, becoming this new power through our increased intelligence and participation in the process of creation itself, we are at the threshold of what we used to call gods, the Greek gods, who blow up worlds, create worlds, build new bodies, destroy bodies.

We in the Evolutionary Church are accepting the process of co-creation.

The thirty-six of us actually experiencing this as a microcosm of the planetary body—the planetary body which is moving towards an evolutionary democracy in which each human being is co-evolutionary.

Through saying *yes* to the intention of creation in us, which awakens the genius, the supra-mental genius of evolution, we are declaring here and now that this church is a vehicle in which the new humanity is finding its own voice and its capacity to express itself spiritually, socially, and in democracy.

If every one of us is unique as who we are, it is no longer feasible for us to look through the eyes of confirmation bias[15], and to declare each other as this race, or that religion, or this type of sexuality, or that type of creativity, because we are all unique.

The uniqueness that we all are is coming from the source of creation, or the supra-mental power, or the core of the spiral that is bursting out into the Evolutionary Church for the first time.

That means to say the Evolutionary Church is the vehicle in which the core of the evolutionary spiral is bursting through the hearts, minds, and souls of its members who are being affirmed in their capacity as co-evolvers of their own lives, and of the lives of democracy, and the lives of the world at the time of the existential risk. This is my thesis:

The reason that nature creates terrible risks, as happened five times before in mass extinctions, is to create evolutionary drivers of such enormity that the species involved have to evolve or die. That has happened in the past.

Billions of species have gone extinct. We are the first species who is aware of this on this planet. We have been hearing that we could go extinct if we don't do *what*? Attune to the core of the spiral, which is Spirit alive in us.

I would like to make another declaration: that the Evolutionary Church of co-creation is to incarnate the impulse of evolution, leading to higher creativity, greater love, and more synergistic order. That we are exponents of the core of the spiral. We are incarnating billions of years of genius.

---

15   The tendency to interpret new information in ways that confirm one's preexisting beliefs, expectations, or stereotypes.

When we are aligned with Spirit inside us, and with one another in love for the purpose of the evolution of our culture, our world, our life—the core of the spiral is saying *yes*. This is not just a personal *yes* from each of us, great as that is. It is a collective *yes* to the next stage of evolution in the first Evolutionary Church of co-creation.

Since the Universe is responsive to request, I am declaring that it is happening through us now, that we can take what we have called for here to the most awesome scale. The Universe has awaited groups of people to do this, because without groups of people doing this the Universe cannot be itself.

With the declaration that we are a church, an Evolutionary Church of co-creation incarnating the genius of the impulse of evolution in each one of us, and uniting with and praying for, the source of power is now given. As we believe it, so it is done. Thank you.

OVERCOMING CONFIRMATION BIAS AND RECLAIMING INNOCENCE

This week, Barbara so gorgeously laid out the beautiful framework we developed together to hold the big vision, to hold the possibility. So now, let's begin to make it real.

How do we make it real in our lives? How do we actually apply it in a way where we can feel into what this means?

We are celebrating democracy and the values of democracy for which millions and millions of men died, and millions of women were widowed, and children were orphaned on the beaches of Normandy and throughout the history of democracy and particularly American history.

I want to celebrate democracy. Democracy is an evolutionary leap.

Democracy is a momentous leap in consciousness.

How do we take this notion of evolutionary consciousness and democracy and bring it together and celebrate it in a way that *changes the way we live,* so that the Evolutionary Church becomes the thirty-six? We become the incarnation of the new consciousness. We become the ones who offer up our lives, our holy and our broken *Hallelujah,* for the evolution of love. That is what we stand for. **The Evolutionary Church stands for playing this larger game, and for together participating in the evolution of love.**

Let me introduce what Barbara alluded to, this idea called *confirmation bias.* What does confirmation bias mean? It means something very deep.

First, let me give you the simple definition: Confirmation bias means that if I hear something about a businessman who is crooked, I hear a story in the press, then there is a crooked businessman. I assume that he must be guilty. Why do I assume he must be guilty? Because my meme is: I am a liberal American, I live on the west coast someplace, and I think corporations and businesses are evil, greedy, and bad. All of them. So, when I hear a story about a businessman who is accused of crooked dealing or corruption, I believe it, *even though I don't know anything about him or her, nothing about their lives.*

I haven't examined any evidence. I haven't looked at the story. I haven't looked at the unique situation. That is confirmation bias. I confirm my previous bias, which is *all businessmen are crooked.* **That idea violates the god of American democracy, the ethos of this evolutionary moment called democracy.**

It was against that confirmation bias that we died on the beaches of Normandy. Because the core evolutionary idea that lives in democracy is newness. Every moment is new, and I have to look at every moment, and I have to look at every person with fresh eyes.

- Every moment is innocent.
- Every person is innocent, never *was* before.
- Every situation is innocent unless proven guilty—and proven guilty requires proof and evidence and cross-examination.

We approach every moment innocently. We re-virginate. We become new versions ourselves.

We unfurnish our eyes. Not "Revelation"—'tis—that waits, But our unfurnished eyes—. . . My favorite poem, some of you know, from Emily Dickinson[16] "not revelation 'tis that waits, But our unfurnished eyes." When we deconstruct confirmation bias, we unfurnish our eyes, and then we are witness to the glory of revelation, which is the innocence, the beauty, the complexity of a particular situation with the particular movements of love that are happening in it.

The core evolutionary invitation is to see with fresh eyes; to see a person with fresh eyes; to see a situation with fresh eyes; and to see ourselves with fresh eyes. Because the idea of evolution is the *possibility of possibility*. That is the great evolutionary declaration.

Evolution stands for the possibility of possibility.

Evolution is a memory of the future which is the possibility of possibility.

That is the Dharma. And evolution is a memory of the future that I can access in myself by imagining the possibility of possibility and I only can do that when I open the doors that have been closed.

Confirmation bias means I have closed the doors; I haven't looked, I am not curious. **When you let confirmation bias grip your soul and let its malaise poison and shut and infect your open eyes, your fresh eyes, *then* evolution dies and closes.**

---

16 Emily Dickinson, The Poems of Emily Dickinson, ed. Thomas H. Johnson (Cambridge, MA: Belknap Press of Harvard University Press, 1955), poem no. 1234.

Evolution means, right, every moment is new. Every moment can be loved open. Evolution means that yesterday doesn't determine today: that I get to be totally new; that I can re-imagine myself; I can re-imagine my vision of reality.

- What is racism? Racism is confirmation bias. I view an entire group of people through a bias I have, *and* I view every person through that bias.
- What is anti-Semitism? Confirmation bias.
- What are our limitations, our limiting beliefs about ourselves? Our limiting beliefs about ourselves are confirmation bias about ourselves.

Does everyone get that? It is huge! When we say all men and women are created equal, well, that's okay. It is a good step. It gets rid of artificial hierarchy. But it is not true! All men and women are created with equal fundamental value. That is true!

But afterwards, we are all completely *unequal*; unequal in the sense that we are *different*, that we are *distinct*.

The second we fit ourselves into some cookie cutter mold of what should be based on the information bias about what our lives should be handed down to us from our parents or from culture and **we stop being innocent, we lose our virginity which is our fresh ability to love the moment open and let the moment love us open**, then we are gone!

The recognition and rejection of confirmation bias is an affirmation of innocence. It is an affirmation of innocence.

That is a result not of the first Big Bang. The first Big Bang is cosmological evolution. The second Big Bang is biological evolution. The third Big Bang is cultural evolution.

Cultural evolution yields levels and levels of consciousness until we finally get to democracy.

Democracy is this explosion of evolution which says we affirm the innocence of every moment and the innocence of every person.

We free ourselves from the vise-like grip of shut eyes. We *unfurnish* our eyes. We let go of confirmation bias, and we begin to *see* each other and *love* each other. Because love is not an emotion. Love is a *perception*.

LOVE IS A PERCEPTION

Love is to be able to *see* someone, right? One of the phrases that I have tried to bring back into reality is Evolutionary Love and Outrageous Love.

So, if you want to think about what Barbara and I are trying to do, we are trying to merge Conscious Evolution with Evolutionary Love. When evolution awakens, it is Conscious Evolution that awakens. It means love is awakening to itself, which means *evolution is opening its eyes* because Evolutionary Love is a *perception*.

- It means I can see you. It means my eyes aren't shut.
- It means I haven't decided who you are before we had a deep I-thou exchange. Even if we have had a thousand I-thou exchanges and I meet you this morning, I say, *good morning* and
- I am fresh and open to the new possibility of you emerging in a way that you weren't yesterday.

Wow! Can you imagine what kind of world that could be, right? I am fully ready to have President Donald Trump emerge in a new way tomorrow. I am not going to put him in a box.

It is one of the things we are doing. I want to say something which is unpopular. No one is going to like this, but I want to say it, President Trump has been a disaster in so many ways in terms of exhibiting leadership, it has been actually painful to watch. But I have to say, and as a liberal, I say this, the viciousness of the liberal attack on him has also been a horror to watch. Just an absolute horror. The mean-spiritedness of it has been a horror. So, let's open our eyes! Confirmation bias: *Trump is bad. We are going to show you that he is bad. We are going to show you, we are going to prove it to you because we have already decided.*

When you decide someone is evil, and then you go to prove it, they might actually meet your demand. Call someone a snake and they will be a snake. Call someone beautiful . . .

I said in Evolutionary Church some 20 weeks ago, Barack Obama is an Outrageous Lover; Donald Trump is an Outrageous Lover. All sorts of people positively retweeted it. Then a bunch of negative people said, *look what Gafni is saying! Donald Trump's an Outrageous Lover. He was a sexual abuser, Donald Trump. What's Gafni's trying to say?*

Really? Is that what we do? So let me say it again: Barack Obama is an Outrageous Lover. And Donald Trump wants to be an Outrageous Lover. And then Melania Trump wants to be an Outrageous Lover, right? And Michelle Obama does, and Hillary Clinton does.

Stop confirmation bias! Let Hillary be someone new and let her emerge. Let's all emerge!

Confirmation bias means we are all guilty and we can never prove our innocence, not even to ourselves, my friends. Confirmation bias is not a detail. It is not like *what are you talking about; it's not grand, it's not exciting?* —It is the most exciting thing in the world, my friends!

Love is in the details. Love is a perception.

It means I can see you for real.

It means I am not blind to you.

It means I am not occluded to you.

It means my heart is not blocked from seeing you.

When my heart blocks, I can't see you. It is only when I unguard my heart, I drop my agendas, I disrobe, that I can see you.

What we have to do in order to get this is: **we have got to be willing to go into the pain of our lives and let go of the things that stop us from being able to see.**

We have got to say, *I want to know what love is, and I am willing to go through all the pain* and actually say, *wow, this is what love is!*

Love is Evolutionary Love. Love is to unfurnish my eyes. Love is to let go of confirmation bias.

I and we can make all the declarations we want. But then, when we get out of church, and we start talking about somebody—confirmation bias. What are we doing instead?

We are not bypassing. *I want to know what love is*, and *I've got heartache and pain*, and I am going to bring it all together. I am going to let go and unfurnish my eyes. I am going to see with God's eyes. Because to be a Lover is to see with God's eyes. It is to see with God's possibility. And God *is* the evolutionary impulse.

The evolutionary impulse says that today is not yesterday.

Today is new. It never was before. Evolution is the possibility of possibility.

We affirm the innocence of every moment.

Let's build the innocence of every moment.

Let's reclaim the infinite dignity and beauty and innocence of every human being.

Let's let go of confirmation bias to ourselves.

Let's re-virginate.

Let's reclaim our own innocence.

Let's *cast out the remorse* of all the stuff that went wrong.

Our favorite poem in Evolutionary Church: *When such as I cast out remorse*[17] (final stanza)

> *When such as I cast out remorse*
>
> *So great a sweetness flows into the breast*
>
> *We must laugh and we must sing,*
>
> *We are blest by everything,*
>
> *Everything we look upon is blest.*

We can dance and we can sing. We are blessed by everything. And everything we look upon is blessed. That is the innocence of the moment.

And in that innocence, I want to invite everyone. Let's build Evolutionary Church!

RE-SOURCING THROUGH GIVING

I am thinking of, for a moment, the very earliest churches, the amazing reality of those early churches where they gathered in small groups and experienced love and the communion.

They had this expectation of what they call the Second Coming of Christ. When I was teaching with the Catholic sisters, who I love dearly, they would say to me, *Barbara, when did you become Catholic?* And I said, *I am not a Catholic. Why do you say that?* And they said, *because you have a sense of expectancy.*

The Evolutionary Church has a sense of reality in the moment and a huge expectancy which would be the Second Coming of Source in enough

---

17 William Butler Yeats, "A Dialogue of Self and Soul", *The Collected Poems of W. B. Yeats*, ed. Richard J. Finneran (New York: Scribner, 1996), 247.

people to be co-evolutionary, to evolve our democracy, to actualize the powers of *Homo deus* that we have been given by our genius, to create a new civilization, a new species even in the universe of billions of galaxies.

I am asking us to re-source this church, that means to give from your source of being that you are choosing to be and to become. *Re-source the church.* That gift resources you, and it resources everyone else who is part of this church and resources the evolution of democracy toward the planetary awakening in love. That is a new way of saying 'the evolution of love on a planetary scale'. Thank you!

CHAPTER FIVE

BEYOND THE GRIM ERA OF DEMONIZATION: THE POSSIBLE SHARED STORY OF THE 146 MILLION (75 MILLION BIDEN, 71 MILLION TRUMP)—CALLED BY THE SAME ANGELS

Episode 213 — November 8, 2020

WHAT IS THE SHARED STORY THAT BRINGS US TOGETHER?

Welcome, everyone. It's been a big weekend. I'm in the United States of American in Miami, Florida, and there was an election, as some of you might have noticed in the United States of America.

First off, congratulations to Joe Biden and to Kamala Harris on being declared the winners of the election.

And we're going to talk about the significance. Clearly from a political, spiritual, emotional, psychological, historical perspective at this moment poised between utopia and dystopia, this is a moment of enormous significance and we have to actually thread the needle,

feel the joy, feel the possibility and come together in this moment of transformation.

It's easy to get it wrong. It's easy to miss it.

So we need to tell the story today in light of shared story.

What's the shared story that brings us together?

- ◆ What's the shared story that brings together the 74 million people who voted for Joe Biden, which is the largest voter turnout for any single candidate ever?
- ◆ And what unites those people with the 70 million people who voted for Donald Trump, which is the second largest voter turnout?

As Joe Biden said in his talk last night, *it's time for the end of demonization.* That's what this is about.

Today is dedicated to those words in Joe Biden's speech, which is about reclaiming soul and about the end to demonization.

How do we do that? How do we do that both within the Democratic and Republican side in America and how do we do that around the world?

OUR INTENTION TODAY IS FOR HEALING; TO MAKE WHOLE

This is a moment of healing and healing is Eros.

Eros always means becoming whole. In our Eros formula that we've written now 12 volumes on that are going to slowly come out.

What is Eros? It's not just a word. Eros means something very specific.

> *Eros is the experience of radical aliveness seeking ever deeper intimacy and ever greater wholeness, ever greater wholes.*

So this is a moment for coming together. This is a moment of Eros. This is a moment of healing. When Kamala introduced Joe Biden, the first thing she said about him was *he's a healer*. What does a healer mean? A healer means *we've got to make it whole*. To make it whole means everybody's included, no one's excluded.

The demonization ends—but it's not that the demonization ends of *those people but not those people*.

All demonization ends.

Not that we don't take stands. We do take stands. We take fierce stands for goodness, truth, and beauty, for integrity—but we move beyond demonization. We're going to talk about what that means today.

Our intention today is healing.

Our intention today is making whole.

Our intention today is honoring not just the American nature—we're all Americans, we're all human beings around the world—but since the eyes of the world in this moment are on America, so **we're going to use this election as a microcosm** and we're going to look for *what's the shared story?*

Beloved Barbara Marx Hubbard and myself together, what we've been saying and all of us together here in *One Mountain, Many Paths* have been saying is *there's a new shared story*.

It's beyond Republican and Democrat.

It's beyond conservative and liberal.

It's a deeper shared story of humanity in which we understand that *that which unites us is much greater than that which divides us*, that we have a shared *daemon*.

FROM DEMONIZATION TO DAEMONIZATION

Daemon means destiny. We don't just have a covenant of fate: *we're stuck on planet Earth and we've kind of got to get along.*

We have a covenant of destiny.

Get the difference? It's not just a covenant of shared fate. It's a covenant of destiny, of *daemonization*.

Daemonization **means we have a shared** *daemon.* **We're called by the same angels.**

We have a shared vision.

We have a shared purpose.

We have a shared truth.

We have a shared goodness.

We have a shared beauty.

And actually it's so gorgeous, my friends.

There's a shared beauty, there's a shared story that unites almost all of the 70 million people who voted Republican and all of the 74 million people who voted Democrat. Underneath all of the divisions, there's something huge and big and beautiful that's emergent.

It hasn't yet happened.

It's bubbling near the surface.

We sense it. So we're going to look for that today. We're going to go deep and we're going to wind a tricky path, a beautiful path—but **our energy is celebration.**

I want to just say I cried yesterday and I haven't cried in an election since I was in Kennedy Airport and I watched Al Gore after the conflict with George

Bush—and there was a whole question about what actually happened in that election—and Al Gore conceded the presidency to George Bush and he said, "Democracy is bigger than any one person."

The orderly transfer of power and the beauty of that made me cry.

I watched on Friday and then last night and I watched the replays of everything that happened yesterday and I watched commentators on Fox News and writers in the *Wall Street Journal* which are on the Republican side of the American political divide.

I watched them stand for democracy and I watched Republican legislators stand for democracy, **I felt the power of democracy.**

Joe Biden won the election. And Donald Trump has complete appropriate legal recourse, as Democrats have done many times, to challenge the election in courts. As the Biden campaign people said correctly, *he should.*

That's the gorgeousness of a democracy.

And when that's over—I want to say something dramatic—I trust that Donald Trump will gracefully concede to Joe Biden and exit gracefully.

I trust that that's what's going to happen.

And I trust that underneath Democrat and Republican—this is what Joe Biden was saying last night—*there's a shared vision.*

And it's deeper than a shared vision of America; *it's a shared vision of what it means to be a human being* and that we actually know that *that which unites us is far greater than that which divides us.* So I cried yesterday.

Now, I want to say one more thing in just setting intention and I want to just say this in the beginning.

That doesn't mean that we think that there are not significant differences.

That doesn't mean that there's not enormous pain. It doesn't mean that the pain can't be transformed.

We're going to take a ride today and we're going to listen to different voices and we're going to weave together something new.

Who's ready? Are we ready to actually evolve the source code?

Who's ready to step in and go beyond the mainstream media and beyond the right-wing media and beyond the left-wing media and beyond the Twitter mobs?

Are we ready to actually be evolutionary mystics? Are we ready to be outrageous lovers? Are we ready to actually raise the resonance, take this to the next level?

That's what Joe Biden called for last night.

He called for a return of soul.

He called for an end to demonization.

You can't end demonization
unless you have daemonization.

When we don't have a shared *daemon* then we demonize, then the other becomes a demon.

So today everyone's in the circle.

Today no one's left out.

Today there are not *74 against 70*; there are 144 million people who have a shared story, who have a shared vision.

And, yes, they disagree about things that are fundamental—and some of those are worth staking everything on.

And underneath that there's a shared heart.

There's one heart and there's one love. And that's what we're going for today.

EVOLUTIONARY LOVE CODE: THAT WHICH UNITES US IS FAR GREATER THAN THAT WHICH DIVIDES US

That which unites us is far greater than that which divides us. We are united in a shared Story of Value. That does not make us perfect expressions of that value. We are all imperfect vessels for the light, holy and broken *Hallelujah*s. We must move beyond demonizations to *daemonization*. It is only the loss of *daemon* that turns us into demon. When we are not inside the circle together we place others outside the circle as a way of pretending that we are inside. Only a shared story based on first values and first principles serves as the ground for a global ethos for a global civilization.

It's from demonization to *daemonization*.

It's a shared *daemon*.

It's a shared unique cultural, spiritual pattern.

It's a shared set of values. That's what we mean by a new story.

You cannot move from demonization, which is what Joe Biden correctly called for last night, unless you have *daemonization*.

Daemonization means *I know who I am*.

I have a shared value.

I have a shared story.

Since I have a shared story it means I'm in Eros.

When I'm in Eros then there's room for all of us.

We can actually find our way.

We can find our deeper shared story.

But if I don't have a *daemon* then only by making you a demon do I have an identity.

If I'm not inside the circle, I'm not in Eros, only by casting you outside the circle do I become inside the circle.

That's not Eros. That's pseudo-Eros.

So a shared story is the essence of the whole thing.

We're going to go so deep into this today. We're going to change the source code together. I'm so honored and delighted—and we're all so honored and delighted just to be here with each other. Can we just love each other in the chat box? Let's just love each other. Who's just up for it just to say, "Oh my God, I love you. I'm so happy to be with you today."

That love means something.

It doesn't mean I'm going to marry you. It's not ordinary love. It's outrageous love. It's the love that's the heart of existence itself. Let's let that love explode, that love that says that *that which unites us is so much greater than that which divides us.*

That's *Amor.*

That's Homo Amor.

That's *I'm a unique incarnation of the LoveIntelligence.*

I have a shared identity. That's the beginning of a shared value.

That which unites us is far greater than that which divides us.

We are united in a shared Story of Value.

That does not make us perfect expressions of that value. We are all imperfect vessels for the light, holy and broken *Hallelujahs.*

We have to move beyond demonizations to *daemonization*, that shared vision, that shared destiny.

It is only the loss of *daemon* that turns us into demon and then we turn everyone else into demon. We project our own sense of being demon, because we've lost *daemon*.

When we are not inside the circle together we place others outside as a way of pretending that we are on the inside.

Only a shared story based on First Values and First Principles serves as the ground for a global ethos to a global civilization.

Now, I understand that politics isn't there yet and we need to get there. It's not there yet. There is not a shared set of first values and first principles that have been articulated, not on the conservative side or the liberal side.

But now we've got to go deep. We're going to go on a ride. You're going to think, *Wow, okay, now I get where we're going*, and then we're going to take a turn in the complete opposite direction.

We're in celebration. **Our mood is celebration and it's also we're trembling before evolution as evolution itself.**

We are the leading edge of evolution. In this da Vinci moment between utopia and dystopia, we are actually responsible for articulating the next level.

There are lots of people who are responsible to protest and all the Trump people have every right to protest and say *Trump should go to court*, as one of the key Biden officials said last night, and support the legal process in a democracy, which allows for recounts, which is fantastic, so, gorgeous.

And all the people who are celebrating should totally celebrate. Of course, the court challenges are going to amount to nothing. They're not going to actually change the result, but it's a fair and beautiful process. That's what's so beautiful. It's gorgeous. That's holy. So let's stay in this together.

TRUMP UNDERMINED FUNDAMENTAL SHARED VALUES

We're going to now take 10 steps. Here's step one. I want to try and do this carefully. I want to tell you *I voted for Joe Biden*. I'm going to tell you why. I read regularly the *Wall Street Journal*. I listen to Fox News in America, but, more importantly, I read more serious position papers of both the right and the left.

There is an entire set of issues that are far more complex than they seem.

There are things that are ascribed to Trump that Obama was doing as well.

There are China policies.

There are all sorts of issues.

There is deregulation, the ability to start a business.

There are lots and lots of issues on which one could take a complex set of positions and I understand that.

I'm neither Democrat nor Republican.

Nonetheless I made a decision.

I went out of my way to get a mail-in ballot to vote for Joe Biden and to take issue with something. Here's what I wanted to take issue with.

My colleague—we've had dinner at his house and we've driven together and talked—Dennis Prager, I haven't talked to him in many years, but we were friendly for a period of time. We come from the same village, if you will, in the world of American culture. Dennis runs something called Prager University.

A *Wall Street Journal* editorial, one of them that I read this morning, Dennis's basic position is something like: "You don't have to believe a single word of the media's hysterical hyperbole about Trump these last four years to think this man is lacking in character. He's lacking the character of the men and women who made this country the greatest nation on Earth. You don't have to think he's Hitler's heir to be massively alarmed by his cavalier disregard for small matters like the independence of the judiciary, the proper use of power or even just truth. You don't have to think he takes personal joy in incarcerating children in cages to worry that his underdeveloped capacity for empathy has made him especially unfit for the crisis of these years. You don't have to believe he's Bull Connor in Alabama"—who was a racist—"to worry that his rhetoric and manner have done harm to the nation's fragile social contract." This is the *Wall Street Journal* writing.

What they're basically saying is, "Yeah, we get that there's a lot of hyperbole and hysteria against Trump, but there are four or five things in which the dude is bad news."

Then they say, "Yet for all his faults, for all the legitimate fear stoked by the last four years, it's not immoral or irrational to think that the incumbent Trump still represents a better alternative to what's on offer."

Then they explain why despite all that they supported Trump.

The basic argument, which I think is wrong and I think it needs to be said clearly and I want to say it clearly, is, *yes, Trump is a massively flawed disastrous leader*—wow!—*nonetheless, we think for these next 10 reasons he's a better choice than the alternative.*

The basic argument is we're interested in the policies of a president, not his character.

So, in general, I believe that argument to be true, meaning the personal conduct of a president, let's say a president has an affair, that's between him and his wife and his partner and that's not our issue. There is a whole series of issues on which you could say legitimately *we're interested more in that person's policies.*

I liked John F. Kennedy. John F. Kennedy was not a paragon of virtue. And his father Joe Kennedy stole the 1960 election, as we know, on the

Democratic side, but you could actually say that Kennedy's character issues were of a personal nature.

> *Trump crossed a line. And the line that he crossed was a kind of abusive undermining of fundamental shared values.*

I'm just going to give you one example.

It was the second presidential debate between Hillary Clinton and Donald Trump and quite a few people that I knew that are very well-known libertarians and liberals were actually supporting Trump. Then Trump basically responding to a question from Hillary which was basically about, "Why don't you pay contractors? You have people come work at your different projects, let's say you have a painter, but then you wind up not paying them. You don't pay whole slews of people and you do it because you can get away with it, because you've got more lawyers than they, and you do it as part of your business deal. You actually stiff people that you owe money to who have worked for you," and he basically said, "That's good business. That's what good business is."

At that moment he lost me.

That's good business? That's a violation of an essential structure of value in Cosmos.

Tragically, *Trump has stepped over the line of the personal moral character of the president* as divorced from their policy.

He's actually violated core structures of value that can't be forgiven.

So therefore I had no choice but to actually step up, mail in my ballot and vote for Joe Biden, which is what I did.

TRUMP LOST THE IMPORTANCE OF HYPOCRISY

Now, I want you to stay with me. When I say *we all have to create a shared story*, it doesn't mean we have to agree on everything.

That's not the point. This is not *we efface all distinctions and we all kind of link hands together and sing Khumbaya*. That's not how we create a shared story. That's nonsense.

We've got to create a shared story from the depths.

I want to go the next step and it's really important to get this. It's not that the Democrats all through history do not have their massive shares of corruption, including invading states, assassinating people, covert CIA operations, corruption on every possible level. Of course there's corruption on both the Republican and the Democratic side. Anyone who intelligently reads the *Wall Street Journal* carefully—brilliant writers—knows that's true. Of course that's true. Of course corruption is not a Democrat or Republican thing.

But I want to say something. It's subtle and it's deep and I want you to get it.

Trump lost the importance of hypocrisy.

Of course there's hypocrisy, but Trump actually removed hypocrisy. I want you to get what that means.

Hypocrisy means *I've got a set of values and I don't live up to them*. So *there's a standard of value and I'm a hypocrite.*

So *even though I hold that standard of value I become drunk with power, I become ambitious, I become greedy, I'm making tradeoffs*. That's what's always happened in politics.

Trump crossed a line. And the line he crossed is he said, "I'm not a hypocrite," meaning, "I don't have any of those standards of value."

That's tragic.

Give me a hypocrite any day, but when you actually undermine the core category of shame, which is, *I'm ashamed that I did that, because that violates our shared standard of value*, then you've crossed a line.

Then what you're actually doing is you're infusing into the world body politic an undermining of the core notion of value itself. You've undermined value itself.

You can't undermine value itself. That's not okay.

So I just first off want to say that. Because if I don't say that then we're doing *Khumbaya* here, so I think it was necessary.

And therefore I think there's cause for celebration for that reason.

Forget about all the policy issues. Trump needed to be removed from office. That's one. I'm going to show you an entirely different perspective in a couple of minutes, but first I want to see if we can grasp that together.

So I want to show you, just so you get a sense of it, a clip from Van Jones who's an American activist who's responding to his experience yesterday when Biden is declared the victor.

[Video clip: CNN's Van Jones brought to tears as Joe Biden wins US election]

I want to say that we can make this a good day for everyone. But I want you to feel the depth of what Van Jones said and that's important. He's expressing something that's important. No one in the United States—when I say no one I mean virtually no one obviously—would want to say to their child, "I want you to grow up and be Donald Trump." That was not a set of values.

The evangelicals who supported Trump did not say, "I want my kids to grow up to be Donald Trump."

The entire world of the United States, whether or not they thought the alternative was worse, felt in some fundamental way violated by one dimension of Trump, which is the tragic dimension of Trump, which is the impulsive, demeaning, insulting, the extemporaneous insult.

For example, the saying to a widow, "Your husband is not going to heaven because of what he did," a level of meanness. That level of meanness, by the way, exploded in the first presidential debate.

I know a whole group of people who were going to vote for Trump as a protest vote and when they saw that meanness in the first presidential debate it just shocked them.

It was tragic. **It fundamentally insulted value.**

That's really important.

Now let's take it the next step.

Now we're going to flip perspectives and we're going to realize that *the people that supported Trump, it's not that they were against value* .

It's not that it's a bunch of what we call in America rednecks or it's not what Hillary Clinton called *a basket of deplorables*.

No, actually, the people that support Trump are actually, the vast majority, wonderful human beings on many, many levels and clearly there's a shared story that we have, that we all have together.

So let's take a look now at the other side of the story. Let's actually do it together.

We're going to take a look at a woman who is a supporter of Bernie Sanders who's far left, who's a liberal, psychotherapist, who did not change. She's still a supporter of Bernie Sanders. I want you to get that. She's still a far-left liberal supporter of Bernie Sanders, but—she's going to tell her story in a second—she went to a Donald Trump rally and I want you to listen to this carefully. Don't listen to it and figure out why she's wrong, especially the

91

last couple of lines. Figure out what she's saying. Take us inside to [Karlyn] Borysenko who will now speak about her experience. Let's open our hearts and let's raise this up.

[Video clip: The Rally That Changed My Mind, Karlyn Borysenko[18]]

Now, remember, I'm not suggesting that we endorse Prager University. I've already said that I disagree fundamentally with Dennis and I sent in my mail-in ballot and I voted for Joe Biden, so I've made my position clear.

And who gets why that video is important? Do you get why that matters? That matters enormously.

We demonize the other.

That's what Joe Biden said last night, *an end to demonization.*

I'm sure he would have loved this video. It's an end to demonization.

The demonization of the other is only when there is no shared *daemon*.

One of the things that lives, that exists is

There is a meanness in woke culture. There is a meanness in progressive culture.

A VOTE FOR TRUMP WAS A VOTE AGAINST WOKENESS

Actually, to really get this, the Democrats are actually correct when they analyze the vote for Joe Biden, which was in part a vote for Joe Biden, which he clearly deserves—he's a man that's filled with compassion who's given a life of service and he deserves our every respect.

And the vote for Joe Biden was one kind of vote.

---

18 QR code is unavailable because the video is listed as private.

The vote for Trump was not a vote for Trump. It wasn't: "Wow, we love Trump."

The vote for Trump was a vote against the overwhelming majority of people—based on the best analysis today if you collate it and integrate it, which I have been doing for about a year; I must have read a thousand pieces, but not newspaper pieces, deeper level pieces—**it was a vote against wokeness.** It was a vote against what was perceived as a woke left political culture.

The feeling was that that political culture was fundamentally violating.

Now, I want to get why this is a big deal. The word "wokeness""is a word in America which means *politically correct culture that says, "We're woke, we're awake. Everybody else is not awake. Our politically correct way of seeing the world is the right way and anyone who doesn't see it our way is just a bad human being."*

That's called wokeness.

I want to give you a guys a painful example. A bunch of people sent me a dialogue of Sam Harris. Sam Harris is an American public intellectual, a larger conversation who he is and what he's doing. He's a materialist, meaning his basic notion is that the world is only material—and yet he's an avid meditator, an interesting person who I take sharp exception to on many matters and he's doing a good job in other ways.

I got in my inbox a couple of days before the election a bunch of people had sent me a lone podcast he did and in this podcast he said, "Okay, I finally figured out why anybody votes for Trump. I've never understood why anybody could vote for Trump. Who are these people? Why are they voting for Trump?"

Here's what he said. He said, "Trump offers what no priest credibly can offer, *a total expiation of shame.*

His personal shamelessness is kind of a spiritual salve.

Trump is 'fat' Jesus.

He's 'grab them by the pussy' Jesus.

He's 'I'll eat cheeseburgers if I want to' Jesus.

He's 'punch them in the face' Jesus.

He's 'no apologies' Jesus."

Then he goes on and he says, "The reason people like Trump is because Trump has no sanctimony" —The word "sanctimony" means *he's not making himself better than you.*

He goes on and he says, "Even when Trump is praising himself, still it's very clear that he's *a bundle of sin and gore*"—that's Sam Harris's phrase— "and he never pretends or even aspires to be more, so he offers a truly safe space for human frailty and hypocrisy, a total atoning of shame. That's why people vote for him, because he actually allows them to be with all of their own disgusting nature without being morally superior."

I want you to get this. This is a very big deal.

I came to this conclusion.

A colleague of mine that we worked together in the old days came to the same conclusion.

What Sam Harris just did was he just insulted 70 million Americans and just demeaned them.

Exactly what we're accusing Trump of—Harris just did.

He just said that 70 million Americans, the entire traditional America, the evangelical, traditional, blue collar, working class America, that whole group of people plus all the minorities that voted for Trump (and he got a big bump in minorities)—"the reason they voted for him is because he allows them to get rid of their shame about their own disgustingness."

That's horrible. That's terrible. That's utterly mean. That's mean modernity.

And it's not the case.

Of course that's true about some people. Let's go deeper for a second. If we can go deeper we can actually come together as Joe Biden called us to do and move beyond demonization.

In other words, exactly what Joe Biden said *is don't do what Sam Harris just did*. Don't demean 70 million people and say that *they are basically filled with shame and Trump allows them to get rid of their shame at their own disgusting nature*. **That's a disaster.**

So what should we do? Let's find our way. I want to really get this clear.

Of course Trump has a hard-core group of people who are deeply into the cult of personality of Trump. But for lots and lots of good reason there is lots of information that says **that the overwhelming majority of votes for Trump were votes against something. They felt ignored or they felt that critical values were rejected.**

It's not that Trump himself embodies those values. Of course he doesn't. That's not the point. It's not that he embodies those values, but I want you to get what the values are.

TRUMP SPEAKS TO ETHNOCENTRIC PATRIOTISM

There are two sets of values. Number one, what did [Karlyn] Borysenko say at the end of her video? She said the people at the Trump rally weren't there because they hated someone but because they loved America. What was Trump's motto? *Make America Great Again.* So what Trump stood for was a kind of patriotism.

Now, again, I want to ask everyone to go deeper. Now everyone's going to think to themselves, *But Trump is this and Trump is that.* Let go of Trump the person. That's not the point here. Let's go deeper here. Think deeper.

In essence, the feeling was for those 70 million people that **a dimension of the far left had hijacked the conversation in America**, that the far left had hijacked the conversation for the last 25 years in which *America had become an evil place.*

America was demeaned.

America was denigrated.

America was painted as the paragon of all evil.

And there was a sense that the fundamental experience of being ethnocentric, that *I get to love my country*—not in a fascist terrible way— but *I get to love my country* and *I get to be proud of my country in some fundamental and important way*—that's important.

And Trump spoke to ethnocentricity.

Trump, the way he expressed the ethnocentric—I want everyone to get this really clear—he expressed the shadow version, the terrible version of ethnocentricity.

Trump was the shadow version of ethnocentricity—but he was all people had.

It was very much a religious population. Just like King David in the Book of Kings does many sins but he's the king, so the sense of Trump was: *We don't really care about Trump, but at least he's speaking to this value of ethnocentricity.*

Yes, he's doing it in a terrible way. But the reason those 70 million people didn't go with the left is because *the left refused to actually embrace and love America in a way that they could feel in their hearts and bodies and souls.*

That's one of the important things that I pray Joe Biden will do. And I think he began to do it last night, to actually speak in this beautiful centrist way for loving America. And to the precise extent that Joe Biden and Kamala Harris will embrace that ethnocentric value—because there's a healthy ethnocentrism. I get to love America. That's an expression of love. That's beautiful. And I get to love American men. I don't want to demonize men and I don't want to demonize America and I don't want to give every American man the feeling that they are Islamophobic and they're transgenderphobic and they're racist and they're xenophobic—the basic sense that you're basically a horrible human being.

As Margaret Mead said correctly to James Baldwin, *you cannot hold every America alive today accountable for the mistakes of 100 years ago.*

We can say we're going to go to heal and repair and transform those mistakes. But you can't actually be woke, politically correct and shame everyone.

What's basically happened is **the culture of wokeness has become a shaming culture in which facts are no longer gathered, evidence is no longer properly gathered, fair structures of justice are no longer in play.**

There are positives to the cancel culture, but there are a lot of negatives, which means you don't gather information, you don't check evidence.

The entire notion of justice and integrity has gotten shattered, and America is made evil.

That's what 70 million people said isn't true and that's what Joe Biden agreed with. So the end of demonization is *it's the end of the demonization of those 70 million—but it's also the end of the demonization of America.*

That's one. That's a very big deal. This is so big. This is so important.

We have to embrace a healthy ethnocentricity.

What Sam Harris did is he basically caricatured that whole population.

Now, his caricature is accurate about Trump, but it's not accurate about the 70 million people who supported him.

A VOTE FOR TRUMP IS RECLAIMING VALUES THAT THE LEFT HAS REJECTED

Here's the second piece. The second piece that those 70 million people take super seriously is they take God seriously. They don't just give lip service to God. They take God seriously. That's a big deal. Now, some of them have notions of God that I think are regressive. There are lots of issues with that, but basically their experience of life is that *God is at the center.*

Now, you're thinking, you're saying, "But for Trump God is not at the center. He's a lying hypocrite." That's not the point.

King David did a bunch of lying and he killed Uriah and he slept with Bathsheba. So from their perspective, *Okay, he's this imperfect crazy, terrible guy, but at least he's willing to give lip service, whatever he believes or doesn't believe, to our churches and to take them seriously.*

That's their experience.

Their experience is that the woke, politically correct left actually has no sense of objective value, no sense of devotion to the larger Godforce and actually ridicules and mocks those basic values which for them and for me are a lived experience. Forget about all the ways that they hijack it the wrong way.

The basic experience is that there's a personal Presence in the Universe that knows our name and loves us.

That's it.

There's a personal Presence in the Universe, a Godforce that knows our name and loves us.

Now, again, what we've tried to do here in *One Mountain, Many Paths* is to evolve those ideas. What we're actually doing here—we're going to do this in our section on first values and first principles—*we've actually evolved a shared language.* That's actually what we're doing here.

We're actually evolving that shared language which can be a genuine shared language for all 144 million people.

But just to really get this, it's a very big deal.

The support for Trump is not for Donald Trump the person. It's actually a sense that there are values that the left has rejected that feel vitally important to people.

That's really important to get this.

- There are shadow, mean forms of modernity and there are beautiful forms of modernity.
- In traditional culture, there are shadow, mean forms and there are beautiful forms.
- In postmodernity there are shadow, mean forms of postmodernity and there are beautiful forms.

The reason I voted against Donald Trump is because Donald Trump brought together in one person the shadow forms of traditionalism—meaning he used ethnocentric love of America as a tool, as a weapon, as a violation of value.

He's a shadow form of modernity, which is about business, but for him business was a completely corrupt enterprise in which you could not pay people who worked for you because you could get away with it.

And he brought together shadow forms of postmodernity, because postmodernity is about post-truth, but he made post-truth into a permission to disregard truth at a level that it's never been disregarded in public culture in the United States ever.

Trump tragically himself, in his person, brought together the shadow forms of traditionalism, modernity, and postmodernity.

So there was no moral choice from my perspective but to vote against him.

And I can do that AND hold and understand what [Karlyn] Borysenko, a Bernie liberal supporter, saw at a Trump rally.

It was that, first off, *the person Trump has got complex other sides.* Number one, an enormous amount of energy and a kind of accessibility, but, more important than that, values, ethnocentricity, loving America, loving God. They felt that that had gotten abandoned—and they're not completely wrong.

- The progressive world has demonized America in a real way.
- And there's a legitimate critique of America.

What do we need to do?

We need to come together and create a shared story.

What would the shared story look like?

I'm not going to go into first values and first principles now. I just want to just on five levels, just in two seconds, here's what we can do.

See, woke culture is not bad either. Let's not demonize woke culture.

There's a demonized form of woke culture and there's a healthy, wake form of woke culture.

Political correctness is not all wrong. Some of it's right.

Cancel culture is not all wrong. Some of it's right.

So how would we bring this together? Just in a few sentences, friends, I want to see how could we bring this together and we're going to bring this to a close.

There are going to be five clauses here.

WE NEED A SHARED STORY FOR AMERICA

One, we affirm the greatness of America.

America has given more aid, more investment, died on shores around the world, has acted as a leader in the world in a thousand different ways. One of the things I'm most proud of is people come to America as refugees and historically have been absorbed, integrated. America is a great melting pot. There's a reason why people aren't moving to Russia, they're moving to America. Two million Black people moved to America in the last couple of decades. Why? Because it's a gorgeous place. As Joe Biden said last night, America is a place of possibility, of gorgeous possibility.

I am proud to be American. I am proud of America. I love America. Wow! We can say that.

And in the next sentence I can say, not uniquely but like the rest of the world, America in the mid-19th century had slavery and that's real.

Then America had Jim Crow laws.

Then America had redlining.

America has made genuine mistakes. And even though we didn't do them we're responsible for America. There is a covenant between generations.

We've reached a higher level of moral consciousness—and this is the correct statement of woke left culture.

We've reached a higher level of moral consciousness in which that which was acceptable 40 years ago is not acceptable today.

So you don't get to slaughter animals who are tortured for three months so you can have a lamb chop. That's not awake.

You don't get to actually have a country in which a disproportionate amount of its resources go to one population and there's not at least equal opportunity. Equal outcome no one can guarantee, but there has got to be a fair playing field. If there's not a fair playing field it's not okay.

It's not okay that Google pays no taxes.

It's not okay that Amazon virtually doesn't pay taxes at all and pays its workers $14 an hour.

In other words, *it's possible to be madly proud of America, to be proud of American history, to be proud of American accomplishment—and to be fiercely demanding, as Barack Obama has said, that America is a dream in progress.*

And we've got to take America the next step. We've got to make America accountable to its own higher self.

We can say that there still are vestiges in this country, even though in the history of planet Earth as a multicultural country it probably has less racism historically than any other country. That's not enough.

There still is systemic racism in America. That's a fact and that's not okay.

We can embrace both of those. **So we can actually correct American misdeeds and have full American pride.**

WE STAND FOR THE IMPORTANCE OF A VIBRANT GLOBAL ECONOMY

Let's go another step. We can stand for a huge necessity for a vibrant global economy, because global economy creates human dignity and creates jobs.

- I can stand for the importance of a global economy. It's not just money. It's dignity and jobs for billions of people.
- And we can stand absolutely for the utter necessity to protect the environment.

Those are not contradictory values.

That's not a left/right. The right says, "Global economy." No, we can stand for both of them.

We can actually be fiercely honoring and venerate the legacy of the best that we've received with huge honor. And a massive commitment to the memory of the future and to what's possible and what's our moral obligation to do, because we have a new level of moral consciousness.

Here are the last two sentences.

- We have to embrace the United States, the best of progressive culture, and to critique its shadows.
- We have to embrace the best of modernity and to critique its shadows.
- We have to embrace the best of traditional culture and to critique its shadows.

We have to weave those three into something larger than the sum of the parts.

A PRAYER FOR THE POSSIBILITY OF POSSIBILITY

Here's a prayer. The prayer is that, oh my God, this is a new moment, that, oh my God, let the 70 million people who actually didn't support Donald Trump the person but wanted there to be recognition of loving America and recognition of loving God—**let loving God and loving America be, in their most beautiful form, legitimate and gorgeous and beautiful values at the center of American and world society.**

And when we say *loving God*, the god you don't believe in doesn't exist, not a xenophobic god, not a homophobic god.

We need to actually evolve and clarify our perception of God. Wow!

And let the new leaders of America embrace this new vision, in this new vision of value, in this new possibility.

In the end, God holds us and God lives in us.

God is the possibility of possibility.

America is the possibility of possibility.

Europe is the possibility of possibility.

Humanity is God come alive in human form, the intention of Cosmos.

Evolution is the possibility of possibility.

This is a moment for a greater vision.

This is a moment for a greater possibility. Wow!

I want to end today with something really beautiful which was from Aeschylus. It was a poem that Biden has quoted and it was actually a poem that my childhood hero, Robert Kennedy—who was a man who went through a transformation, came from a privileged family, was mean spirited on a thousand different grounds and probably corrupt, and when his brother was killed between 1963 and '67 he went through an incredible transformation and changed the world, his heart opened in a big way—so Kennedy used to love this poem. I'm going to read it to you.

> *Even in our sleep, pain which we cannot forget*
> *falls drop by drop upon the heart*
> *until, in our own despair, against our will,*
> *comes wisdom through the awful grace of God.*

What we're trying to do is say, okay, *how do we actually do what Biden invited us to do which is to move beyond demonization and find a shared Story of Value?*

What I just did in my closing articulation when I said, "Okay, now, what's the shared story?" I articulated the best values of the left, *the recognition that there's systemic racism.*

AND there's the greatness of America which is an important version of not Trump but healthy ethnocentricity.

We've got to integrate the best values of the left and the best values of the right and bring them together into a higher vision.

In the end if we're really wise and really smart and we're really listening and we're really thinking, we won't be either right or left, we'll be some new integration, some new whole greater than the sum of the parts.

So let's pray.

Let's find each other in the chat box and let's offer every prayer we can for a new vision.

Let's offer every prayer we can to Joe Biden and to Kamala Harris to actually take this next step in leadership.

Let's offer every prayer for ourselves to be courageous and to be actually warriors in taking this next step.

Let's pray.

I think we're going to hold here. I think we included today first values and first principles along the way and I think we need just to hold what we've done. It was huge. Oh my God, what a day and what a place. Let's find each other in the chat box and just love each other, like we started. We're just loving each other, sending mad prayers to Joseph Biden and to Kamala Harris the president-elect of the United States and vice president-elect.

We're sending mad blessings to the shared story, to the best values of the healthy left and the healthy right.

When those two come together, something gorgeous happens beyond imagination.

And—I want to get this clear—we're not doing *Khumbaya* and *everything's good and everything's equal.*

That's why I started and said Trump himself needed to be voted out of office, because he was a violation of value.

Van Jones's description of Trump as being fundamentally abusive is accurate.

- I said he's a shadow of postmodernity; he moved post-truth to a whole different level.
- He's a shadow of modernity, not holy business but corrupt business.
- And he's a shadow of traditionalism, hijacked ethnocentricity into borderline racism—all not okay, all reasons we had to vote against him.

So I disagree with the people that voted for him. **But I can actually hear and feel what drove them.** That's what Joseph Biden meant when he said *we move beyond demonization.* We begin to create a shared *daemon,* a shared vision that includes love of every other and includes love of country and includes love of God—and the god you don't believe in doesn't exist. That's the possibility.

Oh my God, thank you, everyone. Thank you for being with us. Thank you for being the revolution.

CHAPTER SIX

EVOLUTION NEVER FORGETS A BREAKTHROUGH: A LITTLE BIT OF LIGHT DISPELS A LOT OF DARKNESS

Episode 218 — December 13, 2020

HANUKKAH: THE ABILITY TO REJOICE IN PARTIAL FULFILLMENT

I want to share with you this particular moment, this particular time. We're in Hanukkah. You don't have to be Jewish to connect with it.

The Hanukkah story is about the Greek Seleucids about 160 years before the Common Era, who go on this Hellenistic mission—Hellenism means the spreading of Greek culture—and they go to deconstruct, to defile the Temple in Jerusalem.

Temple as in *Raiders of the Lost Ark*, Temple as in Ark of the Covenant.

The Temple stands for the great tradition of mysticism that sees Reality as ultimately meaningful in every jot and tittle and sees the ethos of the human being as participating in the Eros of the Cosmos.

That movement is challenged by Greece. Greece views man as a spectator to time and existence. Greece removes from the center of the Cosmos the throbbing and yearning dignity of the individual human being, with all of their pathos.

There's this movement of Hellenism. They go and defile the Temple.

And most of the Hebrews of the time feel that *this is where it's going, this is where the power lies, this is where the energy's going*—and they become Hellenists.

There's a small group—it's always a fringe group—there's a small band, it's a band of Outrageous Lovers and they call themselves Maccabees. They come from a little town called Modi'in, which is still, today, a village about 20 minutes from Jerusalem, and they challenge the priesthood which wants to join the Hellenists—and they recapture the Temple.

The small band of Outrageous Lovers, who have no political power and they barely have a budget and they're struggling—there's a group of 20, 30, 40, 50 of them at the center and a few hundred people around them—they organize this bottom up, grassroots rebellion and they manage to retake the Temple.

You've got these Maccabees, this band of Outrageous Lovers, and they're victorious.

Great victory. Fabulous, huge, gorgeous victory. They reconquer The temple. They reconquer Jerusalem.

The only thing is that if you study history, you realize that their victory lasted for about—ready for this? 25 years, 30 years.

Then the Greek Seleucids send other armies and, ultimately, they conquer Jerusalem and the Hebrews lost.

And yet we have this holy day, this Hannukah, which is this great and gorgeous celebration that people are doing all over the world today, which tells the story of this great victory. Again, if you check history, it turns out

108

that, *Oh, not exactly true. That's not exactly what happened.* So how do we put it together? Let's just open our hearts. It's so beautiful.

You see, the masters who established the holiday of Hannukah, they weren't unaware of the history.

They knew the history.

They knew that the victory was short-lived.

They knew the victory was a partial victory.

They knew it was partial fulfillment.

But now, let's open our hearts together.

To be an evolutionary—

- To pick up the torch
- To participate in the evolution of love
- To know that it's ours to do at this moment in time

—is also to be able to celebrate partial victories.

We don't need a total victory.

We almost never get a total victory.

Our fulfillments are partial, our victories are sometimes short-lived.

The ability to be an evolutionary, the ability to be an Outrageous Lover, is to rejoice in partial fulfillment, to rejoice in short-lived victories.

To be an Outrageous Lover is to know that those moments in-between when we're victorious, they add up.

Those points of light become a thousand points of light.

It's just like the new imaginal cells in the caterpillar that's hanging in a chrysalis and turning into a butterfly. There are only individual imaginal cells and they all get wiped out by the immune system of the caterpillar.

But one by one those imaginal cells begin to link together until you get clumps and clusters and configurations of imaginal cells and, gradually, the caterpillar turns into a butterfly.

Each imaginal cell—even if its wiped out, even if it doesn't seem to last—**leaves an impression, leaves an imprint, and participates in the evolution of love.**

I want to see if we can get this because it's so gorgeous from the perspective of history. Let me just ask you a question.

Where are the Greek Seleucids? The great Greek Seleucid empire, where is it today? Nowhere.

It exists no place in the world.

The mightiest power in 160 BCE has disappeared.

But that little band of Outrageous Lovers who came together, who fought the good fight, who stood for integrity, who stood against the wave of Hellenism that sought to depersonalize the infinite dignity and gorgeousness of the Unique Self individual—

That band of Outrageous Lovers that retook the Temple and lit the menorah, lit the candelabrum in the Temple—they established Hannukah. All over the world today people are lighting Hannukah candles.

That's the power of the band of Outrageous Lovers.

As we come together, we are here as revolutionaries, we are here in this moment between utopia and dystopia to realize that:

We are Evolution coming awake to itself.

We are Conscious Evolution incarnate.

We are Evolution realizing its true nature as Evolutionary Love.

That's who we are.

And each of us, in order to take our seat at the table of history and participate in this band of Outrageous Lovers, is living an individual life someplace, somewhere in the world.

How many of us live lives of absolute fulfillment? *No one.* Not one person.

And anyone who says they are is lying. You're lying. There's not one person on this call who's living a life of absolute fulfillment.

Absolute fulfillment is not the nature of the relative world. We live lives of partial fulfillment.

Our brilliance, our light, our wonder, our evolutionary nature is that we have the capacity to have utter, radical joy in partial fulfillment.

The masters declare Hannukah a victory to be celebrated for generations even though it's only a partial victory, even though it's ephemeral, even though it seems to last for a short time, even though for a moment it seems like we might be tilting at a windmill.

There's a sacred text, which reads, *keivan she'ala, shuv lo yored -once you ascend, you never descend*

It doesn't mean you never contract, it doesn't mean you never fall down. But once you open up a door and open up a new portal and establish a new structure of consciousness, then *that structure of consciousness coheres, links to, allures to itself, attracts to itself other imaginal cells.* Those imaginal cells—those points of consciousness, those points of light—come together to form

- a mighty torch of liberation
- a mighty torch of humanism

- a might torch of caring
- a mighty torch of Outrageous Love

Hannukah's an Outrageous Love victory.

It's a partial victory. We're not there yet and we've got a lot more of this partial victory to realize.

We've got to expand and deepen and bring more people into the center and create many more cascading waves. We're at the very beginning of the beginning.

Every single one of us, every place that we are. And anyone who wants to step in is wildly, completely, and absolutely welcome to step in and to step up and to participate and to give everything you have. Let's give it all together.

But we're at the beginning and it's partial fulfillment.

Every time we love each other more madly than ever before—

We stand in the breach.

We articulate the evolutionary love codes.

We speak the new language of the future human.

We speak the language of the new human and the new humanity.

We realize that we are in this da Vinci moment, we're not asleep in this da Vinci moment. Just like in the Renaissance, we're at a time between worlds and a time between stories.

We come together.

We articulate the source code

We evolve the source code of culture and consciousness together with these evolutionary love codes.

We do it by feeling each other, by loving each other.

That is a victory. It's a great and triumphant and wondrous victory.

Is it partial fulfillment? Yes, of course it is.

Is it, in some sense, ephemeral? Of course it is.

And yet it's inscribed in the heart of Divinity. It's inscribed in the heart of Reality.

Something new is engraved.

Our lips impress on the lips of She. And something new is born in that space in between us as we *arouse the feminine waters*, in the language of the mystics.

nashkei ar'ah ve'rakiah - earth and sky kiss

Hannukah's the celebration of partial fulfillment.

A LITTLE BIT OF LIGHT DISPELS SO MUCH OF THE DARKNESS

Here's the next sentence: a little bit of light dispels so much of darkness.

Who's familiar with the Miracle of Hannukah? What's the Miracle of Hannukah? That the candelabrum in the temple, which has eight placeholders for candles, requires pure olive oil to light it.

They come back to the temple, these Maccabees, this band of Outrageous Lovers. They burst into the temple. They retake Jerusalem, they retake the precincts of the temple. They want to light the menorah, they want to light this candelabrum, but they only have enough pure olive oil—because you can only light the candelabrum with pure olive oil—for one day and once you light, you're supposed to continue lighting. You can't just light it and stop.

They say, "You know what? We're not going to light," but somehow they do and then the light burns for eight days instead of one. They just had enough oil for one day and the light burns for eight days instead of one day, so we celebrate the Miracle of Hannukah, an eight-day miracle.

But one second – that's not true. Everything you just said, Marc, is just not true because let's just do the mathematics. Simple math. If there was enough oil for one day and it lasted eight days, so the miracle was *how many days*? How many days was the miracle? Seven days.

Why are we celebrating eight? It should be a seven-day holiday.

The question the mystics ask—and you can get the way interior scientists speak, they speak in their own code, so in the interior, sacred text they always open with the question—is, "What was the miracle of the first day?" That's a *terminus technicus*, that's a technical term, in mysticism.

The mystics turn to each other and they say, "What was the miracle of the first day?" Stay with the question. Before you go to the answer, just be with the question. "What was the miracle of the first day?" It's so deep, it's so beautiful, and there are thousands of pages written in texts of interior science to answer this question: what was the miracle of the first day?

It's the great evolutionary question.

There are two approaches to the answer and they're both equally beautiful.

First, they're sitting there that day and saying to each other—

Remember, everyone had thought that the temple was over.

Everyone had thought that—according to all the currents of history and CNN and all the different internet sites, everyone had reported—*Jerusalem is over. Outrageous Love doesn't have a chance.*

Dr. Phil says, "*What is Outrageous Love? I don't even understand what that is; that's ridiculous. We have no idea what that is. That's a silly idea. Let's get real, let's get pragmatic, let's get practical, let's get strategic.*"

Hellenism has won. And no one thinks, after the Hellenists take the temple, that there's ever going to be a return, a new Renaissance, a reenchantment of reality: *we're never again going to use and be able to access the pure oil.*

Shemen, S-H-E-M-E-N, "oil" is the same word as *shemoneh*, which is "eight." Eight is that which is beyond nature—

The cycle of seven is nature. Eight is Outrageous Love.

Ordinary love is seven.

Outrageous Love is eight—that which transcends nature, the spark that animates the whole thing, that's not explainable or reducible to measurement.

It's the immeasurable, it's the priceless, it's the precious beyond precious. *Wow!*

Everyone's completely sure that we're never going to get back to the pure oil.

Everything's now commodified.

Everything's now measurable.

Everything's now priced.

Everything now fits into a particular algorithmic calculus designed to elicit more profit to a very narrow band of stakeholders.

We're never going to get back to the pure oil, we've got no chance and so there's no reason to actually hide a cruse, a little vessel, of pure oil. It's never going to be used again.

All the priests in Jerusalem have joined the Hellenists. All the establishment, all the hierarchies, have joined the Greek Syrians, but there's a little band of people, a couple of priests, and they say it's not over. They say *Netzach Yisrael lo yi'shaker*. That means that:

Eternity, the thrust of evolution, is going to birth this oil anew.

The thrust of evolution is going to generate new possibility.

They take one little cruse of oil, just enough for one day, and they go and hide that cruse of oil.

They know that in their lives they may not live to ever have that cruse of oil be found, but they hide it for the next generation.

Then the next generation comes and there's this moment of triumph and they need the pure oil.

They search and search and they find, in the hidden place, a cruse of oil that was hidden by the previous generations.

Every generation participates in its evolution of consciousness and every generation has to hide a cruse of oil to be discovered by the next generation.

Wow! That's the miracle of the first day.

Are we actually hiding a cruse of pure oil and will it be there for the next generation to pick up? Will we ensure that there is a next generation? Will we ensure that there is a future?

In everything we do together, whenever we come together and we open our hearts in Outrageous Love and we create new bodies of work, we evolve the source code, we're in this great Da Vinci project – *that's the pure oil.*

It's partial fulfillment. It's not funded the way it needs to be and it doesn't have all the resources it needs, but *it's a cruse of pure oil that we are guaranteeing with our hearts, with our commitment, with our sacrifice, with our dedication* that it's going to be there to carry on, to light the next torch, and to bring us towards the fulfillment of *Homo sapiens* and *Homo amor. Wow!*

That's the first answer to the miracle of the first day. That at a time when it seemed hopeless, there was a band of Outrageous Lovers that knew that the pure oil would be lit again in a new and evolved form and they went and they hid that little cruse, they hid the little vessel of oil, so it could be lit in the future.

That's the covenant between generations.

But here's the second miracle of the first day.

> Imagine the scene there in Jerusalem. There's these groups of priests and groups of politicians and groups of entrepreneurs and groups of strategists and they want to light this great candelabrum and there's just enough oil for what? Just enough oil for one day. What do people say? They say, "Don't start. How can you start? There's only enough oil for one day.

We don't have a budget.

We don't have researchers.

We don't have enough staff.

We don't have enough resources.

We just can't do it. It's not real. We can't get it started. Let's wait til everything's ready. There's too much controversy around.

In other words, *let's just not start because it's just not going to work.*"

Then there's one group of people—just a few of them—who speak against the majority, and against the wise voices of pragmatism, and against the intelligence strategists, and against the wise SEO people, and against the marketing experts, and against the people who say, "We need four or five people on staff to do this. We can't do it ourselves." They say,

"No, you're right.

We do need all those things, but we're going to start anyway.

We're going to leap and the net will appear.

We're going to make a decision that we are going to trust the goodness of possibility and we're going to trust the possibility of possibility.

We're going to trust each other; we're going to trust each other's commitment.

We're going to know that a little bit of light dispels a lot of darkness and we're going to light the candle on the first day."

The miracle of the first day was the trust, the commitment, the sacrifice, the dedication, the knowing, that allowed that small group of people to speak against all the wise majority and to light the candle even though there was only enough oil for the first day.

Friends, that what we do together.

We don't have enough oil for eight days, that's true.

But it doesn't matter.

We know that the oil's going to come.

We know that the Miracle of Hannukah is real and we know that the miracle of Christmas is real.

—I love this time of year. Don't you love this time of year, friends? You can feel it alive. Bethlehem is alive. Jerusalem is alive. The visions of Scrooge are alive. —

Friends, it's so good to be with you. It's so good to be in the Miracle of Hannukah together. It's so good to be together participating in the evolution of love.

It's so good. So much gratitude for all of us. So much gratitude for the utter, radical need for what we're doing here.

We have to celebrate partial fulfillment.

We have to celebrate partial victories.

We have to step in and light even though we're not sure how it's ever going to possibly last eight days.

SCIENCE ENABLES US TO SEE THE CONSCIOUS INTELLIGENCE OF THE COSMOS

I want to just say something clearly. The notion that the Cosmos is only random and only accidental is simply not the case. That's simply a lie. We need to know just so little about the actual nature of the Cosmos, read one good set of papers, and you'll never again not realize that the Cosmos is fully conscious and intelligent all the way up and all the way down. Not to know that is absurdity. It's only a dogma of reductionist materialism that correctly stood against premodern superstition—but is now completely outdated—that would make any other suggestion. It's really important to get that.

There's a good book by a guy named Perry Marshall, who I spoke to a couple of days ago, called *Evolution 2.0*. Perry's a very good writer in the world of ethernet and in the world of complex engineering.

He's very good at first principles from the perspective of first principles of calculus from Newton on down; he's created and built a lot of stuff based on that. So he's a serious engineer and he brought engineering together with— it's a beautiful bringing together—biology, particularly in DNA.

You realize that DNA is what we call a code. A code is a very specific thing; it has five or six characteristics. It's designed as a code. It's designed to exchange information in a particular way to accomplish, under particular conditions, particular results. No code ever emerges from random mutation. It's not a question of random mutation generating more complexity. That is possible in limited conditions. Random mutation never, by itself, accidentally generates code. Never happened, never will happen—and actually Perry offered a $5million prize to any community that could demonstrate otherwise. It's really important to get that.

Sometimes we try and be very sophisticated and we get caught up in the dogmatic materialism of the time. That's just not true.

The Universe is alive.

The Universe is conscious.

The Universe is intelligent.

The hard facts of science make that very clear.

And the universe operates through the natural principles of evolutionary enfoldment and unfolding. And science is at the center of that.

It's really important not to just say, "God did it," because if you just say, "God did it," you actually miss science. You actually stop looking at the layers and layers and layers of infinite, elegant complexity and coherence that are the layers and layers of science. Those are critically important.

The practice: God, give me the strength to light the first candle

We now turn to the infinity of intimacy, to the Personhood, we turn to the Designer, to the Intelligence of Cosmos, to that principle that has a personal face, that knows our name, that designed us through this gorgeous and stunning evolutionary process.

We turn to Evolution itself and we say:

> "Could you receive all of me? I know you know me. I know you're waiting for me. I know you intended me.
>
> You intended me. You, evolution, intended me. You manifested me. You incarnated me. You made me come alive.
>
> You chose when I should be born. You're going to choose when I should die. You chose where I should be born.
>
> You chose the capacities I should be born with.
>
> None of that was me. It was all you. So please, please let me be received by you. Hold my hand. Let me feel you holding my hand.
>
> Give me the strength to light the first candle.

Give me the strength to make the miracle in my life of the first day.

Give me the strength to rejoice in partial fulfillment."

That's what we pray for. We pray for radical joy in partial fulfillment so that we can actually take our place in that great evolutionary torch, without which we won't survive at this moment in history.

Without taking our place, there will be no future. That's the nature of existential and catastrophic risk.

Our prayers are different from any other prayers before because what's at stake is not just us. It's our ability to stand in the breach of this moment and light the candle on the first day is what we need in order to have a future at all. *Wow!*

Let's pray like we've never prayed before with the light of Hannukah. Leonard Cohen, holy and broken Hallelujah. Take us inside. Here we go. Oh my God.

[Music: *Hallelujah* by Leonard Cohen]

CHAPTER SEVEN

CELEBRATING OUTRAGEOUS ACTS OF CIVIC VIRTUE, TRIUMPH OF INTEGRITY: TRUSTING EACH OTHER AGAIN

Episode 223 — January 17, 2021

RESPONDING TO THE GLOBAL INTIMACY DISORDER THROUGH A SHARED STORY

When I was in a different world—there was a world that I lived in for quite a while before I really got the concept of existential risk and that we're in an actual moment in which we're poised between utopia and dystopia—I was teaching what I thought was the best vision we could have about what it means to be a human being and spirituality, but without the context of existential risk or what we've called the Second Shock of Existence.

The First Shock of Existence is the realization of the death of the human being in Dawn Man, where prehistoric man and woman realized we're going to die. The Second Shock is the potential death of humanity, which we're facing today. That began to dawn on me in a real way when I started studying in 2010 or 2011.

But before then, when I was doing this earlier version of teaching, I would teach in both synagogues, but often

churches and all sorts of venues around the country and around the world. But the place I loved to teach most was in an African-American black gospel church—there's nothing like it—because *they let the word move in them*. There's a reason that the black gospel church animated the revolution of the Civil Rights Movement.

So we have to understand what in the fractured plotlines of that narrative are the generator functions that are the cause right now, in this moment, both for catastrophic risk and existential risk. If we can't understand that clearly, then we can't actually create the right medicine.

The right medicine is to heal the global intimacy disorder through a shared story; one that lives within us, that lives within Reality itself, one that actually begins to tell us that *that which unites us is so much greater than that which divides us*, and that actually, **just like shared intimacy creates coherence in a couple, in the world, shared intimacy creates global coherence**. We desperately need global coherence today, because we need to act globally, because all of our challenges are global.

Because just like da Vinci—at this moment between worlds and the Renaissance, as the Black Death swept Europe—knew that telling of a new story about the human being and the divine, about nature and about reality, about who are we and where are we, what's there to do and how should we do it—**answering those essential questions based on the best information and the best validated insights available, integrated into a larger whole, which is the new story; that was the only thing that could respond.**

- ◆ He responded successfully—and that birthed all the dignities of modernity.
- ◆ But in part, the response was wrong.

There were fractures in the new story, there were travesties in the plotline which need to be rewritten, and that's the new story. We re-articulate that in our setting of intention, in some sense, every week, in order to locate ourselves.

We're going to feel it. And we're going to talk today about feeling.

This is how we're together, this is our planetary awakening in love through Unique Self Symphony. This is a new way to call each other. *Don't walk in front of me, I may not follow. Don't walk behind me, I may not lead. Just walk beside me, and be my friend. Together we will walk in the path of the Name.*

The Name in all the great traditions means the Tao, the Spirit, the ultimate Value underneath Reality, and it is ultimate Personhood.

EVOLUTIONARY LOVE CODE: UNIQUE SELF IS WHERE MEANING IS DISCOVERED UNIQUELY IN EACH PERSON

> The Unique Self is the inward space of uniquely lived experience from which meaning is discovered.
>
> The Unique Self is under attack in multiple ways, including the assumption of Big Tech and Big Data that the human being is no more than a social self, the assumption of spiritual traditions that the human being is either a True Self or an obedient self, and the shared assumption world over that the human being is a Separate Self.
>
> The cultivation of Unique Self is therefore the overriding moral imperative at this moment in history.

"The Unique Self is the inward space of uniquely lived experience from which meaning is discovered." I've got to be able to sit and to place my attention inside, place my intention on the conversation, place my attention on each other, and rest in the space. There I create a cauldron of creativity, a cauldron of ecstatic urgency, a cauldron of Outrageous Love, from which the revolution emerges.

Unique Self means *my personhood matters*, the quality of my personhood matters; my unique personhood is valuable. Because that's what personhood means, personhood means it's personal to you and me. It's not impersonal, it's not generic; it's personal.

PRAYER AFFIRMS THE PERSONHOOD OF COSMOS

Prayer affirms the personhood of Cosmos.

We are unique and discrete expressions of personhood, but we're part of this larger overarching Personhood of Cosmos. Is there a personal God? Of course, there's a personal God. But personal God is not Santa Claus, it's not a particular vision of Buddha, it's not even the Christian vision of Christ, it's not Hanuman.

Those are all expressions of the face of Cosmos which is personal. And we call that the Infinity of Intimacy that knows your name.

When we pray, we have this realization that Cosmos is not just third person: the four forces animated by the force of Eros, although it's all of that.

It's not just Reality that lives in me, my own experience of self, and if I'm awake and alive, I can taste my enlightenment; I know that my self participates in the ultimate Self of Cosmos—that's first person.

But Reality is also personally holding me. Every place I go, I fall into the hands of the infinite Personhood of Cosmos that calls me. That's a primordial perspective of the Cosmos.

1. First person, It lives in me.
2. Third person, the Forces of Reality.
3. And I-Thou, the great Personhood of Cosmos that calls me and knows me uniquely, infinitely, ultimately, and irreducibly.

Let's ask for everything. Prayer affirms the dignity of personal need, and unless I affirm the dignity of my own personal need, I can't ask for anyone else's. I've got to be able to feel my own need and clarify my need, and then ask for the world.

WE NEED TO ACKNOWLEDGE SHADOW

So I want to talk a little bit with you today about two things, and it's kind of part one and part two.

I want to talk about how we have to celebrate our heroes and critique our heroes that need critiquing.

I'm going to start with the first part and go to the second part. So here's the first part.

Something happened in the Capitol of the United States and I want to talk about it for all the reasons I said in the beginning. Because it's a world event, it's not an American event.

We could talk about it for hours. There's an enormous amount that actually needs to be said, there's an enormous amount of confusion around it around the globe. But I want to just limit it to a couple of points that are key to *how we actually develop and evolve our very humanity, evolve the very core of who we are, evolve our public culture.*

It's the deepest way how we actually avoid dystopia and enter utopia, and create discourse that matters.

So I'm going to start with what's somewhat the unpopular side for most of our community, and then I want to go to the second side, which you'll be able to hear a little bit easier.

But I'm going to start with the unpopular side, because it's really important. It's very clear that Joe Biden won the elections in America, and it's very clear that the courts checked for voter fraud and decided in 63 out of 64 cases, that there was no voter fraud that was sufficient to overturn the election.

Is there voter fraud in elections? Yes.

I've studied voter fraud extensively, done quite a lot of research. One of our board members and our senior scholar, Dr. Venu—who's a leading doctor in Eastern Texas and a man of enormous integrity—did an extensive first person and third person study of voter fraud, and there absolutely is voter fraud in American elections that needs to be dealt with. We would have been wiser to actually acknowledge that, "Yes, there is voter fraud; voter fraud is an issue that needs to be dealt with."

It's not a trumped up issue, it's not a fabricated issue.

- There's a history of voter fraud which takes place in multiple ways, and we recognize that.
- But in this election, we've checked very clearly, and whatever voter fraud there might have been on both sides, Democratic and the Republican side, it was minor, and in no sense was grounds to overturn the election.

But what happened was—and I tracked this through multiple media posts—there wasn't an essential acknowledgement of shadow. The acknowledgement of shadow where you recognize the lower self in the individual person and the lower self in society, then you can actually say, there's an issue, voter fraud is a real issue.

One of the ways that Donald Trump was able to rile up his base in a frenzy of disinformation was because the mainstream news channels denied that voter fraud was an issue in American society.

It is an issue. There's an enormous amount of data on it, and it's an extensive and complex topic that deserves real attention.

Had we said that and owned the shadow, then we could have dealt with the issue far more powerfully.

That's a very big deal, I want you to understand that.

Let's say you're living in Montana and you hear this whole conversation about voter fraud coming out of particular echo chambers on Parler—which is one social media platform on 4chan, which is another social media platform—and they're talking about voter fraud, and they actually bring extensive evidence for voter fraud; not in this election, but there's been voter fraud issues since at least 1960, in terms of major structural issues.

What actually happened in the 1960 election and did the democrats actually steal the 1960 election? Was Joseph Kennedy responsible for fixing and rigging of voter machines? Those are all very real questions which there's real historical debate on.

But what happened is, when you then went to the liberal mainstream news channels, everyone says *there's never any voter fraud*. But that's not true at all.

I could send you chapter and verse now for a half hour. But that's not true.

There is voter fraud, and it's lived on both sides of the aisle; it's not a Republican issue, it's not a Democratic issue.

Had we acknowledged that shadow, then people would have said, "I trust the mainstream media, because the mainstream media is actually acknowledging that shadow, it's a real thing, and we're now ascertaining based on the best information and investigation by the courts, that actually there was not sufficient voter fraud on either side to change the results of the election."

It's a very big deal: acknowledge the shadow, acknowledge lower self; it's what makes you trustable.

That's number one.

ISSUES OF MORAL EQUIVALENCY

Here's the second thing, and I want to say a couple of really important things. It's really important to get that what happened in the American Capitol was a horror, there's no justification for it.

You can't say, well, in Black Lives Matter rallies, things got unruly—and things did get unruly. —And the press didn't hold Black Lives Matter rallies accountable. That's actually true, and there was looting and burning that cost many poor and lower-income families their livelihood for generations;

it ruined people's lives. There was unimaginable and horrific violence in sometimes 12 cities at once, that's all true; it was out of balance.

Even the Black Lives Matter movement itself at its core is speaking for a deep integrity, and speaking at systemic racism, which is a dimension of reality that needs to be addressed in a real way.

But actually, you don't get to say, "Oh, because rallies at shopping malls or even at state capitals got out of hand, that's actually comparable with what happened in Washington." It's not comparable!

What happened in Washington was not a rally that got out of hand.

I want to get this straight, because it's really important just to say clearly.

It was a deliberate part of a larger attempt by a sitting American president to not allow a peaceful transfer of power.

That just needs to be said, and we need to say it clearly.

Trump was given many opportunities to allow for a peaceful transfer of power, he was asked six or seven times, but he refused to commit himself to a peaceful transfer of power.

That's number one.

Number two, his son that day says, "We're coming for you. You're not heroes, you're zeros."

Rudy Giuliani, his lawyer says, "The people who are voting the wrong way should be subject to trial by combat," which is a medieval phrase, which indicates that if you engage in combat and you die, therefore you're guilty. That's just unconscionable.

Trump himself says that same day, "We're never going to take back our country with weakness, we're not going to take it anymore." Earlier on, in many tweets, he said, "January 6th, big stuff coming down the pike." In his situation room, he was initially watching and cheering what was happening.

That's a travesty. That's not the same thing as riots that got out of hand—which were unconscionable, I want to make that really clear. And when that wasn't acknowledged by certain dimensions of the media and the destruction, which was horrific, which cost people their livelihoods, that's a big deal.

Having said that, that's not comparable.

The comparison that's being made all over the right-wing media, "The Democrats are hypocrites, because look how they didn't speak up in the Black Lives Matter rally as that got out of hand." First off, the Democrats did speak up, Biden spoke up and Harris spoke up. It was too little, it was too late, but they did speak up. So they're not comparable.

Breaching the Capitol with the intention to possibly get yourself killed—because the people who went to breach the Capitol were willing to give up their lives, but for a false cause—causing five deaths, violating with intention to disturb the essential process of government and the peaceful transition of power, screaming "Hang Mike Pence," wearing t-shirts that said "Camp Auschwitz," essentially undermining the integrity of America's capacity to act in the world; that's a horror.

There's no way to justify that. There's no comparison between that and anything else. And that has to be held accountable. So I want to just say that as clearly as we can. Five people died that day. So that's number two.

WE NEED TO BE ABLE TO CRITIQUE OUR HEROES

Number three and four.

I want to offer something really important about how we critique our heroes and how we celebrate our heroes.

With your permission I want to share this with you today, because it's an enormously critical message in building our public culture, and actually creating the new human and the new humanity.

One of the things I love about the sacred text—which is called *Torah*, the biblical text—is that it critiques its own heroes.

It's unbelievably important to critique our own heroes. The left has to critique its heroes, let's say in the United States, but it could be in France, it could be in Holland it could be in China; it doesn't matter where it is.

> *We have to have the ability both to celebrate the victories, even the partial victories, to celebrate our heroes, which we're going to do today, and to critique our heroes.*

If you're a die-hard liberal and you think that everything that Joe Biden and Michelle Obama and Barack Obama and Kamala Harris says is right, and you won't critique them when they're dead on wrong, *then you've become a puppet; you've lost your inwardness.*

If you're a Republican—I don't want to compare it to Trump because Trump is *sui generis*—and you're not willing to critique George Bush or Ronald Reagan, or any of your other Republican heroes, or the Republican Party, but you're always critiquing the other side—*then you've lost your interiority, you've lost your capacity for discernment, you've lost your freedom, you've become a parrot; you've lost something essential in your humanity.*

WE NEED TO AVOID IDENTITY POLITICS

So although I voted for Joe Biden, and thought that Donald Trump needed to be out of office, I want to just say that—Barack Obama has been guilty of this in this particular cycle, as has Michelle Obama, as has Kamala Harris, as has Joe Biden—Joe Biden was the most egregious when he said, "No one's going to tell me that if those protesters in Washington had been Black Lives Matter, they wouldn't have been treated differently." Now, what that meant was that **actually it was a racial issue, that the reason that they were able to take over the Capitol is because they were white, and therefore, they didn't meet real resistance**. If there's evidence for that, we should put it forth. But based on all the evidence that's in the public square today, *that's actually not the case*. There was actually a black police officer who clearly feared for his life. There was a white woman who was shot at point blank range, one of the insurgents; she needs to be shot at tragically, *you were trying to breach the Capitol*. And they were screaming to hang Pence and to hurt Nancy Pelosi.

It was the job of the Capitol Police to stop the crowd, and the Capitol Police was clearly overwhelmed. Unless there's other evidence to the contrary, which hasn't been put forth, they were clearly unprepared and fearful for their lives and didn't know how to handle the situation. There's an enormous amount of material that indicates that's true. The Capitol police did the best job that they can.

We have to actually empathize with the Capitol Police—one of them died—and not suggest that they're racists.

That's one of the tragedies of the left today, it's called identity politics, where we make everything an issue of identity politics; that's a problem.

Identity politics can be, "All women tell the truth, men lie." No, that's not true. It's not a man and woman issue, it's about human beings.

It's not about Jews, or it's not about African-Americans. Although there are Jewish issues.

There are African-American issues, there are issues which are feminist issues and masculinist issues. Of course, there are.

But at the core, we've got to be so careful. **I understand that Joe Biden was elected because of the African-American vote, and particularly the feminine African-American vote that came through for him**. That's beautiful. **But Biden has to be careful like any precedent of pandering to**

his base, and suggesting that the Capitol Police are racists. That's a big deal, can't do that; that's identity politics.

I say this in the spirit of democracy, not as a God forbid Trumpian insult. I have the greatest respect for Joe Biden, for his decades of public service, for his goodness, for his integrity, and therefore he's thrilled that I'm offering this critique; this is respectful dialogue. That's how it works, respect means that we can disagree. Just like the biblical texts that I grew up on, critiques its heroes; Moses gets critiqued, Abraham gets critiqued.

When we're able to love and critique our heroes that we have enormous respect for, then we can create an actual dialogue. That's a critical point.

WE CELEBRATE A RECORD TURNOUT OF AMERICANS WHO VOTED

We've talked about critiquing our heroes, now I want to talk about celebrating our heroes.

This is a big celebration moment. There are two sets of heroes to celebrate here. The first set of heroes to celebrate is, I want to celebrate—starting with the Women's March in 2017, the Me Too movement, and the enormous amount of activism in the Democratic Party which actually activated a groundswell movement—the 160 million Americans who voted. That's unbelievable!

I also want to energize and honor the 74 million Americans who believed in the importance of *Make America Great Again*, which I believe in as well, although I believe that that critical value has nothing to do with Donald Trump, and that Donald Trump actually stood and stands against *making America great again*. He was the wrong symbol, he led his own people astray, and he broke his covenant with his own base.

But I actually believe that the majority of people, the 74 million who voted for Donald Trump, is because they believed in a vision of America, which actually most of us share; an important vision of America. It's not a redneck vision of America.

It's a vision of free elections, it's a vision of family, and it's a vision of value.

Actually, that *what unites us as citizens of the world and as participants in democracy, and for those who live in America, as Americans, it is far greater than that which divides us.*

I want to wildly honor the 160 million Americans—that's a record turnout—who participated in the democratic process.

That's a gorgeous victory for democracy, which is why I also want to honor all of the Republican officials who said that Donald Trump has a right to go through the courts and offer evidence of voter fraud; every Republican who said that deserves to be honored. Because it's true.

So we went to the courts, and 63 judges, many of them Republican-appointed—we'll talk about that in a second—threw out Trump's claims.

Then it's over, then democracy worked.

Then after going through his due right to challenge the elections, what Donald Trump needed to do was to get on television and say, "I exercised my due right, and now I want to congratulate my opponent, Joe Biden, for fighting a hard fight, and winning, and you have my full support." It would have blown my heart open, it would have blown all our hearts open; that's the moment that we needed.

WE CELEBRATE THE UNSEEN HEROES

But here's the thing. There were great heroes that need to be recognized. These heroes are really important, and I want to share with you a couple of these heroes. Kristina and I were talking about this yesterday, and we were crying. We've critiqued our heroes, but I also want to celebrate this unseen group of heroes. Because really, there's virtually an unseen group of heroes whose names actually will be sung in history, who actually held our democracy together.

I've always believed in our democracy. I said to my dear friend, Sally Kempton, who's a wonderful teacher and a brilliant liberal activist. And I was very afraid of all sorts of things that she said would happen. "Sally, none of them are going to happen. Republicans and Democrats are good, they believe in democracy. People are going to do the right thing, and I'm absolutely sure of it." Friends, that's what happened!

So I want to just cite some people who are heroes, who deserve celebration.

Here's the thing, they're Republicans.

First, **Brett Kavanaugh, and the new Chief Justice, Amy Barrett.** Everybody thought in key votes before the election, because they were appointed by Trump, that they would vote the way Trump wanted to. They did it decisively and clearly. **Kavanaugh and Barrett voted their integrity and their reading of the law and defied Donald Trump.** Thank you, you guys were awesome. We trusted you, and we disagreed with you about so many things, but *we can actually recognize that you stood in integrity, and we can celebrate you.*

Number two, **William Barr**, who I've said consistently that he's been demonized. I've studied him, I've studied his writings, and his background. I think he made some significant mistakes along the way in the Trump presidency. I get why he stayed and why he wanted to be an adult in the room. But he actually not only refused to lend the Justice Department's backing to Trump's fabricated claims, but he declared publicly, "I see no evidence of fraud that could have changed the result." **He went way beyond the call of duty.** He could have been a Trump henchmen, because Trump was still at that point the most popular person in the Republican Party, but he said *I'm not doing this*. William Barr, thank you.

Number three, **Fox News**. Fox News calls Arizona for Biden, and then calls the election for Biden. It's very clear that Trump was putting enormous pressure on Fox News not to do that, and Fox News clearly and unequivocally said *no* to Trump; lost an enormous amount of its own viewership, acted against its own self-interest, and actually called the election appropriately, and critiqued Trump. They've reported on the voter fraud claims of Trump, but they have not veered from that position. That's a huge *Yay*. At least for the first time, had they not done that, then we would have had split the universe of America, but they did, and they behaved with great integrity. That's number three.

Number four, **all of the Republican politicians** who actually said, "Trump deserves his day in court, but after his day in court is over, we have to uphold whatever the court says." They deserve a big *Yay*. Thank you for doing the right thing. Thank you for not succumbing to what you thought was the interests of your separate self.

But let's go deeper, I want to go deep here for a second because it's much more dramatic than even that. What Trump needed in order to make this work from his perspective is he needed a court to rule what's called technically that *the states had failed to make a choice*; that's a technical legal structure.

He needed that in order to move key people, GOP Republican legislators to refuse to certify elections. He needed a couple of courts to go his way. **It was court after court with Republican-appointed judges who ruled against Trump.**

So I want to give a huge applause to all the Republican judges who ruled against Trump.

You guys came through, you guys upheld the law; that's fantastic.

But now go to the next step, and here's where it gets even more dramatic. Trump assumed that he would be able to pressure legislators not to certify the elections. Now, had he been able to do that, then what would have happened is—had he been able to get key Republican officials not to certify the results of the elections, let's say in three states—the Republican legislators could have appointed new electors to be in the American Electoral College, which could have voted for Trump. Now, this is an amazing story.

All the key Republican officials—even those whose career is completely dependent on the Republican Party, which was then and is still to a large extent controlled by Trump—**they all said *no*.**

I want to just say to you heroes, *this is a very big deal.*

There's a man whose name should be remembered in history, his name is Aaron Van Langevelde. Aaron Van Langevelde is the man who was needed by Trump to refuse to certify the results of the election in Michigan. There were two Republicans that Trump needed for certification. One had already agreed not to certify, and Trump put enormous pressure on this man. He's Dutch it looks like, and I want to just read you a description of them. The man in the rimless glasses and a Paisley tie who clutched a pen as if in self-defense. Van Langevelde, a boyish-looking forty year old held a part time position in Michigan's election bureaucracy. By great misfortune, he had attracted the attention of Donald Trump, who was three weeks into a desperate struggle to erase his defeat at the ballot box. Trump wanted him and put inordinate pressure on him through so many means to block the certification of Michigan's presidential vote. **The monstrous pressure that descended upon Van Langevelde is not easy to convey.**

He was one of two Republicans in the four-person Board of State Canvassers. Trump needed them both to sabotage the certification, and one of them had already signed on to the Trump team.

State and National Party leaders are broadcasting lies about *enough fraud to overturn the election* all over.

The President himself and a parade of the leading figures in the country on the Republican side sent messages to Van Langevelde that he must follow along or bear the consequences. He ducked their calls, didn't take their calls; he goes off the grid. The observers and everyone thought he would resign, but he didn't resign.

All 83 county authorities reported in Michigan—Michigan is made up of counties or sub-sectors—**valid election results, meaning there was not fraud to overturn anything.**

The entire country's looking, he's been subject to enormous pressure. He's asked, *are you certifying these results?* Van Langevelde leans forward, holds the mic, and he says calmly, "The board's duty is very clear. We have a duty to certify this election based on the returns. I've had a pretty good chance to look at the law these last few days, as you can imagine. I found nothing that gives us the authority to review complaints of fraud."

He said, *we have no authority, I'm not going to actually be a pawn.* He came through!

But not only did he come through, I want to just keep going.

Emily Murphy, who's the head of the General Services Administration, she was pressured by Trump not to release funds. Once Langevelde came through, she issues a statement that she had ascertained that Joe Biden was the successful candidate, that the certification of election results have now happened, and she's releasing the funds against Trump's wishes to allow the transition to take place.

Emily Murphy and Aaron Van Langevelde, let's give you guys a huge applause.

Let's keep going. In Georgia, the Republican Secretary of State, **Brad Raffensperger**—total Republican, had supported Trump—**made a decision.**

He was ferociously assaulted by Trump. He was insulted, mocked in public, and everything dear to him was threatened. Trump demanded that he actually recalculate the result, and Brad Raffensperger utterly refused. Then Brian Kemp, who was a major Trump supporter—Governor of State, Republican, who will probably lose his reelection because of this—supported his Secretary of State.

Even though Trump said that *if you do that, I'm going to do everything I can to bring you down*. And in Georgia, it could well be that Trump could do that. **So both Brad Raffensperger and Brian Kemp went against their self-interest in order to support the doing of the right thing.**

Here's the last one—I know you're not going to like this, but I'm going to tell you anyways—even Mike Pence. There's a reason to criticize for sure over the last four years. But at the moment of decision, **when Trump demanded that he use unilateral power to strike down the state election results, he refused**. That's why there were the shouts of "Hang Pence" at the Capitol. This is a big deal. I want to get this straight, these are heroes.

I want to go to the last step here, and the last step here matters enormously.

So why were they heroes, and why were there so many other Republicans that weren't? For example, 18 Republican state attorney generals who signed a symbolic letter, and two thirds of the Republican caucus in the House of Representatives signed a letter challenging the election results.

Why did those people do one thing and these people did another thing?

I think there's two reasons, and I think we need to understand both of them.

CHARACTER MATTERS: LISTENING TO THE VOICE OF INTEGRITY DESPITE PRESSURE

One is character; character matters. Meaning stepping out of the bubble of pressure upon you, finding the value that lives inside of you, and listening to that voice of integrity.

So these men and women—from Amy Barrett, to Brett Kavanaugh, to Brad Raffensperger, to Brian Kemp, to Aaron Van Langevelde—all these people who did gorgeously, *they had character.*

But it's even deeper than that.

The Republicans that moved to support Trump, for the most part—I'm not talking about the people on 4chan and Parler who themselves were victims of a broken information ecology, where they were actually doused with lies. They actually believed they were saving their democracy, but they acted in ways that need to be countered and defeated with full force. They were acting as insurrectionists.

- The Republicans who signed all these letters, they did it because they thought what they were doing was only symbolic.
- Almost unilaterally, when it came down to doing something that would actually change the game, the actual republicans that I just mentioned, eight of them—whether it was in the Supreme Court, whether it was in the legislators, whether it was governors, whether it was state attorney general—they actually acted with integrity.

That's a big deal, because democracy worked.

In this moment, we got to celebrate partial victories. We've talked about this before. We don't only celebrate a complete victory, we celebrate partial victories. Remember, we talked about the story of Hanukkah, which is one particular holiday in the Hebrew wisdom calendar. Hanukkah was a partial victory. But we celebrate partial victories. So this was a huge and gorgeous partial victory for democracy.

The mistake of the Republicans, both throughout Trump's term and those who supported him in this moment in these symbolic acts, was not to understand that symbols matter. They thought, *these are just words, these are not actually policies.* I can't tell you the amount of Republicans that

I respect, who told me *we're backing Trump because his policies in these particular sets of areas matter*, even though his words are terrible and I'm completely embarrassed by him.

That's a mistake. We forgot that words express our interiority, words express the feeling tone of Cosmos.

When a President makes fun of handicapped people, that's not just words, that's a violation of the integrity of the Cosmos; it's not okay.

People like my friend, Dennis Prager, who I've known for many years—I haven't talked to him in a long time—who supported Trump throughout, he said to me at his home one night, 15 years ago, "The reason I support Trump is because we don't judge a president on character, we judge a president on their policy." That might have been partially true up to Trump. It was no longer true; Trump broke that rule. **Because in him, character became policy.** A child in America couldn't grow up with a sense of a model for what it means to be a human being, which shattered American youth.

America couldn't stand in the world, because it didn't have the integrity and moral authority it needed to stand. You lose moral authority when a president makes fun of handicapped people, when a president publicly says, "I'm a good businessman, and therefore, I don't pay my contractors, because I can get away with not paying them and save money on contracts." Trump said that in the second debate against Hillary Clinton. The second he said that, I was done. I was sitting at Terry Nelson's house, and I said, *that's not okay.* Interiority matters, character matters, values matter; policy has to be put aside.

DEMOCRACY IS A MOMENTOUS LEAP OF EVOLUTION

We got to understand that *that which unites us is so much greater than that which divides us*, and that we're part of a world-centric movement towards the Good, the True, and the Beautiful. It's not about Democrat and Republican. We want a strong Republican party that stands for the true values of the Republican Party—and the huge test today is for the Republican base to actually shift and take the party back; that's utterly essential.

We want a Republican Party.

We want a Libertarian Party.

We want a Green Party.

And we want a Democratic Party.

We want a pluralistic democracy that functions in an exciting and potent and powerful way.

We want to be able to celebrate heroes and critique our heroes.

Democracy is the most important institution. It took 10,000 years to get to democracy.

Democracy itself is a momentous leap of evolution, and so we have to protect it.

DEMOCRACY MEANS THAT THE RIGHTS OF EVERY HUMAN BEING ARE BASED ON THE INDIVIDUAL FACTS

Democracy means two things. It means number one, **we don't do identity politics**. Democracy means that **every human being has individual rights**. Our rights are not based on being black or Jewish, or a man or a woman, they're based on the individual facts in a particular case; we judge each person based on their humanity.

In that sense, identity politics is a regression to a pre-democracy era, in which people are judged not by the content of their character, but by the color of their skin or by their gender anatomy. That's critical, we got to stand against that. We also have to stand against anyone who would allow a sensible policy, as important as it is, to actually suffer a violation of integrity and decency in the public square every single day—which poisoned the very fabric of American democracy for four years. The people that supported Trump, ultimately, after he crossed all those lines: *it's not okay; we've got to draw the line there.*

We have to celebrate our heroes.

We have to celebrate the incredible integrity and goodness, where people did what they should have done.

The reason we have to celebrate and we can't let it go is, everyone thought that wouldn't happen. All of my dear friends who are staunch Democrats were sure that this wasn't going to happen, and the mainstream media listed a whole set of things that would happen; none of them happened.

Democracy stood because people stood in their virtue, in their goodness, and in their integrity.

Let's trust each other again.

Let's reach our hands around the world, across party lines, and let's trust good people to stand.

We can trust good people to stand if we actually stand for those virtues and we make them real every day, all the time.

CHAPTER EIGHT

CELEBRATING THE FOURTH OF JULY: A NEW DECLARATION OF INDEPENDENCE

Episode 247 — July 5, 2021

RE-VISIONING FREEDOM IN THE DIGITIZED WORLD

Happy Fourth of July for those of you in the United States, and happy Fourth of July for everybody around the world—and happy freedom!

What a day! What an incredible day!

There is so much happening in the world, and there is so much joy, and there are *billions* of times more people committing acts of goodness now than there are people committing acts which are not good, which are contracted, which are ego-driven, which are causing pain in egregious ways.

I want to celebrate the good because we have structured our society to celebrate destruction. *If it bleeds, it leads.* News is an entertainment business, it has been that way for several decades, and news is driven by ratings. Then, news got translated into the internet, in which everything is driven by click-bait and hijacking of attention. We all know that attention is more instantly focused by negativity, by jealousy, by fear.

145

So, naturally, the structure of our *gnosis sphere*—of our interconnected global nervous system (because this is what the internet *is*)—is reinforcing the depths of fear, and contraction, and the lowest common denominator of human actions and interactions.

That's a tragedy. It is a tragedy that doesn't lead to freedom, and it is a tragedy that doesn't lead to the celebration of democracy.

So we are in a complicated day.

We are in a day in which the United States, which has been a leading democracy in the world, is here to *celebrate freedom*—and yet it's not easy to celebrate freedom, and things have changed, and we are living in a different world than the world of the Founding Fathers.

What does it mean today to celebrate freedom?

We've got to *re-focus* on the Good, the True, and the Beautiful, and celebrate the gorgeousness that human beings are doing across the planet, and the Outrageous Love that's unfolding in billions of interactions across the planet.

This is not, however, what is driving the digitized environment that hijacks attention and uses addiction strategies to create long-term customers in order to feed a tiny elite of the billionaire class, ignoring the larger good of all of the end users. The end users of the internet are not considered legitimate stakeholders whose deeper well-being must be honored. A plethora of studies shows us what our grandmothers already knew—that you can hijack attention much more effectively through negativity, fear, hate, and polarization than through love and depth. Because **love and depth need to be *cultivated* while negativity is the default mechanism of the superficial. And the opposite of the holy is the superficial.**

In fact, the end users of the internet are *not* end users. They are instruments, objects who are fed into machine intelligence to garner data and personality profiles, and, more particularly, to garner predictive analysis about how you will react to specific sets of stimuli in terms of buying and other key decision-making moments—including *voting*. This information is then sold to third-party customers; this is the structure of the internet. **The structure of the internet is *not* the town hall that the Founding Fathers were thinking about. It is *not* the township.** It is *not* the citizens that know each other. We are in a new world, and we need to think deeply about this new world.

So here is our intention:

- Let us re-vision **freedom.**
- Let us re-vision what we mean by **independence.**
- Let us declare not just a Declaration of Independence, but a Declaration of Interdependence.
- Let us understand what it means to **recreate freedom in the digital age.**
- Let us understand **how we avoid the existential risk of digital dictatorship**, what my friend and colleague, Zak Stein and I are calling "TechnoFeudalism."

TechnoFeudalism is where our attention is stolen and our opinion formed by polarized, broken information ecologies—all beyond the pale of our conscious awareness. How do we move towards true freedom in the digital age? How do we avoid a kind of numbing digital instrumental totalitarianism that views us as nanobots in the larger system of data?

We must re-vision freedom, and re-vision what we actually mean by *independence.*

We must revision our core identities and see how those play out in the digitized spaces.

We must realize that we are not *objects* to each other, but *subjects*.

We are interconnected and intimate with each other.

We must realize that we all need each other, that *no one* is separate from the whole. That we are not nanobots, but irreducible Unique Selves. **We are**

nodes in the great system of immeasurable value, in a world ruthlessly seeking to reduce everything to measurement and commodification.

Let us declare not just a Declaration of Independence, but a Declaration of *Interdependence*.

This is a very different kind of freedom than being free to do whatever you want. It is more like the freedom to be your most authentic and gorgeous Unique Self that reality willed into existence *in you*, *as you* and *through you*. To know that you do not exist independently of everyone and everything. That you are needed by *All-That-Is*. **Everyone and everything literally *needs* you.**

Let us understand how we **move towards a true freedom in this digitized age**:

- the freedom of **interdependence**;
- the freedom of being my deepest expression of authenticity— and **unique authenticity**;
- the freedom of radical, ecstatic joy;
- the freedom of **loving each other**, and caring in the most deep and poignant and powerful way for each other, and staking our lives for each other. Looking in each other's eyes, and being face-to-face, and re-engaging friendship the way it needs to be.

What would it mean to re-vision what democracy means?

What does it mean to celebrate freedom in a post-postmodern digitized world? **A world in which our information ecologies are broken and we have lost our trust in the legacy institutions that govern our sense making.** A world in which our collective decisions are manipulated by digital split testing beyond the pale of awareness, to an extent that easily has the capacity to change the result of an election.

What would it mean to receive the baton today from the Founding Fathers (who left out the Founding Mothers) and be, today, the Founding Fathers and Mothers—and *re-vision*?

Because that's what the Founding Fathers did. The Founding Fathers were highly educated. They had read most of the books available in their day and they tried to think forward. They tried not just to solve the local issues, but to re-vision what it would mean to create a reality that was good, true, and beautiful. **The Founding Fathers were a great evolution of love in a thousand different ways and they were wildly important—but now we've got to pick up the baton**. The world we live in now is fundamentally different from the world that they envisioned. We have to receive the best and the most beautiful that they offered us, but we have to take it to the next level.

Let us see if we can commit to play a larger game in a particular way that we never have before: let us re-vision democracy today; let us re-vision what it means to be human being.

So let me just ask you a question:

- ◆ Are you ready to play a larger game?
- ◆ Are we ready to re-include *everyone* who was left out of the original democratic vision?
- ◆ Are we ready to be the Founding Fathers and the Founding Mothers *today*, and vision again, and write the new documents, and reclaim freedom, and reclaim independence, and reclaim interdependence, and take responsibility to evolve the source code?
- ◆ Are we ready to do what the Founding Fathers did, as the Founding Fathers and Mothers, and **participate together in the evolution of love?**

Because that's what the Fourth of July is.

That's the explosion. *That's* the fireworks of today—that we step into our digitized world, into our world that doesn't *have* town halls—and **recreate friendship and town halls, but at a different level of consciousness, in a new way.** In a way that meets the reality of today, which is wholly different than the reality of the Founding Fathers.

So *are* you ready?

Can we love *that* much? Can we be *that* audacious? Can we be *that* tender? Can we be *that* fierce together? Are we ready to do this for real, fierce and tender, all the way, taking responsibility for the re-visioning of the story, for telling this new story together?

Now is the time.

This is the hour.

We are the people.

DEMOCRACY CANNOT EXIST WITHOUT A SENSE OF SHARED VALUES

The Founding Fathers stepped into a world in which there was *shared value*—**a shared sense of the Good, the True, and the Beautiful.** That shared value was, in some deep sense, drawn from the great traditions, it was drawn from the traditional period, from *pre-modernity*. The great traditions had a lot of things wrong with them. They had an enormous amount of corruption, but they also had *insight*, they also had *practice*, they also had *realization*. There was a sense in which **modernity, after pre-modernity, drew from the great traditions a shared sense of value.**

Now, not all of modernity did that. There were major strains in modernity that believed that there was *no* intrinsic value in Cosmos, but no one really made that the center of the conversation. Even the people who believed that, like David Hume and, later, other major thinkers—who, in the end, gave birth to postmodernity—no one quite *said* it that way. There was a set of what I call *Common Sense Sacred Axioms* that everyone lived by. At the center of the conversation were thinkers like Adam Smith, who talked about *the invisible hand of the market*, and Comenius, and other major thinkers who *knew* that there was intrinsic value in Cosmos. **They understood that this sense of intrinsic value, which was at the center of the great traditions, now has to be re-accessed in new ways.** Even though they had broken with the great traditions—there is a clear discontinuity between the traditional and modern periods—for these thinkers, **there was also a *core continuity* in the discernment and knowing that we live in a value-laden Cosmos, and that value itself lives in us**. And *that* modernity was responsible for the evolution of that core value beyond the ethnocentric claims of the traditional period. **This was the great movement of modernity at its best.**

Because the ethnocentric claims of pre-modernity were along the lines of:

> *It's my God and it's my religion and I own God, and no one else's*
> *God is real, and God is outside of Reality and not inside of Reality.*
> *I'm a small, paltry human being, and my only job is to be obedient.*

The traditional world claimed that God is *outside* of Reality, and not *inside* Reality; it failed to sufficiently recognize the dignity of the human being: "I'm a small, paltry human being, and my only job is to be obedient." The majority of great thinkers in the modern period realized that these notions of pre-modernity were limited, and **modernity tried to extract a set of *universal* values from pre-modernity, beyond the limited ethnocentric claims.**

The Founding Fathers lived in that world. **They *assumed* that we have the sense of universal values that we all share, and therefore, we can create democracy.** Because democracy is based on *sense-making*, and you can only do sense-making if you have a shared ground of value upon which it rests. **If we have shared values, we can make sense of the world together.**

- ◆ We can make sense of the world together, and we can educate a citizenry to do sense-making, and to make decisions.

- ◆ We can have voters—and we can trust our voters because our voters are going to be well-versed in these values that live inside of them, and they are going to be educated, and they are going to participate and become the holders of the power of government.

It is government for the people, by the people.

That was the Founding Fathers. That was their view.

Thomas Jefferson writes in a number of places, *Only the people themselves are the safe depository for the ultimate powers of society.*

We cannot trust government by itself, we cannot trust corporations, we cannot trust kings—only the people themselves. Famously, when Benjamin Franklin was asked, after the Constitutional Convention in the United States, what kind of government was produced, he answered: *We produced a republic, if you can keep it.*

A republic means a democracy as we know it, but—*if you can keep it.* Can we keep that democracy? It was Jefferson who said: *If I could have a perfect newspaper and a broken government, or a perfect government and a broken newspaper, I would take the perfect newspaper.*

What he meant was, **people need information**. They need to be *able* to do sense-making—and if they can do sense-making, they can fix the government. They can correct the mistakes. They can claim power in the citizenry.

Government—for the people, by the people.

George Washington understood this very well. He said that **the most important goal of the federal government is the comprehensive education of every single citizen in the science of government.** That's shocking, and it's the goal of the government itself was to educate the citizens in the science of government. Why? Because we relied on the citizens to do sense-making. The citizens can do sense-making if they can look at the issues, understand them, get a really deep sense of them and then bring their shared values to bear; they can *evaluate*.

You need *values* to evaluate, to discern and to make decisions.

There can be no sense-making without shared values, without what I call *a Universal Grammar of Value*. And there can be no *Universal Grammar of Value* without some recognition of *intrinsic* value at some level of reality. Not eternal unchanging value, not eternal in the sense of *everlasting*, but eternal value meaning *beneath time*. And that eternal value also *evolves*.

Eternal and evolving value. Being and becoming always live together as the two faces of the one. We need eternal evolving intrinsic value in order to articulate a shared ground of value, from which we can do shared sense-making.

VOTERS HAVE NO IDEA WHAT THEY ARE VOTING ON

The world of early democracy that our Founding Fathers lived in no longer exists. It has been completely evolved and in some ways *destroyed* by the technologies of modernity. One of the implications of this new vast and infinitesimally intricate world, **is that we now live in a world in which voters have pretty much no idea what they're voting on.** The issues are simply too complex to understand. That is why we deploy actuarial tables and machine intelligence algorithms to approach so many issues.

We live a world in which the issues are so complex that meta-modernism calls them *hyperobjects*:

- There is too much interlocking complexity to be able to make sense of it through any natural linear process.
- There is too much subtly interlinked cascading causation for an individual to track without a guiding algorithm.
- There is so much interconnectivity between sets of highly

complex issues that only a very small cadre of experts, often aided and abetted by machine intelligence, can get a sense of what is unfolding in real time.

And even these experts disagree with each other on major issues of policy across fields like education, governance economics, health care and so much more.

How should we approach **jobs** in a world of artificial intelligence which is moving to make jobs obsolete?

How should **healthcare** be structured?

How **defense** should be related to **social investment**?

How should we handle the **interconnected economies** of China and the United States?

What does it mean for the dollar to be **the standard of world currency**? What did Nixon change in this regard some decades back?

How do **complex financial instruments** work and directly affect our own lives?

How does **the stock market** and its linkage to six or so major investment behemoths impact thirty other seemingly unrelated domains? Why does that matter?

How to correlate **federal reserve policy** and the implications of fractional reserve banking with numerous issues that seem unrelated?

How does inflation really work, and **what is money** actually, and why is that so impactful across almost every dimension of reality?

What about **virology**?

And gain-of-function research?...

The list goes on.

In other words:

---

*Every major issue is very
sophisticated and complex, so that
non-experts really have little clue
about what's really happening.*

Richard Dawkins, the famous evolutionary biologist, when he went to vote about whether Great Britain should stay in the European Union or leave— what was called the Brexit vote in Great Britain—he said, *This is absurd. The level of complex issues involved in the Brexit vote are way beyond my understanding. The economics, the monetary flows, why am I voting on this?*[19]

We have a new situation where voters **don't really have the capacity or expertise to grasp many of the key issues of the day**. We are asking people to vote on that which they fundamentally don't understand, and the understanding of those issues is hijacked—by necessity—by groups of experts, who fundamentally disagree with each other.

In the last fifteen years, we have been unable to create virtually *any* common ground in democracies around the world. We live in a moment of increased polarization between experts.

What it would take for an individual human being to wade their way through the available information—to be able to vote in a serious way? It is nearly impossible for almost all of us. So why are we voting? What is democracy doing?

How can we trust the democratic process to deliver good decisions on core issues of catastrophic and existential risk or on anything that truly matters?

---

19 Richard Dawkins. Ignoramuses should have no say on our EU membership—and that includes me. In *Prospectus Magazine*, July 2016.

THE KEY ISSUES OF OUR DAY ARE NOT BEING VOTED ON

The second reason democracies are failing is that **the key issues that affect our lives are no longer voted on by democracy.**

For example, how many people who are here voted on the internet? Who voted on the internet: whether we should have an internet, what kind of internet it should be, how the internet should be structured? How many people here are voting on how we should handle artificial intelligence, one of the most essential issues of our day? Who is voting on artificial intelligence? Nobody.

Another example. The COVID-19 pandemic was probably caused by *gain-of-function* research done in partnership between the United States and China. We are not sure how the virus exploded, but it is pretty clear today that it didn't explode just through someone eating a bat in Wuhan, China. It's pretty clear that the virus was developed intentionally by what's called gain-of-function research. We are not sure if it was released accidentally or intentionally. It's unclear. Probably accidentally, but it is not clear.

Now, how many people here voted on gain-of-function research? Who voted on whether we should be doing gain-of-function research, which means intentionally creating viruses? It's a very controversial form of research, and there are enormous financial incentives that are driving that research. How many people voted on that here? Nobody.

> *The key issues of our day are not being voted on at all in any sense, shape, or form.*

What democracies are voting on today are not the fundamental issues that challenge us. They are *not* the issues that threaten our existence. They are not the issues that challenge our existential reality, our very being on the planet. We vote about the border issues between countries, but not about cyber warfare, or about key climate issues, or about data sharing—or anything else that really matters. The issues we vote on are not the issues that are going to cause catastrophic or existential risk. We are not voting on the key issues that—if we get them wrong—are going to cause massive unnecessary suffering of enormous intensity to the least privileged among us.

The issues we are voting on are overwhelmingly decoys. We are not voting on key issues.

WE VOTE IN THE CONTEXT OF NATION STATES, BUT REAL ISSUES ARE GLOBAL

When we vote today, we vote within the context of our nation state. America, Holland, France, Great Britain etc., around the world. Africa, Asia. These different democracies vote, but what democracies are voting on today are not the fundamental issues that challenge us, that threaten our existence, and that challenge our very existential reality, our very *being* on the planet. They are not the issues that are going to cause existential risk—which is the end of the future, the obliteration of the future—because **we are not in a world today in which nation states are controlling the future of the planet**.

We do not have a system of global governance that would allow for nation states to work together in any effective democratic fashion. And as it stands now a world government would have too much power almost by definition. Remember Palpatine and the republic in *Star Wars*? That did not go well.

The future of the planet is controlled or determined by a set of interlocking issues. Whether it's climate change or control of rogue, terrorist nuclear threats, whether it's peak phosphorus or dead zones in the oceans; whether it's artificial intelligence or techno-feudalism that we've talked about extensively this year; whether it's dealing with an international refugee crisis of an insane proportion—**none of those issues are local.**

They are being decided not by nation states but rather by international investment or equity funds, venture capital and research teams that choose what project to take part in, in large part based on what will be funded in the most dramatic fashion.

Take the pandemic, for example. A hundred years ago, an epidemic in Wuhan would have been a local issue—not even a Chinese issue, just a very particular local province of China. But because we live in an interconnected world, which maximizes efficiency over health and wholeness, with jet travel and instant mobility, that virus in Wuhan became a pandemic instantaneously. **In order to deal with it effectively, we needed *global coherence*—and by *not* having global coherence, we increase the death threat by the second and third order cascading effects of the pandemic,** closing down whole areas to jet travel. Because we couldn't provide for agricultural needs, it was causing cascading starvation for tens of millions of people and killing more people through the second and third order effects of COVID than through COVID itself. That's just one example.

In other words, we live in a global world. The nature of the technologies that have been developed in the last 120 years have made local decisions essentially irrelevant to the catastrophic and existential risks that we face. **We can only affect decisions by having a genuine degree of global coherence.**

Without global coherence, you cannot address global issues, so nation states cannot vote on the most essential issues.

Not only are nation states not voting on the local expressions of the essential issues, but nation states *cannot* deal with the essential issues, so voting in a nation state is all but irrelevant.

WE CANNOT CREATE GLOBAL COHERENCE WITHOUT GLOBAL INTIMACY

We can only solve global issues if we create *global coherence* in order to do shared sense-making between the nation states all around the world. **If we cannot do shared sense-making between the nation states around the world, we cannot generate global coherence. If we cannot generate global coherence, we cannot create global action.** Is everyone tracking that?

That's why we are living in what we might call *global action paralysis*. There's global action *paralysis*—number one, and number two: there's global action *confusion*. Either we are paralyzed or we are acting in confused ways. (Both of those happened, by the way, during the COVID-19 pandemic.) Now, what's the source of the global action paralysis and the global action confusion? **A breakdown of global coherence, or what we have called here a *Global Intimacy Disorder*.**

> *In order to heal the Global Intimacy Disorder, we need an understanding of intimacy.*

That has been one of our key foci of in the Center for Integral Wisdom over the last decade. We have formulated a key formula in the interior sciences, equivalent roughly to what the relativity formula was in the exterior sciences—**the intimacy equation**, the core equation underlying the new constitution of the Declaration of Interdependence. It is the formula that constitutes the very structure of Reality itself.

> *Intimacy = shared identity, in the context of relative otherness x mutuality of recognition x mutuality of pathos x mutuality of value x mutuality of purpose.*

What does that mean?

- The core of intimacy is shared identity in the context of relative otherness. **If we only have identity as a nation state, we don't have *shared* identity.** We have to have a shared identity. Our identity has to be, *I'm a global citizen. I'm not just ethnocentric, I'm Worldcentric.* **I don't just act for my own sake.** I don't just act for my family. I don't just act for my nation. I act for the sake of the whole.

- **Mutuality of recognition = We *recognize* each other.** We recognize each other as global citizens. For example when we are worried about tens of thousands of people starving in Ethiopia, it means we *recognize* those people. We recognize them and we don't turn away. We recognize that in Tigray, in this moment, there is massive suffering, and *we place our attention there*.

- **Mutuality of pathos = We *feel* each other.** We feel this suffering in Ethiopia, and we raise a hue and a cry. It's not okay, and I cannot go about my day when that is happening in Tigray, in Ethiopia. I cannot do it. I cannot do it when boats of refugees are sinking all over the Mediterranean Sea, and no countries in Europe are willing to organize and take those people—and *we cannot do it*.

- **Mutuality of value** means that, as global citizens, we have the shared grammar of value, that what unites us is greater than that which divides us.

- **Mutuality of purpose** means we have a shared purpose in creating a world more beautiful than you can possibly imagine, in creating a world that's unimaginably gorgeous in which we are participating together in the evolution of love. That's what we need. That's where we are going. None of that is available through only a nation state.

Now, let me go one step further.

So all our problems are global, not local; in order to solve them, we need *global coherence.*

How do we create global coherence? **We create global coherence by healing the Global Intimacy Disorder.** And how do we do that? We do that by generating a shared identity with mutualities of recognition, pathos, value, and purpose.

Here is the key principle: **intimacy generates coherence.**

Now, how do you get coherence in a couple, whether it's two friends, whether it's a husband and wife, whether it's a brother and sister, whether it's a father and a son, a father and a daughter? Any couple, how do you get coherence?

1. You get coherence in a couple when there's a sense of **shared identity**, number one.
2. Number two, there's a sense of **shared intimacy**.
3. There's a **shared value**.
4. There is a **shared stor**y and that shared story is based on a shared value, and therefore in that couple you have the capacity to do **shared sense-making**.

Does everyone get that? You need intimacy, which means shared identity based on shared value, based on mutuality of recognition, based on mutuality of purpose and mutuality of pathos, so we begin to have a *shared story.*

> *What we need today is a shared story, we need a common story. But it has to be a shared Story of Value not just at the human level, but with all of Reality.*

We need to realize that the Intimacy Formula applies all the way down and all the way up the evolutionary chain. The same definition of intimacy

161

operates in the atomic and molecular worlds, in the biosphere, and in the human self-reflective world.

This tells us that we are part of the same One World, the same One Love, the same One Heart. Now we begin to realize that we share identity with each other. **We are all part of the same field of Eros. We are all interdependent.**

If we only declare our *independence*, then we don't realize we are *interdependent*. We are interlocking with each other. There's no such thing as an individual who lives independently of everything.

Yes, we are individuated Unique Selves—but not *separate* Selves. Unique Selves are unique expressions of the entire field. **We are Unique Selves, who are expressions of True Self, and True Self is the interdependent field of consciousness.**

- The interdependent field of cascading economic factors.
- The interdependent field of the plankton at the base of the ocean, that allow us to breathe and live.
- The insects deep in the soil, without which we wouldn't be alive.
- The dead zones in the ocean that need to be healed in order for the biosphere to sustain us.

—it's all one interconnected unit, and we are interconnected, interdependent with each other.

Therefore, we need **a shared constitution. We need a Declaration of *Interdependence* because you cannot create global coherence without global intimacy.** Intimacy comes from a shared story and without a shared story, without a shared sense of identity, you can't create shared purpose. Without healing the global intimacy disorder, we cannot create global coherence.

Does everyone get that? Let me say it one last way.

Every single problem in the world today is an issue that requires global **co-ordination**. In order to have co-ordination, we need to be co-ordinated—and *ordinated* means we are headed in the same direction. **We need shared ordinating values.** That's what we call our First Values and First Principles.

They are not unchanging, they are *evolving* First Values and First Principles, but they have to be First Values and First Principles that are *ontologies*, that is, they are *real*. That's why we say we are ontological activists.

There is a shared grammar of value that that brings us all together.

FROM THE DEMOCRATIZATION OF GOVERNMENT TO THE DEMOCRATIZATION OF ENLIGHTENMENT

We live in the world with exponential technology. We are challenged with the fragility of an interconnected world where the supply chains can break down at any second. Exponential technology is technology that builds on itself, like the algorithm of Facebook builds on itself to maximize your time online and therefore, generates massive negativity—because it's exponential. **The technology itself is developing better and better algorithms to accomplish the goal of the technology.** All of our software and hardware today are exponential, which leads to building more and more sophisticated weapons, which are easier and easier to make, and crisper technologies, more and more widely distributed.

We have exponential technologies, and we never had exponential technologies. (The first exponential technology was nuclear weapons, but nuclear weapons were owned by essentially two states, the Soviet Union and the United States, and it was hard to get uranium, so we could monitor that.) Now, we have exponential technologies widely distributed among many states (some of them unstable), as well as non-state actors who don't have a shared code of honor, who don't have a shared code of noble duty, who don't have a shared vision of responsibility. Do you get that? **We don't have the capacity to do sense-making because the issues are** "hyperobjects" and too complex, *and* because there is no shared sense of value.

In order to enter the world as we know it today—in which we have global issues which require global coherence—we need to heal the *Global Intimacy Disorder*. **We heal the Global Intimacy Disorder by creating a *Shared Grammar of Value* that we all onboard with. That Shared Grammar of Value becomes the matrix of the new story. The new story becomes the ground of a *Global Ethos for a Global Civilization*.**

Within that shared Grammar of Value, there can be massive diversity. There can be different religions, and different systems, and a cacophony, a polarity of different instruments, but **we've got to be playing the same music, the same score.** There can be lots of jazz movements in the score, but we've got to be playing music *together*. We've got to *recognize* it as music. We've got to recognize it as intrinsically valuable because you cannot solve any issue of global coordination without shared sense-making. You cannot have shared sense-making without shared identity and a shared grammar of value. *Wow!*

So **we need not just a Declaration of Independence—we need a Declaration of Interdependence**.

We need a new Declaration of Independence (meaning our *unique* instruments in the Unique Self Symphony) *together* with a new Declaration of Interdependence.

We are not just created equal.

We each have a contribution to make.

We are each creative.

We are each irreducibly unique, but that uniqueness has to play together in a shared Symphony.

We are not separate, we are unique—and each uniqueness is a unique expression of the interdependent Reality in which we all live.

It is not enough to do what the Founding Fathers did. The Founding Fathers stood for the democratization of governance, but the democratization of governance doesn't work unless you move towards a **democratization of enlightenment**. That is what we mean by a new collective intelligence emergent from a *shared Grammar of Value* that fosters the emergence of a Planetary Awakening in Love through *Unique Self Symphonies*

That is huge, and that is what we've been talking about for the last ten years. This is what I have shared for the last ten years with everyone who would listen, and what Barbara shared in her own language. **We need to move from the democratization of governance to the democratization of enlightenment.** Now, that doesn't mean that every person is going to be sitting on a mountain reciting *Om* or chanting, or doing Rumi Sufi practices. No.

But it does mean that **every person has an experience of identity where I know that I act in ways that are omni-considerate for the sake of the whole**. The enlightened person is demarcated by two experiences:

I experience the whole as living in me.

I act for the sake of the whole.

I act in ways which are omni-considerate.

Because if we don't act in ways that are omni-considerate, we act in ways that are, cumulatively, *omni-destructive*. That's a big deal.

This is the Declaration of Interdependence, which is based on this realization:

I don't exist without the whole.

I am not anyone independent of everyone.

I am not anything independent of everything.

That doesn't mean we go to totalitarianism. That doesn't mean that *I* disappear. No, I'm an irreducibly unique expression of that everything. I'm uniquely creative. We are all created equal, and I've got an irreducibly unique gift to give, as does every nation, but **we have to have a shared grammar of value in order to do global co-ordination based on ordinating values.**

What we need to insist on is a new Renaissance. We need a new Renaissance. **We need a new Renaissance of shared values.** We need a universal grammar of value, and those values have to be based on First Principles and First Values that are innate and intrinsic to Cosmos.

REDEFINING VOTING

I think we should redefine how voting works. Voting has got to work in a way in which you cannot have rights without responsibilities. You cannot have the right to vote without making a commitment to get *educated* on what it means, and what the issues mean. **We need to create new structures of education, and voters need to step in, and we need to be able to move beyond polarization.**

Imagine this: in order to vote, you have to get educated—the same way as in order to drive, you've got to train in driving. In order to become a physicist, you've got to train in physics. What did George Washington say? *The single, most important job of the government is to educate the citizenry in the science of government.* What did they say? Benjamin Franklin: *You've got a republic, if you can keep it.*

Voting on issues requires a capacity to do sense-making around those issues. Sense-making can only be done well if we have at least some sense of a shared sense of value. Otherwise, we can never create a shared evaluation of everything. The result of that fatal flaw is tribal polarization, which is the fallback when shared sense-making is impossible.

We live in a world in which, according to most surveys around the world, millennials think that democracy is less and less valuable. Democracy in the last ten years is less valued than it ever was in the world. China is this emerging autocracy. It is doing long-term planning. The United States, Holland, Belgium—we are caught in polarization, short-term governments, win/lose metrics without an overarching vision. Now, China's vision is world domination, as the Chinese Communist Party says very clearly. Autocracies are planning long-term and are functioning more and more effectively, while democracies are mired down in polarization, without an ability to act coherently together. **If the democracies don't come together and articulate a Universal Grammar of Value, then we are going to give up the future.**

This is our moment.

We are the Founding Fathers.

We are the Founding Mothers.

The evolutionary impulse is awake and alive in us.

It's time to move from the democratization of governance—not to leave it behind, but to invest the democratization of governance with the democratization of enlightenment. Minimally, that means **the ability of a citizen to think for the sake of the whole.**

- To feel the *whole* in me.
- To move beyond my *egocentric* consciousness.
- To move beyond my *ethnocentric* consciousness.
- To begin to step into a genuine worldcentric, a genuine Cosmocentric consciousness where *I experience myself as evolution.*

I am the Universe coming alive. Evolution's awake and alive in me. I'm a unique configuration of the evolutionary impulse, and I act as evolution itself.

That's where we are today. The same force, the evolutionary impulse that moved the Founding Fathers, now has to move *us* as the Founding Fathers and Mothers of a global grammar of value, healing the global intimacy disorder by articulating a new story.

I'm going to tell you one last thing. This is shocking.

In brain science, you cannot *outdo* the traumas of yesterday. Once there's an imprint from trauma in the brain, there's an indelibility that can barely be changed. The brain is a self-organizing system, and the brain operates the same way the universe does. The brain and the universe are reflections of each other. Whether it's the veins on a leaf, or the neurons in the brain, or the movements of the universe, or societies, everything operates according to a set of First Principles and First Values. Here's what's true in brain science—and it's always true. You cannot undo the trauma of yesterday. **But what you can do is you can create *new* synapses.**

You can create *new* patterns of connection.

You can create *new* configurations of intimacy.

We heal the global intimacy disorder by creating new configurations of intimacy. *Wow!*

A new configuration of intimacy means a new way of doing democracy. It means telling a new story. The most powerful thing we can do from the perspective of brain science, from the perspective of the social challenges of today, is to **tell a new common story based on universal grammar of value**. That's the move. That's the invitation.

I'm going to say one last thing. Have you guys noticed all the crazy stuff about UFOs in the world?

Well, there's been UFO information for a very long time, but it's gotten very serious and very validated. It has always been validated, but now it's gone into the mainstream. Let me just ask you a question. If you get the nature of Reality—that we live in an Intimate Universe in which everything is interconnected—**how could it be that we are a Separate Self civilization?** It's completely impossible. We *cannot* be a Separate Self. Our sense of being independent, just like our sense of Separate Self—a Declaration of Independence, an independent solar system, an independent planet—*of course* that's not true. *Of course* **the universe is an interconnected set of interlocking wholes that operates according to certain principles, and our solar system is in a world that always self-replicates.** It's one of the principles of science, self-replication.

We are an expression of a larger system, but in order for us to engage that larger system, we've got to come and bring a unique gift, and the unique gift that we have to give is our First Principles and First Values. It is our ability to create a planetary civilization, which can be filled with Unique Self instruments, filled with different religions and different nations, but is living a global intimacy that becomes a model, a *strange attractor* that invites conversation with other civilizations.

We are moving into a different world, friends. The world we live in now, that we recognize now, it's an old world. It is beautiful, it has given us great gifts, but we are here to engage in the next step.

We are here to articulate a new story. We are the Founding Fathers and Mothers. We are ready to play a larger game.

It's not just about a planetary civilization. **We need to become a planetary civilization, so we can act within what's going to ultimately be a *multi-planetary* civilization**, but what's going to hold that together? The coherence of the whole thing is a shared Story of Value, a shared story of intimacy, a larger shared identity.

That's where we're going. It's a glorious future, and that's one that we have to take hold of and stop business as usual. To do that, we've got to come together. Join *One Mountain*. Let's make this revolution real. Oh my God, Happy Independence, Happy Interdependence, everyone, for every human being on the planet.

CHAPTER NINE

SYNERGISTIC DEMOCRACY IS THE NEXT STEP IN THE EVOLUTION OF DEMOCRACY

Episode 248 — July 12, 2021

WE CAN CREATE THE FUTURE—BECAUSE WE ARE THE VOICE OF THE FUTURE

We have a huge day today and we are going to be talking about democracy, and about synergistic democracy. In Barbara's talk we are listening to today, she's going to start with the words,

Mine eyes have seen the glory of the coming of the Lord.

Let me step back a bit—for those of you who are new because I know that a lot of new people come every week. Lots of people listen to the replay. Lots of people are here live. Lots of people come for one *One Mountain*, two or three, four or five. Some stay. We really want to welcome everyone. I really want to make sure, every week, that every piece of language we use is accessible both to people who have been with us for years—and are really building the revolution, and are on the inside of the inside—and those who are new. I want to welcome everyone, so just feel the welcome. Feel the

welcome. **From all over the world, we are here together—and mad, deep welcome.**

We are building this revolution together, and what's this revolution about?

What's our intention, if you will?

First, I just want to introduce Barbara Marx Hubbard, my evolutionary partner in this particular revolution. We started this Evolutionary Church (which we now call *One Mountain, Many Paths*) together, to be the home of the next stage in the evolution of love, which is the evolution of consciousness. We understood, together, that we face a moment in which we are poised between utopia and dystopia. **Business as usual, and synagogue as usual, and mosque as usual, and secular unionism as usual, and polarization as usual is not going to get us home.**

We need to be just like da Vinci was in the Renaissance, which was—like now—a time between worlds and a time between stories. We need to be telling the new story:

- the new story of community,
- the new story of Eros,
- the new story of meaning,
- the new story of identity,
- the new story of power.

We have the powers of ancient Gods, and those powers are exponentially growing. When that power goes exponential, **when the exterior technologies of Reality exponentially explode, but interior technologies don't unfold—then we self-terminate.** We face genuine existential risk. Exponential technology creates existential or catastrophic risk. The very future of humanity is at stake—will there *be* a future? And there is deep research that has crunched the numbers based on about ten different risks and done the future scenario planning—and the numbers aren't good.

That's a very big deal—and *we can change that.* **We can create the future because we are the voice of the future.**

Exponential risk might be the death of humanity itself, or it could be the death of *our* humanity, of what it means to be a human being. Those are two different existential risks and we are here to address both of them through the same move da Vinci made—through **a radical evolution of culture and consciousness**. This is not an *imposition* that we are doing on Reality. **We *are* Reality evolving. Evolution is moving through us.**

The same force of Eros that animates the four forces of science animates the forces of culture. That same force of Eros—which brings separate parts into larger wholes, subatomic particles into new shared intimacies and coherent identities as atoms—moves *us* as we weave together all validated insights and all validated ideas. Not fundamentalist declarations, not New Age declarations, but weaving together the deepest strands of knowledge—as a Mystery School does—because *One Mountain* is part of the Mystery School.

We are the Mystery School together.

We are *revolutionaries* in the Mystery School.

We are *evolutionaries*, and we are standing for the future.

We are radically committed, and we refuse to look away.

There is a spirit that moves through us. It is not the spirit of fundamentalism, it's not the spirit of dogmatism, and it's not the spirit of scientism. It's the spirit of wisdom, the spirit of *gnosis* in which science and spirit come together, in which

- **the eye of the mind** —- reason, logic, mathematics,
- **the eye of the senses** —all our sensory capacities, even when they are amplified with tools like fMRIs and the Hubble Telescope,
- and the third eye—the eye of the heart and the eye of the spirit

—all function together in a new Holy Trinity.

We begin to *see*. *Love is a perception*. We begin to see the future. We begin to see around the corner. We begin to realize that we are *Homo Amor*—we are not *just homo sapiens*. That **the fulfillment of *homo sapiens* is a vision of the new human and the new humanity**.

Again, that is not an imposition. That is not a strange thing to happen. **That is an expression of the natural trajectory of evolution moving in us because evolution is the nature of Reality.** Reality is evolution. Reality is relationships, forms of intimacy, and Reality is the evolution of intimacy. Reality is the evolution of love and today, in this moment, we *are* the next stage.

We have to be the next stage in the evolution of love.

Think Renaissance. Think Florence. Around the world, how many people were involved in the Renaissance, friends? There were about a thousand people total involved in the Renaissance. There have been a couple of thousand of us in *One Mountain* just this year. We can do this, and I want to invite everyone. I want to invite everyone to step in, in every possible way. I just want to say – and just really overtly, with no apology—that we are animated by Spirit , we are animated by God.

Now, the god you don't believe in doesn't exist. The small god, the god hijacked by ethnocentric and homophobic religions. No, not that god.

The God who's *the Tao*. The God who is value, who is spirit, who is *Maat*, who is *Geist*, who is *Atman is Brahman*, who is the Implicate Order. That sense that we know that there is something, rather than nothing, for a reason, that the answer to the riddle of Reality is not, *Oops*.

We avoid all the dogmatic certainties, we dance in the uncertainty— but that uncertainty stands together with a core certainty that Reality is meaningful. We can participate in discerning that meaning, and we can participate in evolving that meaning that Reality has intrinsic value, that *it's tomorrow and tomorrow and tomorrow*—and then *Homo sapiens* becomes *Homo Amor* in the next leap of evolution.

It's not *tomorrow that creeps in this petty pace, day after day, to the last syllable of recorded time*—and then explodes in existential risk.

Reality is not *full of sounds and furies, signifying nothing.* No!

Everything's meaningful. There's nothing that's not meaningful in Reality, in the larger economies of existence.

We are very careful not to superimpose conjecture and say, *that's* the only meaning.

Meaning is filling Reality. There's a plenitude of meaning.

There is massive diversity in the Unique Self Symphony, there are different intimacies, which discern meaning differently—but we are *in a score of meaning.* Reality is ultimately meaningful. It all *matters.* I matter, and you matter, and we matter. And this is ours to do.

If you think that's arrogant—no. It is desperate—but it's desperately alive, and desperately loving, and desperately delighted, and desperately privileged.

We take seriously the threat, we take seriously the promise, and we are committed to be the promissory note of the future.

The promise will be kept.

We are here together with everything we have—with mad humility and mad love—to keep that promise.

OUR HOLY AND OUR BROKEN *HALLELUJAH*

Barbara is going to begin her talk with the lyrics of Battle Hymn of the Republic.[20] *Mine eyes have seen the glory of the coming of the Lord.* Who knows the Battle Hymn? It's unbelievable.

Mine eyes have seen the glory of the coming of the Lord.

---

20 A 1862 poem by Julia Ward Howe.

He is trampling out the vintage where the grapes of wrath are stored.

He have loosed the fateful lightening of his terrible swift sword.

His truth is marching on.

It is about finding meaning in the midst of battle and the horrors of war. I don't know if you remember it, but the Battle Hymn goes on, and it's tragic and heartrending. Do you remember it? Does anyone remember it?

I have seen him in the watchfires of a hundred circling camps.

They have builded him an altar in the evening dews and damps.

I can read his righteous sentence by the dim and flaring lamps.

His truth is marching on.

It is beautiful and it's heartrending, but we need not a battle hymn of war— **we need a battle hymn of peace.** We need, as Barbara loved to say, not a war room but *a peace room.* We need an Office for the Future—which we are enacting here together—to envision and know *mine eyes have seen the glory.* Love is a perception. The glory is every place.

Glory is a Christian word.

You don't like that word? Good.

I'm not Christian either—but I am. I'm Christian, and I'm atheist, and I'm Jewish, and I'm Muslim, and I'm Taoist, and I'm secular humanist. We're all of it together.

So how about *the evolutionary impulse is marching on*?

How about *Evolutionary Love animates Reality?*

How about the Good, the True, and the Beautiful?

We are here to stand for meaning, and to stand for the future—and to do it together. I just want to thank every single person out for showing up, for waking up so that we can grow up together. We can clean this up together. We can do this. We can open up in a way that we never have.

Amor means love, but not ordinary love—***Outrageous Love***. *Amor* speaks to the Amorous Cosmos, to what we call here the Intimate Universe, that **Reality is lined with love**. From the very first nanoseconds of the Big Bang **it is Eros that animates Reality and drives it forward**. Reality is the evolution of love driven by *Amor*, by Evolutionary Love—and we mean that scientifically. We mean that in terms of interior and exterior science, and we are writing a Great Library to validate and to share that next stage of the Universe Story.

So we move to pray now and I am going to just speak a minute about prayer. If you are new, sometimes we expand the introduction to prayer to fifteen minutes. Today, it's just going to be a minute because we've got a huge conversation around synergistic democracy and an enormous amount of new content to share in this next step, but just a second.

We pray not to the god who doesn't exist, not the caricature of the divine, who is only outside of Reality, demanding obedience and slightly sadistic. We pray with and we pray to the divinity who both *holds* all of Reality—the Value that holds all of Reality, the infinite Creativity, and Goodness, Truth, and Beauty that holds all of Reality—and that *inheres* in all of Reality.

God who is not just the Infinity of Power *beyond* Reality.

God who is the Infinity of Intimacy *within* Reality.

God who is *the personhood of Cosmos beyond the impersonal*.

At the highest levels of consciousness, when you are really awake, when your eyes are wide open, you realize **there is no split between ultimate play and ultimate seriousness**. You realize there is no split between the process and the personal; between eternity and evolution; between autonomy and communion; between certainty and uncertainty; even between light and darkness.

It's all part of a larger play. And so we turn to the divine, who is both the *process* of Cosmos and the intimate *personhood* of Cosmos—that knows our name and cares desperately, and needs us desperately, and holds everything—our *Holy and Broken Hallelujah*.

You can feel that divinity is not a dogma.

That's not a dogma. That's not an assertion. It is not a claim.

It is the personhood of Reality come alive.

Just like you can hear me talk because your intelligence hears me—**our intelligence is not separate from the larger Field of Intelligence.** If we could hear Becca, could the larger intelligence of Cosmos in which we participate *not* hear Becca? Of course not. That's prayer. We turn to the Infinity of Intimacy, for which no word is lost, and we offer up our Holy and Broken Hallelujah.

We find each other and we pray. We pray for the Holy and the Broken Hallelujah, and when we pray, we ask for everything because prayer affirms the dignity of personal need. We ask for everything—everything we personally need and everything the world needs—and we offer up our Holy and our Broken Hallelujah. Oh my God. We take every prayer and we weave them together—as the bouquet of roses that they are—and we lift their fragrance to the sky, and pour their fragrance into the earth where it's received and heard by the intelligence of all of Reality.

DEMOCRACY IS AN EVOLUTIONARY UNFOLDING OF THE SOURCE CODE OF LOVE

We talked last week about democracy. Now, democracy is wildly important and democracy is failing us—as Barbara will say today in her sermon, and as I've said many times over the last years—but that doesn't mean that we move *beyond* democracy.

That doesn't mean that we don't vote.

It means that **we vote at a honed level of consciousness**.

It means that **we re-understand what voting is**.

It means that we stand for **an evolution of democracy**, and I want to understand this very well.

Democracy itself, writes Abraham Kook—one of the great evolutionary mystics of the 20th century—*is a quality of revelation*.

We said last week that we need the Founding Fathers and the Founding Mothers.[21] The Founding Fathers understood democracy to be part of the unfolding of spirit itself, and Kook writes that, ***democracy itself is a structure of the new revelation.*** That is how we understand democracy.

- ◆ Democracy is not just a social construction of Reality.
- ◆ Democracy is an evolutionary unfolding of the source code of love itself.

What that means is that democracy itself has to *evolve*. I want to very briefly touch on seven or eight points, and then turn to Barbara, so we understand what's failing in democracy. Why does democracy, as envisioned by the Founding Fathers, not work anymore (it's literally not working), and why do we need to take the next step?

Democracy, as it functions today, is not working. We need an evolution of democracy. We need to include and transcend into the next stage. The evolution of democracy is the evolution of love, which is the evolution of God. If democracy is a thought form in the mind of God—and the mind of God is the infinite creativity and value that animates Reality—then the evolution of that mind form is the evolution of democracy.

We take democracy seriously.

It is time to write the next chapter in democracy.

---

21 . See Chapter 1.

It is time to walk the next step in the evolution of love, which is what Barbara and I want to call together "synergistic democracy."

I want to briefly talk about how we got here, and then turn to Barbara.

WHAT IS BROKEN IN DEMOCRACY?

We talked about three broken dimensions of democracy last week:

First, **for most of the issues today that we vote on, we have no idea what they mean.** The name for that is "hyperobjects." That's true for virtually every issue. Whether it's gain-of-function research, whether it's issues involving core economic policy, whether it's the implications of health care and how healthcare should function in terms of its economics—the issues are so complex. The world economy is so complex that in order to vote on something, you need so much information. You have to consider, carefully, both sides. You have to integrate that information across such a broad spectrum of issues that it's virtually impossible to vote intelligently. That is a huge challenge and we need to address that, and there are possibilities and proposals on the table of how we can up-level.

So, the first requirement is: we need to engage the issues and up-level how we are citizens of a democracy, which is why Benjamin Franklin said, *We've got a republic here, if you can keep it.* That's why George Washington said that, *The science of democracy is an informed and educated citizenry.*

We don't have that today. We have a polarized space in which **voting is an act of war.** Voting is a function of win/lose democracy. Win/lose democracy is a function of the win/lose metrics, which is the reigning story on Planet Earth today—rivalrous conflict, success story governed by win/lose metrics. Six or seven years ago, I was privileged to initiate a conference called Success 3.0 with my dear friend, John Mackey, and other colleagues (John's the chair of *Whole Foods*), where we discussed this win/lose metrics tragedy of Success 2.0 and we talked about moving towards a synergistic vision of success. We called it "Success 3.0," so we need to apply that to democracy. That's number one.

Two: **the key issues that matter are *not* voted on.** The nature of artificial intelligence that replaces jobs as companies blindly push automation, without understanding the implications—the nature of robotics, the nature of nanotech, the nature of infotech, the nature of biotech—**all of those dramatically affect our future. None of those are voted on in democracy**. All of them begin in the entrepreneurial win/lose metrics driven by quarterly profits. That's where those decisions are being made. None of them are being voted on. No one here is voting on machine intelligence. Virtually no one here understands machine intelligence. The algorithms are infinitely complex. You need algorithms to understand the algorithms. So the key issues that affect our future are not being voted on.

Three: **All the issues that affect the essential existential and catastrophic risks—which define the future of our children and grandchildren—are international.** They're not local. They require global co-ordination, but you cannot globally co-ordinate through local democracies that are fighting with each other in the win/lose metrics between states. That is not to say we shouldn't have democracies. It just means that the democracy structure of nation states, as they exist today, is literally obsolete in terms of meeting the challenges so that's international, not local.

VOTING ITSELF HAS BECOME PREPOSTEROUS

The fourth broken dimension is that **the nature of voting itself has become preposterous.** It's an open secret on Facebook that Facebook—through split testing and campaigns—can affect the results of an election. In 2011, Facebook did a campaign to 61 million voters. They were able, through sharing faces of Facebook friends who had voted, to affect the voting patterns directly in key districts, beyond the awareness of those people who were being affected.

Now, for example, Alex Pentland at the MIT Media Lab reports this Facebook experiment in his book Social Physics as a grand success. He is ecstatic about it. Shoshana Zuboff, in her book Surveillance Capitalism, reports this same Facebook experiment as the potential death of democracy. Do you understand how two responsible reporters are seeing something completely different? Pentland is correct in terms of the efficacious nature of the technological grid in causing action. That's what he is ecstatic about. He doesn't understand what Zuboff correctly understands: the implications.

The implications are that you can use micro targeting of undecided voters through split testing. Split testing means you carefully test how to sequence a number of ads and images and songs in a particular way, or whatever the particular sequence is, in order to **cause a statistically significant result among a particular pool of the population.** So Facebook, Google and other platforms have the ability to do that, beyond the realm of the awareness of the voter. In terms of the individual voter, that has relatively little impact, but in terms of statistics—in other words, percentage points— **you can swing any election—and no one is *aware* that you did.**

It means **we have technologies at play that have the capacity to undermine the very structures of democracy.** As a number of key writers have pointed out, they've been deployed around the world in democracies to affect democracy directly. That's a big deal. Does everyone get that? No one is even aware that's happening. That's number four.

WE CREATE RADICAL POLARIZATION BASED ON WIN/LOSE METRICS

The fifth dimension of brokenness is that the structure of democracy itself is *win/lose.*

The structure of democracy itself is: there is a problem, there is a challenge. The problem needs to be solved. One group of people has enough power to formulate, let's say, a referendum, to formulate a law. **That law favors one**

set of values. That law favors one set of people. **That group of people then uses all of their available power in order to pass their law.**

Let's just take the United States as an example; the United States is split pretty much 50/50 between two large blocks. So if one block wins, that means the entire other block has been defeated, and voting becomes a win/lose form of aggression. Does everyone get that?

It's a win/lose democracy, and you've got to win every four years. You cannot do any long-term planning, but every problem, every challenge—engendering existential and catastrophic risks—requires long-term planning. *Wow!* **Democracy doesn't have the ability today, in its current form, to do that long-term planning because it is always involved in a win/lose metrics.** Every Congressperson and every senator, every state representative—all need financing, all are in a continuous win/lose game.

We create radical polarization, which destroys the basic movement of evolution, which is synergy. Synergy means there is value on both sides. Does everyone get that?

- There is value on both sides.
- We inhabit each other's value.
- We *listen* to each other.
- We use mechanisms of technology to create synergy—and synergy means a whole greater than the sum of the parts.

There is a greater whole in America—greater than Republicans and greater than Democrats; greater than left and greater than right; greater than interest groups; greater than lobbyists. **We need to inhabit the value on each side of polarities, and come to the higher integration.** We called that here, a number of months ago—does anyone remember?—*She comes in threes.*

She comes in threes means there is always a polarity: a thesis and an antithesis. Hegel talked about a thesis and an antithesis: a polarity. Then, if you have good information, if you inhabit each other's values, if you inhabit each other's perspectives, you *synergize* thesis and antithesis at a higher level of consciousness.

We need structures of voting in which we vote, but in new ways, which are informed, and maybe we have representatives who vote for us on issues that we don't understand.

- Maybe we require responsibilities in order to exercise the right, and we need to be informed on issues.
- Maybe we have to have conferences all over the country, new town halls, online and in person, where we dialogue directly, and listen deeply, and inhabit each other's perspective and values, and then create together proposals for synergy.

However we do this—and there are real suggestions on the table and important work being done, for example in Taiwan and in Estonia—we need to evolve democracy itself. **We need synergistic democracy, which is the evolution of love, which is the evolution of democracy.**

WE NEED A SHARED GRAMMAR OF EVOLVING VALUE

But you can only get to synergistic democracy if we have a shared grammar of evolving value. That's critical.

When I say *a shared grammar of value*, I mean we have a shared understanding of the Good, the True, and the Beautiful. A shared understanding of what it means to be a human being—not in a dogmatic way, not in a way that eliminates diversity, not in a way which is totalitarian—but in the sense that that we are all part of the same musical score and each is playing our own unique instrument in that score. We become what we call a *Unique Self Symphony*:

- Every religion is a Unique Self.
- Every country, every nation state is a Unique Self.

184

- Every region of the world is a Unique Self.
- Every race is Unique Self.
- Every populace is a Unique Self.
- Every thought form is a Unique Self.
- Every school of psychology is a Unique Self.

We need *all* the Unique Selves, but we need to be playing the same music. It needs to be part of the Universal Grammar of Value that *value is evolving*. It is not *owned* by any one system, but it is only if we have a shared story—a shared global story, which creates global intimacy—that we can create shared sense-making that enacts global coherence. You cannot have synergistic democracy unless, within every democracy, there is a shared Story of Value that's intrinsic to Reality.

That value is evolving.

It is always taking in new information.

It is always widening its field, but it is *value*. It's *intrinsic*.

We are in the Tao. When we are in the Tao, when we are in value—

- We can hold paradox.
- We can hold polarity.
- We don't divide over paradox.
- We don't divide over contradiction.
- We don't pick up one value and say, This is my value and your value's wrong.

When you are in the Tao…

When you are in the shared Story of Value…

When you understand that we are part of a seamless code of the universe (interior and exterior), and that all values are expressions of the larger Eros of Cosmos…

—then we can *inhabit* each other's value. Then, we don't polarize. Then, we can hold paradox. We can synergize. **That's synergistic democracy.**

Mine eyes have seen the glory of the coming of the Lord.

The next stage in the evolution of love. I turn the word, with great joy, to you, Barbara Marx Hubbard. Synergistic democracy, Barbara Marx Hubbard. [*Recorded January 28, 2017*]

SYNERGISTIC DEMOCRACY

Mine eyes have seen the glory of the coming of the Lord.

I want to start with what it means *to have a democracy at all.* To think of what it was like *before* we had democracy.

- People lived like serfs.
- People had no name.
- The monarchy could boil somebody in oil to see who was right and who was wrong.
- It wasn't even *considered* that every individual should have life, liberty, the pursuit of happiness, and the right to vote.

So take a deep prayer of thankfulness for the pioneers that liberated democracy to begin with—in the United States, in England—and how great it has been, this time of liberating individual creativity and potential.

Here, we reside now in the midst of the first Evolutionary Church on Earth, recognizing that **the structure of win/lose democracy through voting— great as it was for its time—cannot *coordinate* us toward a planetary sense of connectivity, wholeness, oneness, and liberate the creativity of ourselves when we *join.*** We have hit a structural impasse because the win/lose structure in all existing liberal democracies is not working. In the United States of America, it has shown up to be the *divided* states of America—in order for one side to win over the other. Meanwhile, I'm just

186

taking this, Marc, for right now, as an announcement, that **the Evolutionary Church is a seedbed for evolutionary democracy**.

The seedbed is a church.

It is growing in the consciousness of the people founding this church.

The black gospel church made it possible for Martin Luther King to speak, *I have a dream*, and his dream was so great and so clear that it was realized.

In the particular frequency that you have set for this church, **we are the first church to announce the origin, and fulfillment, and dedication to** *synergistic democracy*.

What is synergistic democracy being announced by the first Evolutionary Church—whose text is the sacred story of evolution, allurement, quark to quark to quark all the way on up to single cells to multi-cells, to animals, to humans, to humanity—announced to *us* in this sacred church? Let everybody feel, for the moment, the awesome generation of capacity that we have—because Martin Luther King wasn't given this gift by being given a kingdom. He took it *by his love*.

Here is the essence of synergistic democracy, built upon win/lose voting structures that gave us the first idea of individual freedom.

- Synergistic democracy starts with the phrase, **I want to create**. This is what I want to create. This is my unique passion to express, to give, to become. I want to create. Whatever it is, my Unique Self is yearning to create it.
- The second thing that we say in synergistic democracy is, What do I need to create this better than I could do alone? **What do I most need to help me create it?** (Vocationally, Marc said he needed me to help him create the church because he has a passion to create this church.)
- The third thing that we say in synergistic democracy is, **What do I most want to give freely to everyone?** Because I love

to give it. Do I want to give my music? Do I want to give my healing? Do I want to give my humor? Do I want to give my love to caring for children? Whatever it is, I want to give it freely.

Now, imagine, for a moment, the new structure of synergistic democracy as a *Wheel of Co-Creation*. Democracy, as every other human endeavor, has a structure upon which it is built. The parliamentary procedure is the structure upon which the win/lose democracy is built. **Synergistic democracy is built on something that we are all beginning to do, called "rules of synergistic order."**

What are those rules?

They are that when I say, *I'm yearning to create something and this is what I need*—instead of somebody *voting* that they don't think what I wanted to create is any good, somebody in the evolutionary democracy is going to come to me and say,

> *I have a creative input to help you create what you want to create.*
> *By me joining vocationally with you, within synergistic democracy,*
> *I am going to get to be more of who I am.*

In other words, we cultivate *vocational arousal* in the synergistic democracy of people

- choosing what they *want* to create,
- saying what they *need* to create it,
- having others *join them* to create it.

Let's say you have entered, in the Wheel of Co-Creation, into the field of health. You have a new healing process that you would like to have known, but in order to do that you might say,

> *I need media attention to what I want to offer. Is there somebody*
> *in the media section of the wheel, who has what I need in order to*
> *help me create it?*

188

Someone is going to say, *Yes*, and you will have a vocational connection. You will experience *joining of genius to create* because the person that's helping you will also need *you* to help them get what they want. **We start to cultivate social synergy, coming together to *co-create*.** It's a very natural tendency.

Win/lose voting is not as natural as joining together to co-create. We *had* to go through win/lose democracy so that each individual could feel, *I am significant*. But we have come to the end of your ability to be significant as an individual through winning or losing alone. Marc, in sponsoring the evolution of synergistic democracy through the Evolutionary Church—which adheres to the politics of Evolutionary Love, which is following the great story of Evolution as a love story—created an incredible coherence here.

I am going to declare that, today, **it's the first time that I have personally felt that we could collectively demonstrate synergistic democracy within the members of this church.**

We could call for it within our communities.

We could hold small gatherings—we call them *syn-cons*—for *synergistic convergence*.

We can have real-life gatherings—in the back of churches, in small universities, anywhere we want to connect people to co-create.

Within this domain of the Evolutionary Church

- ◆ We are announcing the development of the next stage of democracy: a politics of love.
- ◆ We are going to be calling on the genius of the gnosis sphere, and all these young tech guys that are doing it.
- ◆ We are going to be calling on the Office for the Future, which holds the Wheel of Co-Creation within it, and which carries us through right to the United Nations of this world.

TOWARDS A POLITICS OF EVOLUTIONARY LOVE

This is a huge vision that Barbara and I articulated together. It requires what we called, in one of the first churches, our first *One Mountain* gatherings, "politics of Evolutionary Love." Barbara created what was called the *Wheel of Co-Creation 1.0*, which she referred to in her talk.

Right before Barbara died, I drafted, together with Barbara (at a restaurant in Portland), and we enacted, *the Wheel of Co-Creation 2.0*, based on *The Universe: A Love Story*, and on this notion of the Amorous Cosmos, and the unique impulse of Evolutionary Love that lives in each of us as a citizen. We are going to be bringing that together, and to be bringing this vision of democracy into the world.

As Barbara said beautifully, **the place of this evolutionary communion is to birth the next stage of democracy**. So no, we don't abandon democracy. We embrace democracy. We embrace it not as one powerful voice but as **a Unique Self Symphony of Planetary Awakening in Love through Unique Self Symphonies**.

CHAPTER TEN

SYNERGISTIC DEMOCRACY AND THE INDEPENDENT MOVEMENT

Episode 337 — March 26, 2023
Speakers: Marc Gafni, Christopher Life

BLESSING OF THE FATHER

Dr. Marc Gafni

We are here in *One Mountain*.

We are in this moment poised between utopia and dystopia.

Several thousand of us have gathered in this community, where our commitment is no less than to evolve the source code of consciousness and culture, which is the evolution of love, and to articulate a politics of love in response to the meta-crisis.

In response to potential dystopias, we invoke the most stunning, good, true, beautiful world that our hearts and our bodies and our minds have always known is possible. Fragments and flickers of this vision live in the interior sciences of the great traditions, but—tragically—those flickering visions were often hijacked by their ethnocentric contexts. **Now we are at a moment where they need to be reclaimed.**

We cannot respond to dystopia without a vision of utopia. We cannot respond to the meta-crisis without a vision of what it would look like. At the Center for Integral Wisdom, we've been trying to articulate this new vision, to articulate this new possibility, to feel into what could be, and to articulate an evolution of the source code itself.

My dear friend just lost his dad a few hours ago, completely suddenly. We were in the middle of the normal intensities of life, and his dad passed away—so we've just been in that here for the last few hours. We were sitting, right before I stepped on the broadcast, deep in this space—holding life and death, and sudden death, and the death of the father.

Part of what we need to invoke today is what I would call *the blessing of the Father*.

The blessing of the Father is not just about the personal father. I want to invoke it in a larger way—because the Father is both the father that I was born to, my biological father, and **the Father in culture**.

We used to talk about the Father as *our Father in Heaven*. That was the Father who was dissociated from the world, who was alienated from the world, who wasn't invested in the world but had created it outside of Himself, demanding, in some sense, its obedience.

We know that that's actually a distortion of the Father, that's a corruption of the Father. The Father is invested in the world, He is part of it, even as He holds it. We are used to talking about the Mother, but we're not quite used to talking about the Father.

Our system of governance is the Father. It's the vessel that holds us. That's the Father in culture.

When we have a broken relationship with the Father, then there is no place for the Mother to emerge. We can do all of the Mother rituals we want—

and many people on this call know that I'm madly devoted to *She*, to the Mother, to *Ima*—but the Mother doesn't have a place without the Father. It's *hieros gamos*. And **our system of governance, which is the Father in culture, is broken. So we need to reclaim the Father, we need to resurrect the Father.**

I've invited today, a very dear friend of mine, and of Barbara's, Christopher Life.

Christopher was a key architectural visionary player in manifesting this iteration of *One Mountain*. A lot of the technologies that we created when we created the space of One Mountain, were created together with Christopher. Christopher is both a little brother, and a dear friend, and an evolutionary partner. He is dedicating his life to the blessing of the Father, both personally as a father, and collectively, **working with this broken system of governance in the United States, dominated by a polarized win-lose metrics, in which democracy doesn't exactly accomplish what it's supposed to.**

It becomes an aggressive win-lose metric, in which there is no synergy. We don't have a vision of what a synergistic democracy would look like. It's always that one half organizes, wins and the other half loses, *so we have half of a country alienated in this tragic broken structure*, devoid of intimacy and devoid of Eros, which is an expression of the broader global intimacy disorder.

Christopher is actually invoking a convention here in Austin, Texas, to begin to articulate a new space in culture, what would it look like to move beyond that binary win-lose metrics, **and see a third way, and see a new way, and resurrect the Father.**

This is a day of the Father. And there are no coincidences in the Intimate Universe. The death of a father, the surprise, the shock, the beauty, the poignancy, the pain, the potency, the presence—it's all one.

Christopher is going to do the major talk this morning, and he is going to talk to us about the vision of a new independent party, and what it means to him, and why it is important. He is going to also invite anyone who can come down, in a week, to be present with us, either on livestream or in-person.

But before he begins, we are going to invoke the blessing of the Father by watching a video. Just to say maybe the last thing—and Christopher, I'm going to pull age rank on you now—just giving you, my dear evolutionary brother, the Blessing of the Father. I'm so insanely proud of you. I'm so insanely proud of who you are, and what you're doing, and your courage, and your commitment, and your depth, and your integrity. I couldn't be more delighted and more honored and more thrilled.

We are going to invoke a silence of presence for a second, and we're going to play the video, and we are going to feel the blessing of the Father.

[Music: Fall on Me by Andrea Bocelli]

Do we understand that? Can we feel that?

That's the blessing of the Father.

That's what the convention next week is about.

It's about reweaving that blessing of the Father in culture; this new vision of governance.

TOWARDS A UNITED INDEPENDENT MOVEMENT

Christopher Life

Thanks, Marc. Thank you, everyone, for being here together today.

I love that this Church allows people to come together and worship, and I've really enjoyed being a part of this community for three years now. Thanks to all the openings, the prayers and the remarks. They remind us of the spiritual reality of the moment of evolution that we're all here a part of and participating in. I'm really moved by Marc's remarks, and the mentioning of the loss of the father of one of his key people. And that video also was really powerful, as I reflect upon that sacred, beautiful lineage and relationship, being both the son of a father and the father of a son.

Barbara was a dear friend of mine. We met and came into a relationship late in her life. Her passing was a real shock to so many of us, myself included, because it felt like we were just activating a real synergistic roadmap together. Her age didn't even cross my mind, because when I interacted with her, she just felt like she had the energy of a 25-year-old, so I imagined we were going to be at it for decades together.

I am the founder of the party, One Nation. The purpose of organizing that party was to create a political vehicle to help folks that are in this conversation, that know that we are in a meta-crisis but that, to use Barbara's terminology, *our crisis is a birth.*

There is a crisis here, there's an ambulance running down the road, the siren is on.

But it's not a heart attack, it's a birth, *there's something coming in this urgent moment of crisis.*

The One Nation party was designed to help people who are oriented around systemic transformation, and moving towards holism, and synergy, and integrating diverse perspectives to create new and novel insights and new and novel solutions, to be able to become the mayors, and the state representatives, and the governors and the national congressional representative, and the presidents of the future.

I was really excited and grateful to be working with Barbara on that project, and to receive her endorsement was very humbling for me. And right when we were gearing up to really put a lot of things in motion, we lost her in this world. The only way that I could really make sense of all of that was that she was moving on beyond, to the spirit realm, to evolve that partnership in a broader, even more profound way than she would be able to do in the flesh. I don't think she would have left if there wasn't a greater positioning for her synergy in this moment in time, because she's so *for* this moment in time.

I feel—and I bet many of you probably feel that too—**that Barbara is actually with us.**

Not just as a trite statement so that we feel better or something, but because it's really palpable. Marc mentioned that Barbara even gave him some marching orders last night.

I really believe and feel that she has such a powerful spirit that she's really truly with us, and she is guiding us, and she is supporting us, and she's helping to create the context for all the synergy, all the miracles, all the synchronicities, all the opportunities.

What a blessing!

THE WORLD NEEDS A COORDINATION SYSTEM FOR ALL INDEPENDENT PARTIES

As I presented One Nation to our country and put a couple years into the development of this party platform, I had a very particular insight that helped me to evolve the brand and evolve the theory of change. It was that **as an emerging new party, I was inadvertently in competition with dozens of other emerging small parties, who had a very similar ethos— to be able to move beyond the dominant hegemonic control of the two- party system in this country**. Even the running candidates were then in competition with each other, competing against independent dollars and independent votes, which only reinforces the election outcomes of the existing two parties.

Once I really got that, I realized that I was no longer aligned with that. That theory of change had brought me to a particular junction point of the Dharma, and that produced a set of insights that allowed the next iteration to unfold. What I realized was that

> *The world doesn't need another new party. What the world needs is a coordination system for all independent parties.*

The world needs a coordination system for the hundreds of organizations that are working on democracy reform initiatives, a space for the millions of Americans who will never join a party to still be able to plug into a political vehicle as a context for collective actions.

And so, I founded an organization called the Independent National Union. That's a union as a political concept. It's not like a labor union, but a union of political actors that don't give up their brands, don't give up their agency, don't give up their audiences, don't give up their own particular ideological orientations, to create **a context where they could all actually start to work together with a higher level of coordination**. Like a board of tourism that represents fifty different restaurants in the city, and puts up a billboard that says, *come to our city*—and they come to the city, and then there's more visitors to the city to be patrons of the restaurants. We need something like a board of tourism for the independent sector itself, to be able to concentrate resources—to put up that billboard, if you will. To be able to build a stronger narrative of what this moment in time really holds for us, what it means to be independent. Because *independent* isn't just a political identification, or even just a voter registration status. To be independent is a very profound cultural concept.

INDEPENDENCE ENABLES UNITY

To be independent means that we have gone on the journey of separating from the inertia of the status quo that impressed itself upon us, that told us what to think, and what to buy, and who to vote for, and what to watch, and what to say.

Instead, so many of us—I'm sure every single person on this call—have gone through multiple stages of declaring your own independence from the inertia of the status quo that tried to tell you what to think, what to speak, and how to act.

Independence, at the core, is really the cultural and behavioral ability to think, speak, and act for oneself.

Interestingly enough, this is not a selfish pursuit, or a self-centered pursuit, or a pursuit that allows the individual to just think about themselves. No.

It's when you have arrived at the ability to think for yourself, that you're no longer manipulatable, that you're no longer controlled, that you're no longer tied into ulterior motives.

From that vantage point, you now have the ability to be able to represent the entirety of your community—not just the blues or not just the reds, but the whole of your community.

Independence enables a certain quality and capacity of authentic, responsible, mature stewardship.

Independence, ironically and counter-intuitively, actually enables and begets unity—because from that vantage point, you can represent the needs of different constituencies, and can better help to be able to stitch together those needs, and to be able to depolarize communities as opposed to increase the hyper-polarization.

Independence is that deeper conversation of a practice of being an independent individual who then has the ability, from that vantage point, to carefully consider the well-being and the betterment and the improvement of quality of life of all they represent.

DECLARING INDEPENDENCE

The profundity of the concept of independence goes even further. Because at this junction point right now—at this phase change in the evolutionary trajectory, the phase change of human civilization, the phase change of the ecological and geological systems on this planet—what's happening is, **people are just declaring independence like crazy.**

They have declared independence, as I said, from the systems that they are no longer aligned with.

They are creating new media solutions, declaring independence from Fox and CNN.

They are creating new technology solutions like blockchain, to be able to create a new context of technology. We are holding space exploration and space commerce out of the control of national governments, and claiming independence, so individuals and individual corporations have access to rockets, and satellites, and space travel, and all those other aspects, and the list goes on and on and on.

There is this larger movement that's saying *we are not waiting for permission. And we are not aligned with that system.*

We are going to declare our future, and we are going to set our own trajectory, and we are in our own self-determination to actually direct where we go from here.

We can bring it back to the story of the colonies, the American colonies coming together to declare independence from the systems they were no longer in resonance with. They were no longer aligned with taxation without representation. They were no longer aligned with being controlled by a country on the other side of the Atlantic Ocean. They wanted their own self-determination, they wanted their own self-governance, and they wanted to determine how they were going to govern themselves. And so, these colonies bound together, they came together, to do something that they could not do on their own. They came together to be more effective in their own declaration of independence.

Unfortunately—because at the time, violence was involved—we came together to marshal the resources and the manpower and the capacities to be able to run a Revolutionary War, and be able to assert their independence fully. And then, from that independence, they were able to write their own constitution, and institute their own national government.

Imperfect as it is, there is a beautiful prayer. **The prayer was the prayer of governance of, by, and for the people, the ideal that governance of, by, and for the people could support the pursuit of life, liberty, and happiness for all—that's a very profound prayer, it's a very beautiful prayer.**

Our country has failed in pretty much every imaginable way of fulfilling that ideal—**but because we set that trajectory as our ideal, every failure isn't for naught.**

Every failure is learning. It's a scientific experiment, to determine how we do governance of, by, and for the people, that supports life, liberty, and the pursuit of happiness for all.

Now we have a moment in time to declare independence even from this last 250-year cycle of a national experiment, so that we can inventory all the lessons learned, and from that, integrate that into directing the future from here.

THE FIRST INDEPENDENT NATIONAL CONVENTION

The punchline of all of this is, I believe that there is this trend for individuals to declare independence. Gallup polls say, 20 years ago, 25% of Americans were independents, then 30%, then 35%, in the last couple years, 40%, 45%, and last year, 50% of Americans identified as independent. What's actually happening here is, in a distributed fashion, individuals are intuitively participating in this collective process of declaring independence again—

but this time, it's not against King George III's Great Britain. It's against the two-party system and the entire gestalt of systems tied to that system that have extractive, manipulative, abusive implications around every corner that we look.

We have this movement—a real movement. Not just like, *hey, let's have a movement*—no, there's a real movement. A hundred million Americans are saying, *I am independent*. We now have the opportunity to be able to crystallize, and ground, and solidify what these hundred million Americans are actually moving towards, what they are standing for, what are the narratives and the stories that are most effective at helping to be able to galvanize that potential into an actual effective, formidable, political alternative.

As the founder of The Independent National Union, **the first act of our organization is to run the first Independent National Convention**. It juxtaposes the Republican National Convention, the Democratic National Convention. We are saying, this is a space to support the unification of the currently and hitherto fore fragmented and siloed independent sector into something more like a *united independent movement*, to be able to identify our common ground, to be able to stitch together roadmaps and joint action, so we can actually work together effectively, to ensure that we have the systems and processes in place, to be able to make sure that we have independent election outcomes happening in mass, that city council people, and mayors, and county commissioners, and state reps, and governors are all starting to be moving into the independent sector—

Whether it's the existing elected officials, like Senator Kyrsten Sinema, who are declaring their independence from their previous party affiliation while in office, which we're going to start seeing more and more of, and/or we are electing people in the office that got there through an independent platform.

Then we are also able to really rev up the democracy reform activities that upgrade the technology and the standards and the protocols of government, so the government itself evolves into becoming something extremely transparent, extremely accountable, really baked in to the participatory engagement from the communities, in the sensemaking process, in the joint action process, **so that government can achieve its ideal of being a system of collective coordination that effectively and efficiently improves quality of life for everyone who touches it.**

And that's where we go from here.

That's what this synergistic democracy is that Barbara has been prophesying for decades—**that government becomes a vehicle for the thriving of all,** in its full evolution from the caterpillar to the butterfly.

I believe that if we focus on building this national event platform, and building this national narrative, and building local organizing systems for this United Independent Movement, and we do this consistently and effectively over the next several years, we are going to see **a fundamental center of gravity shift from the two-party system being synonymous with American government, to that system collapsing, imploding, corroding, losing power, losing influence, losing control, and this rising independent sector of our country actually becoming the prevailing presence of leadership and stewardship in our country,** with that energy, that ethos and that culture further spreading around the world.

Thank you very much for giving me a moment and time to share some of those thoughts, and to make that direct invitation. Everyone is invited. Thank you, Marc, for your time.

INDEPENDENCE EMERGES FROM EROS

Dr. Marc Gafni

Christopher, that was fantastic! Most important response, gorgeous and beautiful. I think everybody could feel Christopher, could feel the vision, could feel Barbara.

We were here deep in the middle of this moment of life and death, and stepped out of it because it was equally important to actually be here in this moment, and I couldn't *not* be here. It's so wildly important.

I want to just share a couple of things about what Christopher said. Let me just see if I can frame this a little, because it's so important.

First, we talk a lot about what we call *one world*—and ultimately, one galaxy—so a whole bunch of people texted me, *Why are we talking one nation? Are we going back?*

No, we are not. That's a great question, I really appreciate the question. **The way we get to one world is we first reconstitute the one nations:** every individual country has to evolve its source code, so that they become units of coherence, and intimacy, and Eros, and integrity—that can *then* become part of one world. There is no bypass road. You have to first do one nation before you do one world, and you have to first do one world before you do one galaxy. That's one, that's critical.

Two is, Christopher has made **a very deep shift in his sacred strategy**, which is a mark of maturity. It's a mark of maturity and depth and wisdom, a leader who's able to make that kind of shift. He began running One Nation as a political party. I think there may be a place for One Nation to come back in the future. I, for one, think it's still important, it has value.

But this in-between step is unbelievably important, this coordinating function. **You become a coordinating function by actually creating the space, the ground of being, in which becoming can happen**. That's a visionary move: I am going to create the ground, I am going to be the space in which emergence can happen. That's a shockingly beautiful, and stunning, and utterly necessary move, which requires a *bracketing of self* for this larger self to emerge.

That's number two, and that's wildly important. I think it's a sacred strategic movement, which is brilliant in the sense that it's filled with radiance, it's filled with light.

Three. **This notion of being independent is unbelievably important.** And you remember, we talked about polarity and the causes of polarization, it's been a major topic of ours. Let's just talk about this notion that Christopher spoke about so beautifully, this notion of independence.

I just want to say this deeply, and I am going to try and give you a different image which will bring us back.

Take the notion of a secret. When someone says, *I'm going to tell you a secret*, and then you say, *Yeah, totally, I'll totally keep a secret.* What most people mean when they say they're going to keep a secret is, they'll only tell two other people. That's generally what it means: *I'll keep a secret, let me tell two people.*

Now, in all the lineage traditions, there was what was called the *ba'aley ha'sod*: those who could keep the secret. Why was it that a requirement of an initiation into a great interior science was this capacity to keep the secret?

The answer is very subtle, it's very beautiful: because **you can only keep a secret if you can give up the hit of egoic attention-energy that you get when you share the secret**. There's this moment when you go share the secret, where everyone's like, *tell me that!* And you get that moment of attention, and we feel sometimes so empty inside that we betray a confidence because in that moment of pseudo-eros, I get that hit of attention-energy, I am alive for a second.

You become an initiate into a great tradition when you don't need that hit of superficial attention-energy, because you are so deeply grounded in your own independence—in your own interior sense of identity and self. You have a sense of who you are.

What that means is, **to be independent, I cannot conflate my inner integrity, my being-ness, my inner quality of self with a particular political position.**

What people do today is, the reason we have polarization is that we have conflated identity with political position. Wherever you are, **when you identify with a political position as a way of having an identity, you can never give up that position**. Because that's your identity, and who gives up their identity?

> *To be independent, I have to have an identity rooted in Unique Self, rooted in Eros, rooted in the Field of Value.*

That's why the word independence in the original Hebrew is very beautiful. It's a gift to brother Christopher. The word independent is *atz'maut*. And *atz'maut* means 'inner full essence'.

It's only when I have inner full essence that I can be independent, because then my independence emerges from my Eros. When I don't have inner full essence, I cover up the emptiness with pseudo-forms of political identity.

Virtually no one espousing those positions (and I've read position papers on both sides) has actually investigated deeply. They have, in a kind of knee-jerk way, identified with a position in order to have that position be a pseudo-eros of identity. That's why Christopher and I came together in the beginning, it's why Barbara was so interested, and it's why the three of us were interested—because **you can't have independence without a new Story of Value rooted in First Principles and First Values**.

We desperately say, *I love you* is *I need you*. And *I love you, I need* you means: We need Christopher to be doing this work.

We need this to be happening.

He needs us. We love each other. We love each other. We need each other. We're holding hands. And we're making this revolution together, so thank you.

CHAPTER ELEVEN

THE FUTURE OF DEMOCRACY AND META-CRISIS

Board meeting of the Think Tank of the Center for Integral Wisdom — September 30, 2021

WE LIVE IN A WORLD OF OUTRAGEOUS PAIN AND OUTRAGEOUS BEAUTY, AND THE ONLY RESPONSE IS OUTRAGEOUS LOVE

Marc Gafni: I just want to share something briefly, just of a strange experience that I've had today, with KK and Chahat and Zak and one other person on this call. Yesterday, Gabrielle sent to KK and I the draft of a book she's been working on for a year, which she completed (which is a big story). We call it *The Tailor of Eros*—because we are all the tailors of Eros together. It's this gorgeous and beautiful book, which is about a little bit of the story of the Think Tank and the story of the Dharma. It's a beautiful piece, which is just a very deep highroad into heaven (actually, I have no real idea of what it says, because Gabrielle has not let me see it for the entire year; but I know it's fantastic, that's for sure). At that same moment, I just went through a somewhat excruciating experience in the last day. Just to feel that it was coming together, and to feel them arise in the space, and to feel tears of joy and tears of pain at the same time, and to hold them together. **It's an unbearably beautiful privilege to be alive.**

I got, again, the realization that **we live in a world of Outrageous Pain and we live in a world of Outrageous Beauty, and the only response is Outrageous Love**.

There are few things that make me happier than looking at the quality of the people here, just who has moved to join this revolution and this beauty and this depth, and the maturity of them, and the depth of it. It just blows my heart open. Just feel the goodness and the integrity of the space. This is a place where there are no devotees, other than devotees to She—to truth, to integrity, to goodness—and we are part of a symphony together, and we are trying to write the score of a symphony together.

Zak will perhaps distinguish later between propaganda and education. But we are on the side of education. The self-evident truth is that **we want to everyone to speak for themselves, and to let them emerge, and that we participate in their emergence**. It is such a noble moment, and it is such a noble gathering. *Nobility* is a word that we've lost access to. I can just feel the nobility of the gathering, and the pulse of da Vinci is with us, in this time between worlds and time between stories.

I left a short Vox for Dr. Stein about an hour ago, about the one thing that is a mystery. If you want to ask me *why*, don't. If I ever pretend to tell you *why*, then leave, because I have no freaking clue—**but *why* the world is Outrageous Pain and Outrageous Beauty together?** According to the great mystics, there are fifteen explanations. But *before* all the explanations, and *after* the all the explanations, as the Kabbalists say, is *mystery*—that's the great mystery of Reality. The great mystery of Reality:

- Why does it happen through evolution?
- Why does it happen over billions of years?
- Why is the process of soul-making so excruciatingly beautiful and sometimes excruciatingly painful?

But one thing is absolutely clear to me, which I can claim enlightened realization on. **It's not a bug in the system, it's a feature. It is *not* an**

accident. It's not like, *we wheeled out the wrong model of the world, sorry.* Somehow, this process in which we participate—in which our integrity, and our goodness, truth, and beauty is participatory in the evolution of consciousness—is the great gift that the Infinite gives to us.

In Hebrew wisdom literature, they talk about *lechem d'kisufin,* the bread of shame. It essentially means that there is no free lunch, and **the greatest privilege the Infinite, who loves us madly, could arrogate to us is our capacity to create a flourishing world, to tell a new story, to create a world which is world of love**—a world where we are romancing each other in all ways, each other's hearts, and each other's souls, and each other's deepest depths.

It's just a wild delight to be here at our Board Meeting. It's really a great delight to introduce our Co-Board Chair, Shareef.

IN RESPONSE TO THE META-CRISIS WE NEED A NEW STORY

Shareef Malnik: How does a layman address this group and introduce the greatness that we are about to hear? I will make a humble attempt and be brief. It has been established by Dr. Gafni and Dr. Stein that **we are presently faced with a meta-crisis, with fifteen or more enumerated challenges. And a *meta*-crisis needs a *meta*-solution.**

The problem is that there are people trying to solve meta-challenges with piecemeal solutions. That isn't working, and it's not going to ever work. When you look at solving the problems of China, climate, the wealth gap, nuclear proliferation, and more, there are core generator functions that exist underneath the surface. **The interconnected world is paradoxically opposed to piecemeal solutions**—we are very familiar with paradoxes. In order to fix any of the meta-challenges, you must get to the *generator root causes.* **The root cause is what Dr. Gafni calls *the source code,*** where lasting change happens; it doesn't happen on the desktop.

Dr. Gafni and Dr. Stein and this think tank has been warning of this for the last ten years. The best analogy is the Renaissance. The old pre-modernity world was falling apart while a pandemic was raging, and no one knew what to do about it. In steps, Leonardo da Vinci and his contemporaries identify the root causes, and they realize **the root cause was a failed story about how we understand Reality**. The existing pre-modern story was broken, so da Vinci told a new story—not a made-up story, but a story based upon the best information in the world at the time. The new story created the best of the modern world—but it wasn't quite good enough or complete, which is why we have existential risk today.

We are here to tell a better story, a complete story that takes the best of the Renaissance and the best from all other sources in the universe in order to change the world. What an amazing thing to know! It is mind blowing. I feel so honored, as I know all of you do, to be part of something like this—to be blessed with this knowledge and with the ability to make a change. I have all this gratitude, and I introduce Dr. Gafni with gratitude for this knowledge and for the opportunity to be on the team.

RESPONDING TO EXISTENTIAL RISK WITH A NEW STORY ROOTED IN FIRST PRINCIPLES AND FIRST VALUES

Thank you so much, Shareef. It was just wonderful. You just gave Zak's and my talk; you basically covered everything. So, I think we can chant for the next couple of hours anyways, or maybe just play your guitar, and we'll be good. It's beautiful. Shareef said so much.

What I'm going to do is: I'm going to take a piece of time, and Zak is going to take a piece of time. We are going to talk about related and overlapping issues in two distinct but interrelated understandings. We are going to be dealing today both with the crisis which Zak was tracing for me yesterday, where perhaps the word meta-crisis came from. It is not a word that we generally use, but it is a good way to talk about it, because it is not an ordinary crisis. But *crisis* **has been at the center of evolution's drivers consistently.** Our beloved Board Chair Emeritus, Barbara Marx Hubbard, spent her entire life talking about *our crisis is a birth*, and the notion of crisis as an evolutionary driver.

In the original Hebrew, the word for crisis is *shever*. It is a very beautiful word. At the source of what's called the Metatron tradition, there is what's called Shevirat ha-Kelim, the breaking of the vessels. When the vessels break, the shards of broken vessels, in this mythic image, are spread throughout Reality.

We live in a world of broken vessels. But within each broken vessel, there is a spark of light.

The image is stunning. And Walter Benjamin, among many other people, fell in love with this image, because it is an image which is not a euphemism, it is an image that's a *metaphor*. A euphemism hides; a euphemism lies. But a metaphor *reaches* for something, like poetry, which breaks the boundary of words to capture the depth of the silence that permeates all of Reality.

Feel into it for a second:

We live in a world of broken hearts.

We live in a world of broken vessels.

We live in a world of broken promises.

We live in a world of broken people.

Yet, out of that breaking emerges *wholeness*; there's nothing more *whole* than a broken heart. Out of the breaking of the vessels, when the vessels scatter, there emerges, in every generation, what's called in the Zohar *Chevra Kadisha*, the holy band.

Probably the most excellent scholarly and academic reader of Zohar today is a man named Yehuda Liebes, who I had a lovely exchange with about a year and a half ago. He wrote a number of very important scholarly monographs on the essence of the interior scientific tradition saying there is the *Chevra Kadisha*: **the band of Outrageous Lovers, who come together, loving each other deeply, to fix the broken source code**.

That fixing of the broken source code is called the *tikkun*: the fixing. They go through tribulations, and the tribulations look different in every generation. There are *always* tribulations, but there is also such incredible beauty, and ultimately, triumph—the triumph that **we can, in fact, participate together in evolving the source code**.

From this crisis, the breaking of the vessels, our crisis turns into a birth.

It is not just that we are in what Zak has called a time between worlds, which I refer to as a time between stories. We put those phrases together into *a time between worlds and a time between stories*.

It is not *just* that we are on the brink of a potential dystopia, which we are; there is a genuine sense of catastrophic and existential risk. But it's no less true that the same exponentially developing web technologies have *utopian* possibilities (for example, blockchain technology).

It is not a bad world. **It's that utopia and dystopia are *enmeshed* with each other.** That idea is not a unique idea. In all the great traditions there's a version of *Messianism* or *Armageddon*. That idea is deeply rooted in human culture, this understanding: *there's the Messianic possibility, and there's the Armageddon possibility*.

Sometimes people say to me, *you guys have created this*. No, we didn't create this. Nick Bostrom, who coined the term *existential risk* in early 2000s, didn't create this—the notion that Reality at a certain point is going to come to some kind of climax, and that there are going to be two roads that diverge in the wood; that we are actually going to be able to feel a potential utopia and a potential dystopia yawning before us.

It's going to be our job sometimes to be closer, sometimes to step back, but never to look away; to be willing to face Apocalypse, and then walk through it, and not stay in the pre-tragic mode that denies its existence and lives its comfortable spiritual life—and yet, not get lost in the post-doomer tragic move that our wonderful colleagues like Joanna Macy and Michael Dowd and many others are making; this kind of looking down to say, *we're doomed*, which is also a tragic mistake. We have to move from the *pre-tragic* to the *tragic*.

On the first day of our study this summer we embraced the tragic profoundly, for several hours, deeply—we had an incredibly painful day. But the next day, we went to the *post-tragic*. **We are in a post-tragic moment right now, and we want to look from the post-tragic perspective.**

1. There is a multitude of challenges, one.
2. Two, that's always been true; that's not *new* news.
3. Three, it's not more of the same. It's not just another moment in history.

Even though every generation has said that, we are paradoxically right.

That's because **the nature of technology is such today that we have a globally interconnected system, where everything cascades into everything**. Nothing is separate, which is this move towards this larger union, which augurs towards a potential utopia.

At the same time, because everything is so cascading, so interconnected, it is all a set of dominoes. It is all *inherently fragile*.

It is not a *complex* system that's brought together through a fundamental allurement, in which all the parts are omni-considerate of the other parts and there's a sense of the whole. It is a *complicated* system is a *dissociation* between the parts, an inherent fragility in the system, which is coupled with exponential technologies in multiple vectors, with potential for damage, controlled by diffuse actors.

There is this potential for destruction—both from a technological sense, in terms of weapons, and from the very structure of culture itself, as played out in digital technologies. The exponential destruction *will* actually destroy us, if we continue on the vector that we are on. **That destruction feels,**

not just like a minor possibility, but a very significant possibility. Nick Bostrom's last calculation was 19–20% chance of this, a couple of weeks ago. Now, you'd think that seems not so bad, but imagine you are about to get on a bridge, and there is a 20% chance that the bridge is going to fall. Of course, Bostrom is talking about a genuine existential risk. **But with catastrophic risk, we are talking about 98%.**

> *We are in a moment of unbearable possibility—both dystopian and utopian.*

It's *not* "more of the same."

I was talking to a very significant and beautiful man, 80 years old, who's a leading scholar in one major discipline in the States. I was trying to explain this to him, and he said, "Marc, it's always been this way. There's always been advertising." No, it's one of the things that's just not true. **This is a unique and novel moment, both in its utopian possibility to create a flourishing world, and in its dystopian possibility.** Looking away is not an option.

This is what Shareef pointed towards—what we are pointing towards—**the underlying generator functions.** Barbara spent her life on this. Even before Barbara and I met at the think tank, we both focused on the win-lose metrics in particular ways. We called it *Success 2.0* at a big conference in 2014—the win-lose metrics that generates cascading system failures, this move towards what Daniel Schmachtenberger likes to call *self-termination*, where the system self-terminates.

So that's one.

Second, we generate fragile systems which are *complicated*, not *complex*, as I just referred to. But those are not the root cause, those are two generator functions.

Underneath the generator functions, there is a more fundamental cause, and we're calling that a *Global Intimacy Disorder*. Meaning: in a complicated system, the parts are *dissociated* from each other in win-lose metrics; obviously, that's a fundamental failure of intimacy. That's Global Intimacy Disorder.

Here's the great news. That is really hopeful, and that's what Shareef was pointing to. **The ability to find underlying root causes doesn't lead us to *despair*, it brings us to *hope*—we are actually excited.** If you remember *House, M.D*, the diagnostician on that great show: *diagnosis is everything*.

If we can get the diagnosis right, that's huge.

That's not minor, that's a *massive* break.

That's radically hopeful!

Once we understand there is a Global Intimacy Disorder, then what do we need to do?

We don't need to *restore* intimacy because this level of intimacy never existed. It's not saying: "Let's do this restoration; let's go to the ancient world and restore it." We can't do that, because we never had this kind of intimacy.

There is a new emergent intimacy that needs to arise. We know that every crisis is not just a crisis, it's a crisis of *intimacy*. Therefore, what responds to every crisis of intimacy, in the meta-model of reality, is the emergence of *a new configuration of intimacy*. That's what we have been talking about for the last 10 years.

What's the new configuration of intimacy that can cohere a planet?

Well, the answer obviously is: what coheres people? What coheres people is *language which tells stories*.

Not just stories that are *fictions*, but language which tells a Story of Value rooted in *First Principles and First Values*. That's coherence. **You generate coherence through both the quality of *story* and the quality of *value*.**

If you have a need to, let's say, raise funds for a particular cause, and you put a very well-argued series of First Principles about why a person is obligated to give to this very important cause, you will get very little response. But if you put a picture of a nine-year-old boy or a girl, and you tell their story, and the story incarnates those First Principles and First Values, you will get an outpouring of response. **This Story of Value merged with First Principles and First Values generates coherence.**

A new story means We take the best separate parts from premodern, modern, and postmodern wisdom streams, the best validated insights, and we weave them together synergistically, generating a new whole greater than the sum of the parts, aka a new story. That new story itself generates a new level of political will.

- It's a new collective intelligence.
- It's a new cultural enlightenment.
- It's a democratization of this *omni-considering* quality of enlightenment.

We emerge a new vision of identity, *Evolutionary Unique Self*, which then coheres into *Unique Self Symphonies*, and we move towards a planetary awakening in Eros through Unique Self Symphonies.

That's a new story.

We're not going to spend today telling that story. But the point is, there is a meta-crisis, and there is the other term, the meta-solution. It is hopeful when we get to a root cause, and what we need to do now is tell that story. **But that story can't be via declaration—we can't *declare* the story.** Barbara and I used to laugh about this. We can't declare the story, we have to actually show it to be true, show it to be truthful; to hold both of those dimensions, *truth* and *truthful*. We have to take the Tenets of Intimacy and laws of Evolutionary Love—this understanding of what we call *Evolution: The Love Story of the Universe*—and not declare it, but *show* it to be true.

There's been a kind of disparagement in one dimension of a world that Zak and I have moved in extensively. When Ken and I talked about Eros as a moving force of Cosmos, there was an outpouring of division from references to pseudoscience. No, we've got to look *deeper*—we've got to go into the deepest sciences. **We have to look at all of the *exterior* sciences and all of the *interior* sciences, and draw from them the validated understandings at the leading edge of each of them,** woven together at a kind of Darwin-Freud level.

I mean, when you think of the 19th and 20th century, which politicians do you remember? What really changes history? Darwin, Marx, Freud, Einstein—those are the names of people who had genuine paradigms that they didn't *make up*, but they validated empirically through various forms of empiricism.

That's the level we have to operate at. Not propaganda, as Zack will discuss, but actually, literally **articulating a *genuine new story* rooted in multiple source codes, which are rooted in an underlying shared vision of Reality which allows for maximal diversity**. It's the opposite of totalitarianism. It's the shared score, and everyone's playing their music in the symphony. It doesn't move towards a world government or one religion, nothing like that. But it's one field of music—there's a field of value that we all operate in.

CHAPTER TWELVE

SIX KEY DIMENSIONS OF WHAT IS BROKEN IN DEMOCRACY

Board meeting of the Think Tank of the Center for Integral Wisdom — September 30, 2021

I want to look in a new way at what's broken, and I want to talk about something for which it's a given that *this is okay, that this is not broken.* We don't truly regard it as a genuine possibility to say that this particular dimension is broken; this is our sacred cow in the Western world. **I'm talking about *democracy itself.***

I want to focus on democracy, to see where democracy itself, at its very core, is broken in its structure today, and is not happening. We're actually *not* living in democracies. In order to heal that brokenness, we need everything I've just talked about: we need a new story and a universal grammar of value; we need a shared Story of Value based on First Principles and First Values in order to respond to the brokenness of democracy.

I want to look at six or seven key dimensions which point to the breakdown of democracy. We have never done this in one piece before, and I want to do it briefly, just to allude to it, to set the stage for the next dimension. Each of these is an essay or a book by itself, but I want to try to see them together.

1. VOTERS DON'T UNDERSTAND WHAT THEY ARE VOTING ON

Voters don't understand the complexity of what certain theoretical schools have termed in the last ten-fifteen years as *hyper-objects*. I'm going to use that word not in a very precise way, but in a more "meta" way.

The world is inordinately complex. Richard Dawkins said, "Why are they asking me to vote on Brexit? I have got no idea."[22] Dawkins is an intelligent evolutionary biologist, who I disagree with on multiple counts, but certainly an intelligent man, who reads the papers every day. He says, there are the cascading and interlocking issues of currency, economy, economic policy, social policy, etc. of Brexit—and that leaves him clueless. Brexit was passed in England through an overt propaganda campaign. What that means is, it was an overt movement to use certain kinds of tools to pass Brexit. So, Dawkins says, why am I voting on this?

But let's not talk about Dawkins, let us talk about readers who are less informed than Dawkins. **Why are people voting on things that they have no idea about, and that you can't get a gut feeling for?** We basically have a set of highly complicated systems, and we are voting on them even though we don't understand the issues at play.

- ◆ What is our relationship to China? That's a very, very complicated set of issues.
- ◆ What does it mean when Nixon affixed the dollar in a particular way, and then when he changed it in 1972? How did that change things?
- ◆ What's China trying to do with the dollar, and how is that affecting the United States?
- ◆ China is a totalitarian country, based on a classical Maoist position. How do we relate to that?
- ◆ How do we look at currency in general?

---

22 . Richard Dawkins. Ignoramuses should have no say on our EU membership—and that includes me. In *Prospectus Magazine*, July 2016.

- ◆ What are the implications of current federal reserve policy and fractional reserve banking, and a whole host of issues that relate to education and poverty? Most of us can't even see it.

There are so many highly complex issues that you would need to be expert in to comment on. The experts themselves are hijacked by different partisan groups. The experts are evenly divided, not based on what should be an objective conversation about the issues, but based on political affiliation, which means **we are not getting real information**.

There is this unbelievably complicated ecosystem, where people don't have the capacity or the expertise—or if they do have the capacity, they don't have the time—to become conversant on what they are voting for. At the same time, there are Brexit-like campaigns moving to get them to vote in particular ways, and they are unaware that this is even taking place. That's issue one.

It is very different than getting a sense for whether I think that I should vote for John Adams. I go to a town hall, I hear John Adams speak. I know him, or I don't know him, or I know people around him, or I get a sense of what he stands for. I am for slavery, or I am against it. In other words, the set of issues is completely different.

That's the first issue. **People, the overwhelming majority of the electorate, have no idea what they are voting on.**

2. THE KEY ISSUES OF THE DAY ARE NOT BEING VOTED ON

The key issues of the day are *not* what we are voting on.

- ◆ How many people here voted on the internet, or the structure of the internet?
- ◆ How many people here are voting on AI?

There has been very particular incremental progress in a particular form of AI in the last six months to a year. But who voted on that? No one! That's driven by entrepreneurship, which is driven by a win-lose metrics, and a group of scientists that have been hijacked by entrepreneurship, who are rewarded within that win-lose metrics. Virtually no one is overseeing it, and the implications are beyond imagination. So, who is voting on that?

Those are the most important issues of the day.

The most important issue of the day is not the wall with Mexico. That is an issue that's important, but you can see that, you can imagine that, and you can gather information about that. But what is really going on is that the most important issues of the day are not being voted on.

One of the things that COVID brought to the front was the issue of **gain-of-function research**. (Toby Ord, in his book *The Precipice: Existential Risk*, has a great chapter on gain-of-function research, which is well worth reading.)

- Should you be for it or should you not be for it?
- Who is getting rewarded by it?
- Who is not getting rewarded?
- What are the sets of relationships between the different players in the system?

Unless you are tracking gain-of-function research, you've really got no idea. Certainly, nobody in this room voted on gain-of-function research.

After a year of being told that the pandemic came from a bat in Wuhan, it's very clear that the pandemic *didn't* come from the bat in Wuhan. It almost definitely came from gain-of-function research funded by the United States. Now, I am not saying that's a good thing or a bad thing—that's not our topic here. But that seems very close to what actually happened.

What does that mean? How are those decisions made? Was it intentionally released or not intentionally released? The mainstream legacy media has embraced that as a possibility—after ten months of previously dismissing that possibility. You could actually lose your job in certain places for saying it was a possibility.

This has got nothing to do with conspiracy theory. It's got nothing to do with Democratic or Republican. It has to do with *Who votes on this?*

We could go through fifty more key issues, none of which are being voted on.

To sum up, **one: we don't understand the issues we are voting on, and two: we are not voting on the key issues.**

3. WE ARE VOTING WITHIN THE CONTEXT OF NATION STATES, BUT THE REAL ISSUES ARE GLOBAL

We are voting within the context of nation states. But in reality, **every single challenge we have today is global. All of the existential challenges, the huge ones, are global in nature. You cannot address them within the confines of a nation state.**

That's why many people made suggestions, a decade to three decades ago, of **global governance**. Global governance has lots of shadows; it is a potential totalitarianism. But what motivated those suggestions was that you actually cannot deal with global issues otherwise—even with an issue like slavery. We all grew up around the world, whether you live in America, or Germany, or Sweden, or Holland, or wherever you are. In the United States, we grew up remembering the emancipation proclamation of Lincoln—that we have abolished slavery. In England, it was *Amazing Grace* Wilberforce, who was this incredible figure, who moved with a couple of his colleagues for this heroic battle to end slavery. **But there are six times more slaves in the world today than there were at the height of the slave trade in the mid-19th century.**

You cannot deal with sexual slavery. I spent 2006 to 2008 studying just this issue, madly reading everything I could. **You cannot deal with it without a global congruence and coherence.** Can you believe that there are six times as many slaves in the world today?

Similarly, the issue of data: without a global data commonality of some form, you cannot even begin to address the issue of data.

All the major issues are in some sense non-local issues. We live in a world where there is an epidemics in Wuhan—and in our interconnected jet travel world, the plague is all over the world. **How can a nation state possibly vote effectively to deal with these issues?** It makes absolutely no sense, even dealing with COVID on a nation-by-nation basis. Just ask the COVID virus if it respects the sovereignty of nations. It's a joke! In other words, it is so self-evidently obvious, and it is structural.

4. THE PREPOSTEROUS NATURE OF VOTING

Voting is preposterous by nature. This is a huge topic, but let's understand it very briefly.

In 2011, when Facebook was being naive in what it was releasing, they released a study in which sixty one million voters were micro-targeted by Facebook in order to get them to vote—to move them from non-voting to voting. If you do that in a very particular district, you micro-target voters from wavering in a particular district, the effect on an individual voter might be very little—but statistically, **if you change 2–3% of the vote, you can swing the election.**

It was picked up by several commentators in academic scholarship, including Zuboff's magisterial *Surveillance Capitalism*, but also by a writer named Bill Davidow who talked about surveillance capitalism in 2015 in a series of *Atlantic* articles, and a bunch of other writers. Nicholas Carr picked this up pretty early. Cathy O'Neil, in her book, *Weapons of Math Destruction*, picked this up in 2014.

You've got the situation which is kind of astounding. The joke in Facebook was: we all know we swing elections, or we all know we *can* swing elections (the quote is not clear). Meaning, Facebook is consistently split-testing, and what split-testing means is, they're identifying peer groups. Notice *euphemism, euphemism, euphemism.* Peer group doesn't mean groups of lawyers, groups of doctors, groups of teachers. Peer groups means people who react to a sequence of stimuli that's discernible only through the most sophisticated machine intelligence we have in the world.

You see a cat, and it is a black cat; then you see a one-second pause; and then you see a particular strain of music; then you see blue font of a particular kind—it's a four-second sequence. You split-test that sequence, and you find groups of people who respond to that sequence in a particular way. This is all happening beyond the pale of your awareness; you don't even know this is happening. You can identify peer groups all over the country, and then create particular sequences that affect them in a particular way, beneath the floorboard of the conscious self. This is pre-verbal. This is color.

If you can statistically change enough of votes in particular districts without anyone ever knowing you did it, then you can change elections all over the United States. In fact, Facebook proudly announces how they were able to get to a place which had statistical significance in getting people to vote, or not to vote. That's shocking!

You all remember the *Cambridge Analytica* scandal in 2016, where Jim Wiley became a whistleblower, and we were all mad at Trump. There's a lot of good things to be mad at Trump for, but that's a separate issue. This was not a Trump issue at all. To be clear, Jim Wiley, who was the whistleblower in *Cambridge Analytica*, was trained by Eric Schmidt. Eric Schmidt was the former CEO of Google, who directly and personally oversaw the micro-targeting of wavering voters in the Obama campaign, in 2008 and 2012.

We are not commenting that this is a good thing or a bad thing. It just means that democracy, as we understand it, is truly *not* at play. That's a very big piece of information. But that's just the tip of the iceberg. There were four or five writers who wrote about this in the Obama campaign as a non-political issue—really good liberal writers. It's just that no one paid attention until *Cambridge Analytica* happened.

5. THE WIN-LOSE STRUCTURE OF DEMOCRACY UNDERMINES DEMOCRACY ITSELF

There is a win-lose structure, and the win-lose structure of democracy itself undermines democracy. Barbara was very passionate about this, and she coined the term *synergistic democracy*.

In a classical voting situation, voting itself is *weaponized*—instead of being the way you create a new whole. Voting becomes weaponized as part of the win-lose metrics. So, if you have a polarized country, you basically marshal your people, your troops, to get your laws passed and to hell with everybody else, because you are in power now. We recognize this happening in the United States today, on both sides of the aisle, in different ways. It's a win-lose game. It's a win-lose game all over the world, though.

Voting becomes weaponized, so that, just by definition, you are disenfranchising a huge portion of the population in order to accomplish your goal.

And you accomplish it not because your goal is right, not because you have exchanged information, not because you have inhabited each other's values, not because you've looked for synergistic solutions—but because you *won*; because you weaponized voting; because you were better at weaponizing voting—and creating massive alienation in the system. So much so that a commentator like Ben Shapiro, a right-wing commentator (you can disagree with Ben on a thousand things, but he is not an idiot) says, *I think it's time to have a secession from the Union, or we might be coming to that soon*. He said this two weeks ago. He didn't mean it seriously, but if someone like Ben Shapiro had made that suggestion twenty years ago, the world would be in arms.

The level of polarization is so intense for a number of reasons, but one of them is because voting itself has been weaponized—the structure of voting.

Democracy has become win-lose, instead of *synergistic*.

How do we create communication structures that move us from a broken form of democracy to synergistic democracy?

6. SYNERGISTIC DEMOCRACY ONLY WORKS WITH A SHARED GRAMMAR OF EVOLVING VALUES

Finally, you cannot do democracy unless you have a shared story—a shared Story of Value, based on a universal grammar of value. It has to be real, rooted in First Principles and First Values. It just cannot happen otherwise. Because **in order to do democracy, you need a shared collective intelligence.**

One of the things I've mentioned to some of you in the last few weeks is, Nixon and John Kennedy were good friends. It is a very interesting relationship. They remained very good friends, even after the incredibly bitter, hotly contested 1960 election, which Kennedy was accused of stealing. It's an incredible story. But they remained very close friends because they had a shared bedrock of value together; there was a shared Story of Value that they both held together. We barely see those kinds of friendships anymore.

The reason you need a universal grammar of value is because you can't do *sense-making* unless you can *evaluate*. It's a very simple sentence.

- You can't evaluate anything without a shared grammar of value.
- And without a shared evaluation, you can't do sense-making.
- Without a sense of shared sense-making, there's no democracy.
- The education of citizens towards the capacity to do sense-making is impossible without a shared grammar of value.

227

I just touched on the very bare surface of this.

We are in the context of great hope. But we are trying to actually touch the core issues. We begin to see that this Story of Value, this universal grammar of value based on First Principles and First Values, is not some abstract issue. And this is just one example of ten we could have taken today.

Zak is going to go in a whole different direction, but intimately related, without which the core structure of democracy doesn't work.

CHAPTER THIRTEEN

THE THREE STRUCTURES OF THE META-CRISIS

Board meeting of the Think Tank of the Center for Integral Wisdom—September 30, 2021

By Dr. Zak Stein

We are speaking broadly on this issue of democracy. I am going to walk back across some of what Marc walked us through and point out slightly different . Basically, we are going to end up at the same place, but looking at a few different things.

The first one is this phrase *meta-crisis*, which we have used in the space, and we were throwing in a little bit more; it's become popular. There are a couple ways to think about it, and we are thinking about it in a particular way.

The first time I heard it used was at the Integral Theory conference where it was used to just mean *a crisis composed of many crises*. That's a pretty good definition. There's the oil crisis, the economic crisis, the crisis of ubiquitous psychopathology, the ecological crisis, etc. If you gather them all up, and count them, and draw a circle around them, then all of them combined are the meta-crisis. That's one way to think about it.

There is another way to think about it, which is the way we are going. That is, all of those crises exist, and you can draw a circle around them, and that's fine; that's a bunch of crises. **But underneath them—*before* them, *prior* to them—is this meta-crisis.**

If you think about being lost in the woods—you're lost in the woods, you can't start a fire, you don't know where you are, it's getting cold, you don't have any food—these are all crises. Your organism will be in a crisis soon if you don't solve a combination of those. That's crisis. **The *meta*-crisis here is your own mind**: it is the absence of your capacity to do the things you need to do, and if it gets really bad for you, the absence of your capacity to keep your shit together when you are lost in the woods. Many people, when they are lost in the woods, will run in some direction that they believe is the right direction. They panic, and they run in a particular direction. Or they will attempt desperately to do one thing, like start a fire or find food, neglecting to do other things like finding water or shelter.

So, the many crises combined are just a really bad crisis. The *meta-crisis* is deeper. It is, as Schmachtenberger would say, *orthogonal*, and it concerns the mind, the state of your capacity, and specifically the state of your ability to hold your shit together. I wrote in a paper some years ago that the meta-crisis is *education*; **the meta-crisis is psychological by definition.**

The root cause that we are trying to diagnose isn't technical solutions to any one of those problems. It is solutions to the problem of meaning-making, sense-making, legitimacy, and a whole bunch of other dimensions which can be characterized as *superstructure.*

SUPERSTRUCTURE, SOCIAL STRUCTURE, AND INFRASTRUCTURE

A couple of models have been gaining credence lately. One is a neo-Marxist model, which has been taken out of context, but it puts superstructure at the top: *ideas, meanings, values, why are we doing what we're doing?*

Underneath that there are *social structures*. Social structures are the patterns that we use to cooperate. They are the institutional rules, especially governmental procedures. Voting would be an aspect of social structure. **We justify certain social structures based on a superstructure.** *Why* we vote is based on our philosophy—it's based on our superstructure.

Underneath superstructure and social structure is infrastructure. This is where most people are identifying crises, at the level of infrastructure: supply chains, medical system, economic system, ecological system, the way our computers work, distribution of resources, even the internet (which is one of the many things that I'll talk about later when I describe the infrastructures that make possible computational propaganda). These are all infrastructure problems.

The whole reason to have superstructure and social structure is to be able to have the people, us, bind or control what happens at the level of infrastructure. That was the whole notion that Shareef was talking about—the enlightenment and the birth of democracy, the overthrow of the ancient regime, and putting in place a way of thinking about how to regulate infrastructure that involves us:

It's not the feudal lords and the kings who get to decide the distribution of resources and how it works. No.

We have a whole new way of thinking—a whole new philosophy, a whole new superstructure of ideas and values which forces us, basically by reason, to create a new kind of **social structure**, where there's something that we call **democracy**.

By the way, democracy is rare historically. The vast majority of human societies, especially complex ones, have not been open societies. It is kind of a crazy idea to run a vast, complex society where you let everyone basically weigh in on what's going to happen. It takes a lot to pull that off. It takes a lot of very advanced superstructure and social structure to bind the infrastructure.

We are now in a situation where infrastructure has run amok in many domains, and we can't get our shit together well enough to tell them to stop doing it. It's like everyone *knows* Zuckerberg needs to stop what he's doing, but no one can get their act together at the level of social structure to create the legal mechanisms by which to do that. That's because there is an absence of political will, as Marc noted, because we are confused about what *right* and *wrong* are, as a culture. If you can't figure that out then you sure as hell aren't going to be able to fix the social structure and the governmental procedures well enough to bind an infrastructure that's more powerful and runaway than any infrastructure that's ever existed.

The work we are doing here, as Marc is pointing to, is not targeting technical solutions to infrastructure problems, or even saying, *we need to fix democracy in a particular way*. Rather, **we need to recalibrate First Principles and First Values at the level of superstructure**

- to be able to stand anywhere on a *true moral ground*,
- to be able to recalibrate the social structure,
- and then *rebind the infrastructure* for the purpose of humanity—not for its own self-perpetuation or profit-on-profit returns.

That's an interesting way of thinking about the nature of the work that's being taken here.

A lot of what is normally discussed is *diagnosis at the level of social structure and infrastructure*. But what we're saying is there is an urgency here not for technical solutions, but for the ways of thinking about ourselves as a species that are new enough to give us the level of reconfiguration that's necessary.

That's one ramble through the meta-crisis.

INFORMATION TECHNOLOGIES UNDERMINE OUR PROCEDURES AND CULTURAL DYNAMICS

Looking at these layers of issues that really concern us here, and the ability of our governments to control the infrastructures that are being built by technologists right now is maybe the main fundamental problem. There was recently an *Atlantic* article that said, *Facebook is like a hostile foreign actor*. This is an argument which we're making: **these entities that have emerged, like Google and Facebook, have taken on a dimensionality and a power that is truly unprecedented**.

In other companies, for example, an oil company: *there's an oil spill; that sucks. We need to regulate the oil industry*. But an oil spill doesn't stop our ability to do governance; it's just an oil spill, and we need to clean it up. It's not an oil spill in Congress that stops Congress from meeting, or an oil spill in the mind of the Senators which causes them to think in a really messed up way.

On the other hand, **the externalities of Facebook's business model take root in our psychologies.** It is much more difficult to regulate the unbounded infrastructure of Facebook because **its externalities are undermining our procedures and cultural dynamics**.

That is worth keeping an eye on—that we are in a unique situation, even with regards to being able to bind particular out-of-control infrastructures. These infrastructures are informational, they have co-opted and taken away many of the other places where education and the public sphere used to take place. They are undermining the conditions for the possibility of some of our basic practices.

First of all, remember Facebook alone has more users than any country that's ever existed—ever—a larger population of users in China and India combined. It's the largest on the planet. It's like a large for-profit government that lives parasitically off of the geo-spatially demarcated nation states. It's what is called a large *noetic polity*.

It's a planetary noetic polity that's run for profit, living off of the infrastructures built by actual nation states, and running interference between citizens and their own country's legal systems and public spheres.

THERE IS AN ATTRACTOR IN CULTURAL SPACE THAT'S DRAWING US AWAY FROM DEMOCRACY AND OPEN SOCIETY

Turning to the issue of democracy and trying to point out what Marc was saying, we are in a novel situation with regards to the undermining of the conditions for the possibility of our society.

We find that most societies, from all time, were not open societies. This is like a crazy experiment. When you look at it, there have been brief windows during the experiment that we've really had more or less open societies. For example, if you look at the prelude to World War One, it's hard to say that we were living in an open society, due to the level of propaganda that was instituted to get people mobilized to go to war. There have been these ebbs and flows with more and less openness, even in the history of the United States.

The claim here isn't that there was a golden era of democracy and we've lost it, and we need to return to it. That's not the claim. The claim is that **democracy was always an ideal that we were trying to approximate**; we are always trying to move towards greater democracy. We have always been moving slowly towards democracy (a part of our mouth said, *yes, democracy*—and then: but *not women and not blacks*). But it appears now that **some large section of elites, and specifically a rogue group of technologists, have decided not to do that anymore**.

This is a counter-revolutionary stance that we're taking. **We are saying that we are standing for the principles that we have always been trying to approximate—the move towards greater democracy in a greater open society**. *You guys have the wrong idea, building these tech infrastructures that are actually undermining society.*

234

All of the things that Marc noted—that problems are too complex, that the voting is being weaponized, that we don't even vote about the most important things—that whole list is very real. That whole list is used to justify the emergence of *neo-feudalism*. It's the same diagnosis that Marc stated, but it is being run by the people who are saying:

"Enough democracy! Wouldn't it be great if everyone just thought the same way about the vaccine—if everyone just *agreed*? Wouldn't it be great if everyone just thought the same way about January 6th, or about this policy, or that? Wouldn't it be great that we have a consensus? Wouldn't that feel like a relief to everybody?"

Due to the demonstrable problems with democracy as it is currently run, there is a pull *away from it*; there is an *attractor* in cultural space that is drawing us away from our commitments to trying our best to build an open society, even though it's the hardest thing we could do.

The easiest thing to do would be to *force* consensus, to create a scapegoat, and just have fun being righteous.

But the more difficult thing to do is to fundamentally recreate the informational infrastructure so that we can be educated enough to resume reasonable conversations with one another about the nature of the public good—*which is what's necessary.*

The situation we are in with democracy is one where there are groups who believe that the interest of all people is actively working against maintaining open societies.

They are preferring order to chaos. Many just think the chaos is unavoidable, that we are moving through a bottleneck, and there'd be a small number of people choosing chaos.

But actually, the accelerationists in particular are trying to *accelerate* the onset of chaos and collapse.

THE PROBLEM IS THE ABSENCE OF FIRST PRINCIPLES AND FIRST VALUES

There is a third attractor that says we don't need breakdown, and we don't need authoritarian lockdown to solve this quickly. We need to marshal our energies towards the reuse of digital technologies in the interest of a higher-order superstructure.

The problem isn't the technologies. The problem is the absence of the First Principles and First Values that could inform the technologies.

Imagine the same internet, but instead of all the algorithms being built to *addict* you to stay on screen, the algorithms are built to actually *educate* you. That's all there is.

If you can clarify the difference between *manipulation* and *education*, and you can clarify the normative vectors of value that constitute true educational advance for individuals, then **you can write algorithms that give you the next best step in your educational journey that deepens towards greater perspective-taking, compassion, reason, objectivity, and ethics**.

We can write those algorithms.

Right now, we are writing algorithms to make you addicted and to sell advertisements. The business models are toxic, and we are arguing that these business models are so toxic that **they are undermining the condition for the possibility of democracy.** Therefore, this is a national security threat. But again, **no one can hear it, because the superstructure is distorted**.

Instead of trying to change the law to get Zuckerberg shut down, **we are trying to change the conversation.**

236

This is the Messianic invitation[23] **to raise the level of conversation about what the First Principles and First Values are that we're committed to, how they are ontologically established in the universe vis a vis the science and metaphysics we all love, and how clarifying that at the level of superstructure could then allow us to begin more reasonable conversations, reconfiguring governance structures to potentially bind the infrastructure that's running us up against the limits of our own sanity.**

That would be the way that I would begin the entry into this conversation. There is more to say there about some of the specifics of the propaganda campaigns we're currently seeing, which, again, run and have power because of the absence of the level of superstructure of coherent First Principles and First Values. It creates a vacuum for propaganda to enter.

---

23   The word for Messiah in the original Semitic languages is the same as the word for "conversation."

CHAPTER FOURTEEN

DATA SCIENCE AND THE BREAKDOWN OF VALUE

Board meeting of the Think Tank of the Center for Integral Wisdom — September 30, 2021

By Dr. Marc Gafni

IS THERE ACTUALLY SOMETHING THAT'S CALLED VALUE?

We are working on every one of the issues in a meta-systemic way. We are currently working very deeply on a major work on Anthro-Ontology and First Principles and First Values.

Imagine for a second, the Death Star from *Star Wars IV*, which was the first Star Wars movie made. You might remember that later, in one of the rogue movies, we found out how they stole the plans for the Death Star. That's a very important relationship that you need to know if you're a Star Wars freak, which I am. Even if you're not, you know that the rebels are trying to take down the Death Star, and what do you have? You've got a bunch of little spacecrafts, these little, tiny things. Remember *Star Wars IV*, when Mark Hamill was young, Princess Leia was doing gorgeous, and Harrison Ford was a kid?

So, if you track, you understand that the Death Star is *culture itself.* How do you score a direct hit on culture? That's what Zak and I are talking about; that's what the think tank is talking about. **To score a direct hit *on culture*, you have to affect something in the source code itself that then ripples and cascades through the system.**

One of the direct hits that we have been thinking about for a long time is: *is there something that's actually called value?* Zak, Ken, and I have been in a deep set of conversations about this, and Zak and I have been in a conversation about this probably for three to four years, and Howard Bloom is also deeply involved in this conversation.

There is an assumption that there is an undermining of anything I can call *value.* This happens not just in the postmodern space, not just in the space of the policymaking intelligentsia, but often even in the space of the so-called spiritual world. *If I don't know what a human being is, then I am going to build anti-human technologies, because a human being is just an algorithm.* It's not that human being is *a machine* (that's old news, we are not quite a machine), the human being is *an algorithm,* the human being is a computer—but a human being cannot do as well what a very sophisticated machine-intelligence algorithm can do. *So let's just automate all the systems.*

We all participate blindly in our companies, in our worlds—so let us create a world in which human beings aren't going to have jobs, and systems are all automated.

We're going to get to a place where we don't even need human beings as *consumers* anymore, because the AI algorithms can just trade with each other.

There is an *undermining of value* unless I have a sense of the **irreducible value of human personhood**.

There is an undermining of value unless I understand that **you're not a gadget**, unless I can actually track that there is a **First Principle and**

First Value of personhood, there's a First Principle and First Value of **uniqueness** (which goes through stages from matter to life to mind), and I can articulate a set of First Principles and First Values, that solve the eight or nine major attacks on value (which are, in part, legitimate).

It's not that there are completely crazy people in modernity and postmodernity who are entirely evil, who are standing against value. No, that's not true. There *was* a reason to attack the great traditions; they *did* make some mistakes, which are real.

The great traditions were also in a win-lose metrics with each other. The win-lose metrics didn't start in modernity; the great traditions were already fighting each other. Everyone said, *"We've got an exclusive path to God. You're wrong, and I'm going to convert and kill you for the sake of God."* It was a bad story. *Let's go back to the old, beautiful, great traditions*—that's a really bad idea.

What we want to understand is *what the deep values are that the great traditions knew?*

Not all the great traditions are equal, different ones are better at different things.

- But what are their values, and what are they based on?
- How can I show that those values are actually intrinsic and inherent in reality?

These questions have basically been taken off the table. The assumption until now has been: *you cannot solve the problem of value; we just don't have preordained eternal values.*

That's nonsense! We're saying that's not true.

I'm not going to get into *how* we solve that problem right now, but we are deep in it. We are taking the attacks seriously, and we believe that we need to be able to reformulate what Zak called *the superstructure*, so

241

that the superstructure then reformulates *the social structure*, which then capacitates us to engage *infrastructure*.

I'm going to go one more step. I'm going to try and say this in the most elemental terms, and I want to say it simply—but I can only get to a place to say it simply because I've been thinking about this day and night, I wake up in the middle of night dreaming about this. So, I am going to say it really simply.

DATA SCIENCE ALLOWS US TO RECODE REALITY AS A SKINNER'S BOX

A book called *Social Physics* by a guy named Alex Pentland[24] is the central book that formed the internet. Zak and I have been working for the last year on a book called *From Skinner to Facebook to Google*, where we are not just *claiming*, but *documenting* very extensively, with an insane amount of primary source material, that the vision of technologists of reality is a *Skinner's Box*[25]—not hyperbolically, but in reality.

Skinner couldn't accomplish that. I've read quite a lot from B. F. Skinner, the great psychologist, who was a brilliant man.[26] A bunch of his books are sitting on my desk, and I have spent half the night several times just going through them again and again—so I could *feel* him. I have enormous respect for him as a thinker. He has engaged me—and I think he is infinitely more dangerous than I thought when I started reading him.

Skinner is the hidden source code of the technology world. But Skinner couldn't get it done. Why couldn't he get it done? Because he didn't have what he himself called *the machines and methods*. How are you going to create the world as a Skinner's Box? Along comes data science. Skinner is at the very beginning of that digital moment, and along comes data science.

24 Pentland, Alex. Social Physics: How Social Networks Can Make Us Smarter (2015)
25 That is, the world turns into a kind of conditioning chamber where our behavior is fully controlled by algorithms.
26 See, for example: Skinner, B.F. *Beyond Freedom and Dignity* (1971).

There are about ten thousand great data scientists in the world, and those ten thousand data scientists have been hijacked by a group of technologists for the sake of this rivalrous conflict win-lose metrics.

Coupled with the most advanced machine intelligence, **data science allows us to recode Reality as a Skinner's Box**. There's a kind of epidermal, embracing *skin* around Reality today that is generated by ubiquitous computing which is getting more and more ubiquitous—the Internet of Things, in multiple forms, that's getting more and more dramatic, which enables a worldwide kind of Skinner's Box, creating worldwide surveillance.

But the problem is not even the surveillance. In a 2019 essay, Bostrom[27] makes the suggestion that in order to deal with a complex set of existential risks we might need global surveillance, which he calls the *black ball from the urn*. He talks about four possibilities to solve it.

- One is: get rid of the bad people—that's hard.
- The other is: stop technology—that's hard.
- The third is global governance—big shadows.
- The fourth is worldwide surveillance.

But the problem is not *surveillance per se*, although that is a huge problem. The problem is surveillance *without First Principles and First Values*. It is surveillance which is *not* governed internally (the latter would have Reality self-organize according to simple First Principles and First Values).

I have been studying self-organizing systems over the last decade. Self-organizing systems organize according to simple First Principles and First Values. Maybe the most important thing I ever said to myself, a decade ago—and Zak and I got excited about it together—is:

Just like exterior sciences operate according to simple First Principles and First Values, *so do interior sciences*.

---

27   Nick Bostrom, "The Vulnerable World Hypothesis," *Global Policy*, Volume 10, Issue 4 (2019).

The superstructure is governed by simple First Principles and First Values. But if those disappear—if there is no collective intelligence rooted in simple First Principles and First Values, and you have a privately run onshore group of technologists, governed by a win-lose metrics—then we are developing exponential technology, where the technology itself, or the algorithms themselves, move to optimize in order to create particular outcomes.

PEOPLE ARE NOT NATURALLY GOOD—PEOPLE ARE INHERENTLY GOOD

Tim O'Reilly said that Alex Pentland was one of the six or seven most important figures in the world. Alex Sandy Pentland said to Howard Bloom, our senior scholar, "I created the internet." That's a quote, and he's not inaccurate. His gaggles of doctoral students at the MIT Media Lab are in fact embedded throughout the tech plex.

Pentland makes an assumption. It's this very strange, naive, but understandable assumption that's made across the board. Pentland assumes that people are naturally good. That's not true. **People are not *naturally* good; people are *inherently* good.** You cannot have this conversation without getting this distinction:

People are *inherently* good, but people are not *naturally* good.

To realize and activate my inherent goodness I need *education*—not propaganda. I'm going to leave that distinction to Zak, but what education means is really simple.

Just to understand the definition of education, let's refer to C. S. Lewis who writes about education in 1943[28]: *education means that old birds are teaching young birds to fly.* Flying is a real thing, it's a *real value.* They are not making something up. They are not raising young birds to be slaughtered

---

28   Lewis, C. S. The Abolition of Man; or, Reflections on Education with Special Reference to the Teaching of English in the Upper Forms of Schools (1943).

in poultry farms. There is an actual value, and we share that value through the process of education. But if there is no real value—if value is completely made up, if there is no value of uniqueness, or of the Good, the True, and the Beautiful of personhood—if that doesn't exist, then the superstructure begins to collapse.

If you think that people are not inherently good, but they're naturally good, that's the single most dangerous belief you can have—not to realize the distinction between people's inherent goodness and natural goodness. Because **if people are naturally good, we don't need education**: *people are naturally good, it'll be fine.* But what's happening is that people are inherently good, not naturally good.

We have dismantled a system of strange attractors that we call a Story of Value based on First Principles and First Values that would allure people, and educate people to their goodness.

Here is the key. Now what happens is that people begin to act based on what we call the lowest common denominator of humanity. The reason is because the internet is built on measurement; data science is a science of measurement.

THE RISK OF LOSING OUR HUMANITY

I just clarified this notion to myself when I was talking to Zak in the last couple of days. Ken said something on our phone call which sent me looking for stuff after the call—that measurement, **what you can *measure* is *not* a person's Unique Self**, what's *anomalous* about a person, what's *different* about a person.

You can measure the lowest common denominator, the ways in which people are the same. You measure it through data science by seeing how people respond when they respond the same way to negativity:

- They respond the same way to gossip.
- They respond the same way to mobs.

245

- ◆ They respond the same way to fear.
- ◆ They respond the same way to anxiety.

The entire internet is built around a system of measurement intended to generate exponential windfall profit for about fifteen to twenty people, which is completely unbound by any kind of First Principles and First Values. It is based on data science which *measures*. And it measures the lowest common denominator of the human being—and that's what it drives.

I'll end with just an incredible quote from Pentland's *Social Physics*, which I've read five times because I wanted to feel into it. At the end of the book Pentland has a section which is called *Promoting Freewill and Human Dignity*. The name of Skinner's book is *Beyond Freedom and Dignity*. Pentland is playing with the audience. He calls his major, most important section in his book *Promoting Freewill and Human Dignity*, meaning, "I'm not like Skinner." But why is he even saying that? He's saying that social physics is going to promote freewill and human dignity. But if you carefully read what he says, he is saying the opposite. What he really says is kind of shocking.

He says that *there are some anomalies, when people will act according to inner processes, which will occasionally defeat our models of social physics. But generally, the percentage is so minuscule that it doesn't make a difference.* Then he goes on to say that *freewill is in actuality irrelevant in most thinking.* He uses Kahneman's distinction (Kahneman won a Nobel Prize for distinguishing between fast and slow thinking).[29] Pentland says virtually all thinking is fast thinking, not slow thinking, giving three or four reasons why the slow thinking has become irrelevant. *So, if we can control fast thinking* —which we control through the measurement of data science—*we can control society.*

This is not because Pentland is evil; he's not. Pentland views himself as a utopian, as did Skinner. But utopians without First Principles and

---

29 Daniel Kahneman, *Thinking, Fast and Slow* (2013).

First Values, driven by privatized exponential windfall profit and power, become a very dangerous reality; in fact, *the* most dangerous reality. We've been listening in at the Center for Integral Wisdom, and what Skinner and Pentland are really saying is there are two kinds of existential risk.

We are concerned with the first kind of existential risk, they say, *which is the death of humanity, aka extinction—we're going to kill ourselves; we're going to cause massive suffering. So, what we are going to do is create a Skinner's Box that allows for control—to **save** us from existential risk.* That's the hidden conversation in rooms behind the scenes. I would bet my life on it.

The only problem is, because they've abandoned First Principles and First Values. They are the cause for **the second kind of existential risk, which is the death of *our* humanity**—the death of personhood, of uniqueness, of everything that we recognize as uniquely human, which makes the vast majority of the human race irrelevant.

What happens when crisis comes, and virtually all human beings are irrelevant? To say *it's not pretty* is a major understatement.

CHAPTER FIFTEEN

DISCERNING EDUCATION, PROPAGANDA, AND MANIPULATION

Board meeting of the Think Tank of the Center for Integral Wisdom — September 30, 2021

By Dr. Zak Stein

I am going to focus on the distinctions between coercion and persuasion and education.

The phrase that's used by the gaggles of doctoral students around Pentland, and the people at the Laboratory for Persuasive Technologies at Stanford, is that these technologies that Pentland is talking about—which we are calling Skinner's Boxes—are these phones in your hand, these computer screens. But I'm going to take a different tack. Think about how you make a society that's larger than your family work. What are the modes by which social organisms function? How do people cooperate to do things they couldn't do by themselves?

In family systems, we cooperate because we are educated into the norms of the family, and we all agree about what's taking place, and we negotiate in everyday language who does what and who's responsible for what. But as soon as you get to hundreds of people, let alone thousands of people, if you are trying to build things like pyramids, in ancient Egypt for example, you cannot organize large-scale social cooperation through everyday communication and socialization. So, you invent propaganda, which is the use of the human symbolic capacity—it's a species-specific trait that allows for family, that allows for education. **The use of that symbolic capacity in a very particular way allows for the large-scale control of human behavior.**

One way to think about civilization is to think about the creation of symbolic human control systems. Interestingly, those were always loose around the edges. And—like Moses escaping and wandering through the desert—**there was always an out**. The system was always limited in size and scope, and the techniques were always things you could walk away from, more or less. You don't have to read the newspaper if you don't want to.

What we are looking at is a story similar to a lot of the civilizational-collapse dynamics, which is that we are doing the same thing we've always done, **but the technology has gotten to such an extent that we *just can't* continue to do the same things that we have always done.** As long as we continue to try to organize society through these types of propagandistic social control mechanisms in the current context, it is beginning to backfire and fail. **The propaganda is starting to create more confusion than it's resolving, and it's creating more behavioral-disorganization than behavioral-organization.**

When you think about being in a context like Facebook, reading a newspaper, or whatever, the question is *whether the communication relationship is one that is truly educating me or not.* This is a deep question to ask, **if the informational environments we are in are in reality educational environments, or are they manipulative and coercive environments?**

And we know these distinctions.

If you go to a Tony Robbins event, and there's music going, and there's tons of people, and you haven't eaten in six hours, and you are not allowed to take a bathroom break, and you didn't sleep well last night, and Tony Robbins is talking a thousand miles an hour, and he's coming at you— this combination of sensory overwhelm, disorientation and a whole bunch of other factors, make you susceptible to the input of messaging. That's an environment where one is susceptible to being brainwashed and propagandized.

Here's the important thing. In those contexts, **if what is being done is such that the person can *know for themselves* what is being taught, it is very different than a situation where there's an *unbridgeable gap* between the teacher and the student.** This is the key distinction. There is a coercive context like brainwashing where you're tortured and stuff—obviously, this is a coercive implanting of ideas. But there are other contexts where senses are overwhelmed, rituals performed, and other things that make you susceptible to certain kinds of uptakes.

Then the question becomes: what does a person do when they step into that container? When the symbolic matrix is created, who is it that steps in, is it an educator or a propagandist? How you can tell the difference?

- The propagandist says, "I know things you do not know, and that you will never know." There is a barrier of access to the level of knowledge on which the propagandist stands, and that barrier, the unbridgeable epistemic asymmetry, is specifically guarded against being breached.
- The educator steps in and says, "Hey, I want you to come up right next to me. I want you to look over my shoulder at exactly the same texts that I am reading. I want you to understand this shit better than I understand it, because I have to pass it on to you. You have to take up the mantle of what I'm trying to teach you. It needs to be obvious that we completely understand the same thing, together."

That's a big difference.

As an example of this, think of TikTok. I think TikTok should basically be banned, because TikTok is like the Fentanyl of social media. It is designed to be the very strongest, most addictive, most stimulating and overwhelming and brainwash-y of all the social media technologies. It creates an environment like a Tony Robbins event. It used to be that you needed to rent a whole place to have this whole kind of thing. But now you can just space out eating breakfast and watch fifteen different videos, each professionally produced with something like a hundred sub-cuts each, and something like a thousand bits of information, some of which you are not even realizing you're perceiving.

With a measurement feedback loop, as Marc just said, they are creating operant conditioning; they're creating schedules of reinforcement. For example, they know that you like videos of cute cats. So, every time you stay on longer they will give you videos of cute cats. We know that those mechanisms are in place. It creates that kind of de-realization and susceptibility to manipulation. And it is built into the way things are designed.

The argument ends up being that **you are in a pretty bad spot under those conditions, if the people who are putting ideas into those contexts are also establishing unbridgeable epistemic asymmetries where they know things that you will never know.** That characterizes a lot of the propaganda that we are under presently within the context of presidential elections and pandemic public health campaigns.

There are two components:

- There is the context of communication, which can be more or less manipulative, more or less brainwash-y.
- Then there's the actual structure of the relationship of knowledge: is it propagandizer and one who is propagandized, or is it teacher and student? The educational relationship is different than the propagandistic relationship. That's key.

The vast majority of the informational environments that currently exist on the internet are basically designed to be optimally propagandistic. They are designed to allow for the slipping in of messages and the creation of a context which, under legal terminology, is called *undue influence*. Undue influence is a technical legal term that describes contexts like when you've been kidnapped and brainwashed and forced to rob banks, like Patty Hearst was. Patty Hearst was kidnapped by radical socialists in the United States. She was tortured and brainwashed into believing conspiracy theories, and she ended up robbing banks for the kidnappers. She was arrested and thrown in jail. Clinton pardoned her in the nineties. Why did he do that? She robbed the banks. She ran away from FBI agents and shot at them. Because she was *under undue influence*. She was not responsible for her behavior, because she was so coerced into believing certain things that her mind was being controlled. The decisions she was making were the decisions of her controllers, not her own decisions.

So now we are making the strong argument that **the contexts of social media are creating conditions of undue influence**, because we have created technologies that have gone from persuasive to coercive and negated the possibility of education. It's like asking if anyone who's really addicted to social media is actually responsible for the decisions they make when they vote, undergo a biomedical procedure, etc.? If you're under undue influence the answer is you're not.

Undue influence is a nice way of saying *mind control*, and it's the legal term that is used by expert psychologists in criminal trials to relieve people who've been in cults from responsibility for their actions while they were under mind control. **The argument is that if we have technologies that are powerful enough to exert undue influence, then people basically are not able to be held responsible for what they're doing.** That means that Zuckerberg and crew are so fundamentally undermining national sovereignty that it's a major legal and security threat. But remember, it's not an oil spill somewhere far away in the wilderness. It's an oil spill in the mind of all the senators and congressmen who have to think about what to do with this problem. There's an *embeddedness* of the problem that makes it difficult to solve.

That was a kind of a windy way through. Propaganda has always been around, but **the conditions for computational propaganda, which moved from persuasion into basically coercion, have changed the nature of the game**. And it explains a lot of the behavior that we are seeing in terms of the intensity of the polarization and the dominance of thought-terminating cliches and other aspects of propagandized language in the culture. We ourselves are so used to being exposed to psychological weaponry that we start to use psychological weaponry on other people, and we spread what's called *horizontal propaganda*, where we take up the catchy propaganda line and default knee-jerk reaction and refusal of the counterargument, and we use it bluntly as an instrument, as a thought-terminating cliche, to stop conversation and keep it on propagandistic lines.

Therefore, we are internalizing the grammars of the propaganda. And **the grammars of propaganda are genocidal grammars**. The opposite of a universal grammar of value is a grammar of genocide. It's the grammar that creates the group that *you are allowed to hate*, the group that *we all love to hate together*. That's what propaganda creates.

Many people I know, who would never fall into such a category, *are* in that category now, in the context of the pandemic propaganda. We are actively creating a biomedical underclass that we have every reason to hate and fear and to seek to coerce and control. If you're speaking that language, you are speaking the grammar of genocide that's been handed to you by the propagandized—the opposite of the grammar of value. It's the risk that we are in now, as our languages cease to be our own, and even some of our decisions become hard to be accountable for in these conditions.

CHAPTER SIXTEEN

THE ECSTATIC URGENCY OF CHANGING THE SOURCE CODE

*Board meeting of the Think Tank of the Center for
Integral Wisdom — September 30, 2021*

By Dr. Marc Gafni

I want to add one thing that is super important. What we are saying is completely inter-texted. We have had hundreds of conversations, and we are working on different and shared parts of this. All of this is getting gradually written and organized and put together in hopefully clear ways. We are trying to articulate eight or nine pieces of this picture, *but to articulate them so clearly that they're self-evidently true.*

Because once they are very clear, the actual source code just changes.

Imagine Darwin for a second. Daniel Dennett has written *Darwin's Dangerous Idea.*[30] No matter what you think of Darwin, the set of ideas he put forth were so compelling that it became, as Dennett wrote, *an acid that cut through society and reformulated everything.* Paul Johnson opens his book on the 20th century explaining how Darwin literally reformulated people's essential self-understanding.[31] Darwin had a lot going on, but

---

30   Dennett, Daniel. *Darwin's Dangerous Idea: Evolution and the Meanings of Life* (1995).
31   Johnson, Paul. *Modern Times: The World from the Twenties to the Eighties* (1983).

Neo-Darwinism went nuts. Until we realize that Darwin's ideas got hijacked by Neo-Darwinism, we cannot move on. **Because the model of Neo-Darwinism is actually dead.**

- Getting this realization will then allow us to actually reformulate value. You've got to do *the Neo-Darwinism is dead* move very carefully. We are working on that very seriously. That's one piece.

- Another piece is to show that **evolution itself is driven by value**. But you can't just *say* that. You've got to *show* it in fifteen different ways. You can't just declare it. That's a second piece: evolution is driven by value.

- The third piece is: how do we respond to the ten postmodern and modern critiques of value?

How do we clearly formulate the distinctions between education and propaganda? What is our universal grammar of value and what is not? We must get these things so clear that they become butter. When I say *clear*, I don't mean *dogmatic*. It's the framework that must be clear.

Think about the deists who were the Founding Fathers. (We missed the founding mothers because deism hadn't evolved that far). When they talked about *truths that were self-evident*, that worked! Self-evident truths worked for a while, doing something unbelievably important. The great revolution of democracy was based on self-evident truths, which means *they are intrinsic to Cosmos*. We've got to find those again. That is just another way of saying (I want to say this a little dramatically, just in our own inner circle): it's like finding God. This is what we mean when we say, "finding God".

We say, the god you don't believe in doesn't exist. God is not a cosmic vending machine. One way that god appears is in this notion of intrinsic value in Cosmos, that's really *real*; that's actually *intrinsic*. Spirit is real. Beauty is real. Goodness is real. But the God language is too laden; it's too stuck to solve the problem. We've got to include everybody. And because

65% of the world today lives in God language, you cannot just write people off; they have to be part of the conversation.

There are a lot of pieces to this, but they are all handleable. We can do this. A decade ago, we had no intention of doing this. I want to make that very clear: we didn't *intend* to do this. When Zak and I first started studying in 2009, we knew of each other. I had written *Unique Self*, and Zak was working on education. There were problems in the way people talked about enlightenment, so we wanted to reformulate it, and we wrote *Unique Self, Radical Kabbalah,* and *Self*.

But what we did was, we started handling different problems, but with no intention of doing this. We were going to evolve particular dimensions of the source code, which we took very seriously. Then somewhere around 2012 or 2013 we began to realize the second shock of existence; we read a bunch of books, and we changed. We realized, *Oh my God, no one is noticing, and it's actually **all** at stake, in a real way.* Another bunch of spiritual books are really great, but in reality, that would just be a form of turning away.

What we did though, is we just kept working on each issue: let's look at *relationships*, let's look at *Eros*, let's look at *sexuality*, let's look at *governance*, let's look at *education*, let's look at *identity*. We began looking at these issues, issue by issue, and formulating models and distinctions that allowed for a new language. Somewhere around 2016 or 2017 our friend Daniel joined us and started asking questions, which were good questions, they helped us focus. Then the *Intimate Universe* started to emerge, and *The Universe: A Love Story*. The questions that Daniel asked were: *How do you know any of this stuff? It's changed my life, but how do you know it?* So, we worked on our epistemology—First Principles and First Values, Anthro-Ontology.

We didn't plan this. She did this. And that's why we trust Her. We realized all of a sudden, *oh my God, the world's desperately thirsty, and we've got some water, and it's exactly what's needed.* What it creates anew is not a sense of triumphalism. It creates a sense of what I might call *ecstatic urgency—*

ecstatic in the sense that we are so privileged to hold this, but enormous urgency and trembling in me. It creates a sense of trembling.

Trembling comes from different places. There's trembling in fear, there's trembling in trauma—and there's also trembling before She. There's a text, *gilu bir'a'da* "tremble in joy." This was a kind of *trembling in joy*.

However, without all of us together in this Unique Self Symphony, we cannot do this. We are doing this together. Some people are taking major leadership roles, and there are a couple of major leaders stepping forth. Everyone is taking a particular role, and we are being a Unique Self Symphony. It's real, and we actually love each other.

In the end, this is not a university conversation, although universities are important. Zak and I committed the sins, and we know it, of writing doctorates at Harvard and Oxford, respectively. But in the end, **this** is *Chavraya Kadisha*, **this** is a band of Outrageous Lovers, and we love each other. We know this needs to be done, and we know we need to clarify it deeper and deeper. We are holding it together.

I just want to maybe say that as a last sentence: **You can't say *I love you* without saying *I need you*.** But we have exiled need, we are afraid to need. We have made need a codependency, where need is a kind of neediness. Maybe the greatest mystery of the interior sciences of Hebrew wisdom is that Infinity, She, turns to human being and says, *avoda tzorech Gavoha* "I need you", meaning, the Infinity of Power turns to human being and says, "I need you. I have created a Reality in which I need your partnership; I cannot do it myself." The Infinity of Power is not playing power moves. Power moves have place somewhere in Reality, when the power is deployed appropriately. But the Infinity of Power steps back and says, "I love you so much, I'm willing to say I need you." In the great tradition, we do *Imitatio Dei*, where we try to be like the Infinity of Power.

So I want to be like the Infinity of Power, which is also the Infinity of Intimacy, and say, *we need each other*. I'll say it in the first-person on my birthday: *I need you; we need each other*. Zak just gave his talk—I need

Zak. Can we be vulnerable enough to say, *I need you?* We need each other. And let's love each other more deeply, and more wondrously, and more gorgeously.

Let's do it all together.

CHANGING THE SOURCE CODE THROUGH COMMUNICATION

Mike: It's great to see everybody. I'm blown away every time I listen to you, and Zak, and everybody else. Let's take, maybe, five steps into the future. Say that everything that you were talking about, it comes in a crystal clear format and structure. Because I am assuming that there's some type of movement that has to take place to repress this train that's on its tracks. But I look at the movie *Social Dilemma*, which I watched. I'm in the social media business, online business. I have looked at it. I knew that they were just mind-fucking all of us. Excuse the French. But that was done really well.

It had 38 million views. I don't know what it did. More than half, some people would say "I'm getting off of Facebook." If you're able to do what you said in changing the source code with communication… Maybe a great movie that gets… I mean, 38 million views is a lot. **How does that do what it's supposed to do?**

Marc: That's a really great question. I think Zak and I will both address it. Because I think it's worth addressing. It was actually an important movie. Say, two things. One, it's very clear that it needs to go another bunch of steps. I think there's things in play to move that forward. That's one.

But, two is, in some sense, what *Social Dilemma* movie did very well was address some of the structural issues. I think they did a really good job. But they were operating at the level of what we might call infrastructure and social structure. We're operating at the level of superstructure; **we are providing a different piece of the story.**

I'll just give you one example. **Attention is hijacked.** That's what the movie is about. They are hijacking your attention. We see what happens to the kid is, his attention is hijacked. He winds up at a demonstration, protests the ground with his sister. This creates great polarization. The movie did as much as it could have done. But unless you understand that attention is a First Value and First Principle, and that attention hijacking is a violation of personhood, unless you can *demonstrate* that, you cannot even begin the conversation.

When I say you cannot even begin the conversation—let me say it more accurately: you cannot complete the conversation. You can begin the conversation—Senator Sloan did it and did it very well—but you can't complete the conversation.

Zak and I were just talking, literally, we've talked, actually, I would say, five times this year, having particular conversations with key change agents about the First Principle and First Value of attention. Those conversations are happening. *Social Dilemma* is wildly important. It's insufficient. But insufficient doesn't mean *bad*. It means it is a piece of the story. And we need to create the right alliances, and to make the right moves, you're absolutely right. And that's the direction we're going in. It needs to happen. Right, Zak?

Zak: The Social Dilemma opened many people's eyes, but it's an entry way up into a broader conversation about the meta-crisis. Not just "Let's all grab pitchforks and attack Facebook." Which is kind of what is happening. That's one piece. Which is that, that movie in particular, is actually one of the best ways in. Marc and I almost independently discovered this broader question of the meta-crisis as a *crisis of meaning*, a crisis of meaning-making, and the need to resolve that superstructure.

Then there's a second thing. Which is that, *how does one actually take a bunch of ideas, and have them not only propagate and saturate into the culture but do it in such a way that things actually change?*

There are two ways to answer this. One is that it's a small number of *exactly the right people* changing their minds that's necessary first. The goal isn't to convince everybody. The goal is to convince a very small number of exactly the right people first, and then it starts to go and then eventually there's a critical mass. There is that famous saying which I think Marc has used. It's like there's only a couple of hundred people that were involved in this thing we call the Renaissance. Obviously, the plan is much bigger. It's going to be more than a couple of hundred.

The key thing is direct strategic *metanoia*—direct strategic interventions to try to change significant agents' minds. This is what's necessary. In order to do that, you actually need a whole body of theory behind you, so that when you show up as somebody or broadcast something or write something, they are not like, "Well, who the hell are you?" You're like, "I'm this dude. We have *The Great Library*. We've got this tradition of evolutionary spirituality and Kabbalah, and I'm this dude." Now we are changing minds. There's a downward trickle effect from the highest order. Leveraging.

Mike, this is the strategic question. Because if, by chance, someone solves some technical problems, that's great: thank you, you've saved us time. But this is the hardest problem to solve, with a level of superstructure. I think the most faith and grace is involved. Part of this is also praying that it works out. Hopefully, that helped, Mike.

Marc: What I want to do is have private conversations with key players where we actually do what we would call *Holy of Holies* and study. *Let's study for five sessions. What is the first principle of attention? And how does it work?*

Here there is a very deep partnership with Zak, and myself, and a lot of us in other dimensions. For example, we put up the Unique Self Institute. You put up the Unique Self Institute and, all of a sudden, you've got a place with an enormous amount of information on Unique Self. Now you can refer to that, and it's really beautiful. You're not just making a claim. You create a Phenomenology of Eros. You create what we call *The Great Library*. You create the key work on values, a key work on Anthro-Ontology.

We all have different roles to play in the symphony. We are at different moments in time. Some of the roles are public and some of them are behind the scenes and some of them are private. We've got to be in this place where we are in this egoless yet wholly audacious Unique Self. You need Unique Self here.

We are together giving gifts across a system that can transform the system. And I believe that we can. I believe that we can. I've had, over the last twenty years, any number of transformational conversations with key people that changed their trajectory in life, by actually doing a certain set of source code structure study with them.

But at the same time, Zak talked about, "Okay, let's change a few minds." The thousand people in the Renaissance. And at the same time, we actually want to also turn to public culture itself and be able to change the source code of public culture. We want to go from both ends.

Does that make sense, everybody? Darwin moved in and just changed the elite. It changed the intelligentsia which then trickled down to the elite. We've got to do both of those moves, and we need each other to do it.

SURVEILLANCE CAPITALISM, TECHNOLOGY, AND THE OLD TESTAMENT

Alden: I was reflecting when you were talking about surveillance capitalism, and technology, and data analytics. I find it interesting because in the Old Testament, the devil only shows up a couple times. Each time, he's doing data analytics, basically. He's tempting the king, I think it's David or Solomon, to take a census of the people of Israel, which is a sin. Then he's going up to God and he's like, "Check out Job. Here's the whole list of all of his things." He finds a chink in the armor. I'm wondering, are there clues in there, or keys in there?

Marc: It's a good question, Alden. Thank you. It's a great question. Shareef and I actually talked about this last night when we were preparing the meeting. This exact topic. Which means, *is this all in ancient texts?* To answer is, *it's not*. I just want to be really clear about that. That's a fundamentalist mistake.

One of the things we were talking about, Shareef and I, last night is the notion that penicillin existed, for example, in great sacred texts, the most beautiful ones. It didn't. Reading a sacred text is *not* what you should do when your child needs penicillin, which was one of the great antibiotics. The antibiotics started with enormous promise. Penicillin actually saved people's lives in a way that prayer didn't. But **it's not that penicillin and prayer are *opposed* to each other.** Prayer is one modality, and a sacred modality, and it has its efficacy in Cosmos. And penicillin's another modality.

Penicillin is an expression of the Field of Eros, the Field of the Divine—no less than prayer.

I am going to say this very carefully. There are many superstructure clues, as you put it, in the sacred texts. And those are unbelievably important. That's what we mean when we say, we integrate the best of the **traditional**. And we have a reverence, we bow before, we are in devotion to the great traditional wisdoms. I've spent my life studying sacred texts. For sure. Absolutely. Those texts infuse everything.

Then we embrace the depth of **modernity**. Again, when I said the *depth* of modernity, not *all* modernity, but the best validated insights of the new forms of knowing—*gnosis*, the modality which, for example, produced penicillin. We watch for the shadows. We don't do a blind embrace of modernity.

Then we look at **post-modernity**. What postmodern things did Foucault say that were really important? Foucault pointed out these power games that were happening; he pointed out a lot of very important things. We look at the best of post-modernity.

Then we make the great move: **we integrate it in a new story where all those pieces have a place.** But what I would say is, *under the hood, if you will, it's all animated by She.* It's animated by an integration of the best value we have everywhere. But we have to express it in a way that can penetrate the source code of conscience and culture in a real way.

Zak: I was having a similar conversation the other day with somebody. Jordan Hall, you guys know him. This notion came up that there is an archetypal property to the demon or the devil, which is that their choice architect had a nudger. This is classically when the devil comes up: he's giving you a bargain. He's giving you some options. He's constraining the choice, "You want the apple? I am not saying you could have a pear, I'm saying do you want the apple?" The choice architect, who surreptitiously puts certain choices in front of you presenting the idea that you're choosing when, in fact, the deck is stacked. Then there is a slow, subtle nudging in towards evil or whatever. That notion that it's a nudging.

There's something about that archetypal property worth saying. That's why we get so creeped out about what's happening—it feels almost demonic, in a way, the way some of these technologies have been able to exercise mind-capture, and to actually recruit the people who are being manipulated into supporting the thing that's been manipulating them. There is this strange double-bind. Although there's no way this was foreshadowed, there's a deep structure to certain forms of bad behavior, which is just isomorphically similar to what goes back.

That's what people were pointing out in those texts. Archetypically, there's a way that certain interactions go where the choices and the deck are stacked against you, where there is manipulation, where there is nudging. Those are bad relationships as opposed to the open, transparent, educational, all-the-cards-on-the-table, we're-looking-at-the-same- deck kinds of conversations.

I think there's something deep in the archetypal problems with what we're encountering that goes way back. Humans have been worried about this kind of stuff for a long time, in one way. But in another way, it's completely novel.

Marc: It's that combination. Just like there are First Principles and First Values on the value side of equation, there are adverse First Principles and First Values in the dark matter as it were, on the devil's side of the equation. That's what exists. It's always First Principles, it's always structural. At the same time—that's the key sentence—it is so old, it's time immemorial *and* it's completely new. It's completely, utterly new.

WHAT ARE THE RISKS THAT COULD INHIBIT THE SUCCESS OF THE NEW STORY?

David: Hey, Marc. Thanks for the great presentation. If you're looking at just our group, and the work that you're doing, and the work that Zak is doing, and the whole band of Outrageous Lovers, what might be a risk that could inhibit the success of progress? Are there any blind spots that we should keep in front of us and proactively engage to make sure that we are successful?

Marc: I would say it's not a blind spot. There is a different risk. **The risk is, we don't take it seriously enough,** that in some sense the think tank becomes for people a hobby. We obviously stay fully engaged in the depth and goodness of our lives, obviously. I think the biggest risk is, *we don't actually get what's at stake.*

There's an incredible book that I read that changed my life. Two books actually. One was by a guy named Arthur Morse called *While Six Million Died,*[32] and a second by David Wyman called *The Abandonment of the Jews.*[33] They were formative to me personally. They both describe the American-Jewish community, and the secular spiritual community between 1939 and 1945.

---

32 Morse, Arthur. *While Six Million Died: A Chronicle of American Apathy* (1967).

33 Wyman, David S. *The Abandonment of the Jews: America and the Holocaust, 1941–1945* (1984).

Wyman, a Christian scholar in Massachusetts, describes the amount of information available which told us that the final solution was being implemented in Germany. That there was a genuine possibility to have allies' bombers bomb the railroad tracks in Auschwitz, for example, where twelve thousand people were being gassed on that day.

But no one was willing to get out of their comfort zone. *We don't want to be seen as unpatriotic.* There was a whole set of social issues. In Miami, where I am right now, there were ships off the coast, 931 Jews. The entire Miami Jewish community—like the communities in the rest of the country; it wasn't a Miami issue; Miami is just like every else in the country: Chicago, New York—everybody went about their establishment, *business as usual.*

Now I am critiquing. You can only critique the community that you were raised in. I madly love the Jewish community. Obviously, this happened in the Protestant community, and in the Catholic community, and in the secular. It wasn't a Jewish issue, it was an *everybody* issue. I'm saying, even in the Jewish community, no one was willing to step out of their comfort zone, to cash in the social chips they needed to take a stand—and those people died.

That wasn't what the Holocaust was. Arthur Morse wrote this incredible book, how, basically, **everybody knew, and no one was willing to go out of their comfort zone.** David Wyman writes the same book. *The Abandonment of the Jews.* They document it, step by step by step.

One of the few people who was willing to step out of her comfort zone was Eleanor Roosevelt. And particular elements, paradoxically, not of the modern Jewish community but of the ultra-Orthodox community, who said, "Fuck it! We're taking a stand." The people took the biggest stand because they were like, "We don't care." Because they were most rooted in First Values and First Principles.

Are we willing to step out of our comfort zones?

Are we willing to actually take a stand?

Are we willing to *sacrifice* something?

I know that's a super direct answer, maybe more direct than anybody wanted. It's not challenging anyone in particular, it's just saying that **if we don't stop business as usual, nothing changes.** Just ask anyone who's ever been an entrepreneur. Entrepreneurship only works if you pour your life, heart, soul into it.

Essentially, we are entrepreneurs of the New World. We are engaging in a kind of entrepreneurship. We got to figure this out. How do we actually do it right? We are entrepreneurs of the new Story of Value. But we *have* to be entrepreneurs. Entrepreneurs take risks, and entrepreneurs pour their heart into it. Entrepreneurship is a beautiful thing. **We have to take our unique risks**. To do that, we got to look into it, face it—not with fear, not with trepidation, but trembling with joy at the privilege of it. And there's an ecstasy in that, there's a trembling with joy at the enormous privilege of it. Wow.

David, thank you. That was an enormously great question.

WHAT ARE THE ROLES OF THE OFFICE FOR THE FUTURE, THE FOUNDATION FOR CONSCIOUS EVOLUTION AND THE CENTER FOR INTEGRAL WISDOM?

Veronica: Hello, outrageous lovers. I was tracking everything and, in the interest of time, I'll just jump to my question: Could you point to the role that the *Office for the Future*, and *the Foundation*, and the *Center for Integral Wisdom*, those different actors, what those roles are?

Marc: Fantastic. That's a great question.

Essentially, the Office for the Future is, if you will, the meta-structure holding vision. The Office of the Future kind of holds everything. The Office of the Future is actually a forward-facing, world-changing name. It's not rooted in Integral, it's not rooted in a particular tradition of Spirit. The

Office of the Future. How can you be against standing for the future? We are articulating a memory of the future. Within the Office of the Future, there are a number of divisions, a number of projects: the Center for Integral Wisdom, the Phenomenology Project, the Unique Self Institute, the Foundation for Conscious Evolution—we are all individual autonomous expressions, but we are associated. It's a web of associations.

The Center for Integral Wisdom, in some sense, is doing the structural deep thought of the think tank.

The Unique Self Institute is focusing utterly on Unique Self, because Unique Self is structural to everything.

What we call the Phenomenology Project is focusing on Eros and sexuality.

And the Foundation for Conscious Evolution, which is the place we partner with Barbara, is focusing particularly on the evolutionary dimension.

Then, of course, there's *One Mountain*, which is the weekly broadcast.

The festival is the Dharma lab for everything.

Then there's another piece, just so you get it, it was called the Outrageous Love Project, which is, in a certain sense, the activist arm of the think tank work which revolves around Homo Amor, Unique Self, Eros.

Of course, the Great Library is at the center of everything. It goes across platforms. That's a very short answer to a fantastic question. Thank you, Veronica. It's a great question.

THE POWER OF TRUTH, INTEGRITY AND OUTRAGEOUS LOVE

Dr. Marc Gafni

I just want to maybe say one last thing and we are finished with this. I said in the beginning that the trials and tribulations we go through are a *feature* of the system, not a bug. The ability to create the capacity for us to talk to each other, to move beyond trauma, to take stands.

We had this big conversation about this statement of a German pastor, Martin Niemoellere. He said,

First they came from the gypsies and I wasn't a gypsy, so I didn't speak up.

Then they came for the trade unionists and I wasn't a trade unionist, so I didn't speak up.

And then they came for gays and I wasn't gay, so I didn't speak up.

And then they came for the Jews and I wasn't Jewish, I didn't speak up.

In the end, they came for me, and there was no one left to speak up.

So, **whenever people don't speak up clearly and in truth, they always have a set of strategic reasons to do it.** Those strategic reasons are always good, or for some general larger good. I get that, and I understand that, and I honor that. And there's a certain moment. **We've just got to be in integrity, and we just got to speak truth.**

The kind of *groupthink* that lives both on the far right and far left, in the woke worlds of the left and the woke worlds of the right, that the utter inability for people to say, *No, actually, I'm going to speak truth to power.* Power is generally not, as it used to be, some big institution. Power is on social media. Power is *the fear*. We actually, each one of us, have to decide— and there's no one who can decide it for you. It's a Unique Self decision.

Where am I going to stop business as usual?

Where am I going to let go of strategy?

Where am I going to turn towards?

Where am I going to show up—like you're doing so gorgeously?

Where am I going to actually take my unique risk?

There's no teacher who can tell you where you should do it. But in the end, what we are held accountable for is, *did we take our unique risk*? When we take our unique risks in Outrageous Love we become a *Unique Self Symphony*. Wow!

No one can tell you that you should do it, and all the voices will explain to you exactly why you shouldn't. And you *should*.

That's what makes me alive.

That's what makes me a human being.

I'm addressing this not to anyone here particularly. This is the best group of people in the world who are doing gorgeous unique risks in a million ways. I am addressing it to myself, and I am addressing it to all of us. Where's the place where I can be in more integrity? There are always good reasons not to speak up, there are always good reasons to temper it, and there are always good strategies. **There's got to be a moment you let go of strategy.**

Because I am *in* all the way, standing for the future of humanity. In every little decision, it matters. There was an article that Kristina sent me by Anne Applebaum in *Atlantic* magazine called *The New Puritans*.[34] It was why people in a social system allow for demonizations to happen and don't speak up. And everyone's got a million strategic reasons.

Let go of strategy, friends.

Our power is Outrageous Love.

Our power is outrageous integrity.

Our power is the goodness of who we are with each other.

Thank you, everyone. What an absolute, mad, crazy, delight to be with you. Deepest bow, deepest love, more madly than ever before. Amen. Yay!

---

34 Applebaum, Anne. *The New Puritans*, published in: *The Atlantic*, October 2021.

CHAPTER SEVENTEEN

A PLANETARY POLITICS OF COSMOEROTIC HUMANISM: SIX KEY DIMENSIONS BROKEN IN DEMOCRACY

A conversation between Layman Pascal and Marc Gafni — November 10, 2021

INTRODUCTION

Layman: Hi Marc

Marc: Hey Layman, it's good to be with you, sir.

Layman: You too. It has been a treat to talk with you for a while, partly for your ideas, and partly for your passion, and partly also, of course, for the sense of exciting controversy that's woven into the community's impression of you sometimes. And when I saw your Independence Day remarks on democracy and governance in the context of planetary politics and heroes, I thought maybe this is a really interesting way to the history of whatever Marc Gafni is.

So, this talk is going to be largely about **structural insights into human systems**, which is the theme of this particular podcast. And that will afford us some opportunities to explore the larger ethos of CosmoErotic

Humanism that you want to bring forward. We'll touch on a few other things near the end, that maybe the community want to hear about, but that's not what the focus is today, and maybe that's a jumping off point for a future conversation.

Marc: Sounds like a plan, Layman. We're in.

THE OVERALL META-VISION OF PLANETARY POLITICS

Layman: Fantastic! Why don't you start by giving us your sense of **the overall meta vision for what planetary politics could and should be?** And then we'll start digging into some of the specifics around how you feel democracy operates—or fails to operate—in contemporary contexts.

Marc: That's a great way to start the conversation, and maybe we'll just dive in directly. We started in 2010. I was delighted and privileged to found, with Ken Wilber and Sally Kempton, and some other great folks, the Center for World Spirituality, which morphed into the Center for Integral Wisdom and the reason that's relevant is because Ken and I, in many conversations, talked about *existential risk* (and this is really before existential risk was kind of "in vogue" in a certain sense). We both had a deep sense of it. I had borrowed a term from a colleague who had actually come to a bunch of seminars I'd done, we talked about **the second shock of existence**.

- The first shock of existence is the realization that death grins at the banquet. Not just biological death, but the *existential realization* of death. That first shock of existence presses humanity into the depths of culture, the depths of interiority.
- The second shock of existence is the realization not of the death of the individual human being, but the potential death of humanity.

The realization that hit me very strongly—I remember I was going through the potential existential risks (Nick Bostrom's term from the early 2000), and every one of them was *global*. **There was nothing that wasn't a global issue.** There were no local issues. **It became just obvious that without global coherence and global coordination, it was literally impossible to engage in any of these issues.** I tried to think through how do we create global coherence?

It just became very clear that you can only create global coherence if you have an exterior shared language. I mean, let's say you're working with a couple. (I occasionally work with couples.) If a couple doesn't have a shared story, then they can't actually *ground* their intimacy—if they have a different understanding, and fundamentally different ways of how they understand value. More importantly, **if they have a different sense of what their story is together, then you have an intimacy disorder.**

You actually have to create the ground of shared story, and that's when it first occurred to me that we actually have a *global intimacy disorder* at the very core. I am just finishing a piece of writing now, with my colleague and partner Zack Stein, on the twelve dimensions of the global intimacy disorder. **The realization was: we need to create global coherence.**

I'll just go one more step, and maybe this will be helpful.

An *intimacy disorder*—what does *intimacy* mean? Let's try and define it. We have created what we call *the intimacy equation*. We are now working on 500 pages of primary source footnotes across fields to see how this equation applies. So, here's the equation. Ready? Equation coming at you in the interior sciences.

> *Intimacy = shared identity, in the context of (relative) otherness x mutuality of recognition x mutuality of pathos (we can feel each other) x mutuality of value x mutuality of purpose.*

We are now applying that intimacy equation across the board. Let's just look at it for a second and then get to your question. If we've got some muons and hadrons moving around, subatomic particles,—protons, electrons, neutrons—they *come together*. There is a *recognition* between them, there is an allurement between them, there is a *mutuality of pathos*. That's the prehension that Whitehead was referring to. There is a shared value setting. They are trying to *do* something together. There is a set of values at play, and they come together, they create an atom, which has a new function, new purpose. And so, **the subatomic particles create a new shared identity, called an atom, in the context of *otherness*.** There's still a proton, neutron, electron, whatever that means.

There's mutuality of recognition, pathos, value and purpose between them.

- It is true about an organization.
- It is true about subatomic particles becoming an atom.
- It is true about a couple.
- It is true about Leagues of Nations.
- It is true in theories of economics, in market theory.

That's actually really interesting. In other words—if we cannot create, on the human level, a sense of intimacy, meaning shared identity that generates mutuality of recognition, mutuality of pathos, mutuality of value, and mutuality of purpose, then we are going to break down in the most *core* way.

Now the question is, how do we do that? We've got our intimacy equation. We have, for one second here, alluded to the fact that this works across platforms. We are talking about this meta-meta theory, that will work cross-platform. (That's a different conversation. I know that you're having a different set of conversations on that and maybe we'll get to that at a different time.) How do we address that? **How do we actually generate a response to the global intimacy disorder?** Now you could say, *let's restore intimacy*, but that wouldn't be true either because **we have never had intimacy at that level. It's not a restorative move.**

It's actually what Gershom Scholem and Walter Benjamin call a *utopian* move. Meaning, it is an emergent intimacy, it is an evolutionary intimacy.

We have to *evolve* intimacy, not *restore* intimacy. We have never had global intimacy before. So, how would we do that? (I apologize that this took too long, but just to get the pieces on the table.) The way you restore intimacy is you generate—and this is very a very precise sentence—**you generate a shared Story of Value rooted in First Principles and First Values.**

When I say *a shared Story of Value*, I don't mean what Harari calls *value* in Chapter 2 of *Sapiens*—and Harari is important not because he's a good thinker—he's not, he's a good populist, and he's a lovely man and he's done an interesting job. Harari is important because he is, what we call in scholarship, *uncontaminated material*, meaning he is *parroting* the post-modern conclusions and taking them as givens. Harari's view of value is, he has three phrases for it: *fiction, figment of imagination, and social construction of reality.* That is, there is no inherent value, and there are no First Values or First Principles, and there is certainly no narrative.

What we are saying is: **to create intimacy, you need a shared Story of Value rooted in First Values and First Principles**—and the reason that's important is *you need both*. Habermas, for example, is trying to look at *First Principles* (although he doesn't call it that). People like Mary Evelyn Tucker, or Brian Swimme, are trying to look at a *universe story*, but it is mythopoetic, without inherent value. Brian wants to be really sure he stays within the standard narrative, to make sure he's being mythopoetic, so he's kosher—and he's done a beautiful job, and so has Habermas. But neither of those that are sufficient. Story by itself is insufficient. You need a story of inherent value, combined with First Principles and First Values. Why? Because only those two together create two factors, *will* and *allurement*. For example, Snowden distinguishes between *complicated* and *complex* systems.

- A *complicated system* means there are hyperobjects, the parts are dissociated from each other, therefore, it is fragile (Ferrari is a complicated system, world currency is complicated system, etc.)

- A *complex system* means, for example, Brazilian rain forest. What's a complex system? Let's add to Snowden. **Complex system means there's *allurement* between the parts.** There is an inherent will between the parts to find each other, and there's a sense of allurement between the parts.

So, how do we create allurement and will, whether it is political will or moral will? We create that through a shared Story of Value rooted in First Values and First Principles. George Floyd is tragically murdered. We are in the middle of freaking Covid. The entire liberal community—that actually completely subscribes (and in many appropriate and beautiful ways) to masks and all those important restrictions and lockdowns—all floods into the street, into Black Lives Matter rallies, importantly so, and Covid be damned.

Why? Because we saw what appears to be a murder. We saw the violation of value in front of us. This kind of horrific horror, and it was watched millions and millions of times, and it generated moral outrage, as it should. It generated an allurement that wanted to come together, political will was generated, and a certain amount of action was taken.

That's a general sense of what we mean by **global intimacy disorder is responded to by a new Story of Value**. A new Story of Values. A new *coherence* between parts. In other words, we bring together parts in *a new shared identity.*

That's what a new story is. It's *a new configuration of intimacy*. It's very beautiful, and it brings together the leading-edge validated insights of premodern, modern and postmodern into a new integration, new configuration of intimacy, which responds to the crisis of intimacy.

Last sentence: it has been the movement of evolution all the way up and all the way down. Meaning:

- Evolution is always a crisis.
- The crisis is a crisis of intimacy.

♦ The response to the crisis of intimacy is a restoration of intimacy—or the evolution of a new emergent level of intimacy.

That's the same thing that happens here.

That was a big tapestry, but I hope that helps. Now we can work with it. Now we got to refine it.

Layman: That's very rich. I don't know if it's complicated or complex, but we are going to leave that with people, I will come back to that after we've gone through some of these specific points.

Marc: Thank you for your presence.

1. VOTERS DON'T UNDERSTAND ISSUES THEY ARE VOTING ON

Layman: The first one that was in there is that voters don't understand the complexity of hyperobjects. I think what it's saying there is: when we set up our democratic constitutions and procedures, many of which were formed in the 1700s, we were

♦ (a) not facing the shared complexity of our current international economic and technological realities, and

♦ (b) our knowledge of the world was very simplistic compared to what we know about how systems and interactions and networks function today.

I think it is probably true that **if even experts and algorithms cannot adequately handle the nuanced complexity of today's world, we should stop pretending that the average voter has a realistic handle on these situations,** especially when they are also being lied to, and massaged, and targeted with this information.

On the other hand, a lot of people feel, perhaps rightly, that **their inherited human heuristics for intuitive behavior are actually really smart, maybe**

smarter than they are, and are unconsciously adapted to handle messy complexities very well. So, maybe you could give us a sense of what you mean by *hyperobject*, and also how you view the limits and the opportunities of human capacity to make complexity workable,

Marc: Fantastic. Two things:

One, this first notion that **sense-making is virtually impossible to do for the voter who needs to make a decision**. A good example was Richard Dawkins. Richard Dawkins and I disagree about pretty much everything (although once one accepts Richard's *apotheosis of DNA*, we can go with him anyplace. In other words, what Richard basically does is make DNA God, and then he solves the problem, and then everything works. Actually, once we accept the apotheosis of DNA, we can actually go with Richard), and Richard's a brilliant thinker, and he said something very beautiful.

He said, around Brexit, *why are they asking me to vote on Brexit?* I have no idea of the cascading interplay of economic issues and political issues. He is a very intelligent man, who kind of reads carefully, and basically says, *I can't vote on it. I have no idea.* That's definitely part of what I meant. You said it better than I did, so beautifully stated, and I'm going to get to your juristic question at the end.

Here's the second part. Let's go the second step.

The second step is, what you also pointed towards, which is that we've never had a situation in which **the machine intelligence is intentionally arrayed against you, beyond the pale of your awareness, seeking to create predictive analysis that is being sold to misaligned third parties in order to influence your decisions.** And it is now exponentially—literally exponentially, not figuratively—better than the machine intelligence that beat Garry Kasparov. When Google Alpha Pro, in 2017, played the old version of the machine intelligence that beat Garry Kasparov, back there in Deep Blue days, it didn't lose any matches, won 137, tied whatever the amount.

I was trying to share this problem with someone, a professor, a few days ago, an old good friend, he said, *Marc, Mordecai* (he called me Mordecai), he said, *this is just the same old problem with advertising.* No, it's not. It's not a level playing field with one advertisement going to everyone. It's a personalized system, *personalization being a euphemism for a very high form of machine intelligence manipulation*, whose goal is to actually change how you are going to act without you knowing, at a level of knowing precisely what in your particular peer group will trigger a particular response. That's unbelievable.

By the way, a "peer group" is also a euphemism. We think a "peer group" means something like a bunch of lawyers. What a peer group means in data science, it a group of people, algorithmically generated, who respond to a particular sequence of stimuli in the same way. Let's say there's a particular font with a particular amount of words, which then has a picture of a cat that has a one second interval, then has a tune. Particular sequences are algorithmically generated, split testing happening every second. Generating data science peer groups that only the algorithm can generate.

For example, should the person without a shirt be a girl or a boy? Well, that depends on your personality profile. What are your inclinations? How are we going to actually get you to react to a particular product or particular political decision—and Brexit, knowingly, deployed all these tools. I am not talking about things that *might* be happening, these things *are* happening. That's a very big deal. With that going on in the background—combine that with hyperobjects, and you are in a lot of trouble.

When that's happening, you cannot then rely on the last point that you made, Laymen, which is, well, our natural human capacity to handle and see and evaluate will kick in. No, it's been intentionally deconstructed. It's being intentionally deceived.

The algorithms are designed to manipulate not just my mind, but my *feelings.* Jim Wiley—who was trained by Eric Schmidt, who is, as you know, the former CEO of Google, who personally ran the 2012 and 2008 Obama micro-targeting campaign—went on to work for guess who? Cambridge Analytica in 2016. Eric, of course, blamed the terrible Trump people for doing this terrible micro-targeting, but Jim was trained by Eric Schmidt and the Obama campaign, and it's just a standard practice. When Jim explained what was happening, he said, *we are actually targeting your feelings, your vulnerabilities.*

In other words, the notion that you go inside, and you kind of *feel*—that's the old liberal order. Our consumer and our voter decisions are based on our feelings, but feelings do have a *vessel* dimension, not just *light*. When we can hack the life system, and feelings can be reduced, inappropriately, to algorithms, and you can then manipulate those feelings—so that that default mode that we always relied on is inaccurate—then it actually makes no sense for people to vote.

Now, there are solutions. In other words, we could have *liquid democracy*, for example, which Jim Ross has appropriately championed, where we can have certain educational processes we go through. It doesn't mean we abandon voting. It means we *up-level* voting to require a kind of training—as Jefferson and Washington famously talked about, *we need to train people in the science of government.* That's what the founding fathers envisioned. We need to engage in generating a new training in the science of government, but that's okay for number one.

I think we got a sense of it. Is that fair?

2. THE KEY ISSUES OF THE DAY ARE NOT BEING VOTED ON

Layman: Yeah, that's a fair, that's a good sense. The second one, the key issues of the day are not being voted on.

To me, that brings up the sense—I mean, there is a complaint that **democracy is confined to particular domains**. Wilhelm Reich campaigned for democracy in the workplace 100 years ago, and it is still barely been tried. There are lots of areas like work that are not democratic and there are lots of issues affecting everyone that don't enter into the arena of public decision making. None of us voted on having massive industrial fish boats, pushing ocean species to the brink of extinction and filling the world with nets.

That was not on the ballot. None of us voted on whether to export our vaccine supply lines to other countries, or have these algorithms hacking our subconscious. So, we have to ask ourselves, like, **what good is democracy if it doesn't even have its hands on most of the levers?** So how big an issue is this, and what could we possibly do about it, Mordecai?

Marc: We have to give you a Hebrew name. That's very sweet.

So, Layman, again, you are articulating it beautifully. The second variable that we listed there was, **who votes for the key things?** And let's just nail it. Who voted for Google? Who voted for the Google business model? Who is voting for (and this is really important) what's driving now, let's say, the new advances in the last half a year in AI? What's happening in AI is there are incremental advances in AI's capacity. One incremental advance not such a big deal, but then there are ten or five years, and now we have a changed game. Who is tracking that?

That's been driven essentially by entrepreneurship and research, which are married and which are driven essentially by a rivalrous conflict governed by win-lose metrics, what we called it, back in 2014 when we did the Success Summit, *Success 2.0*. It is a rivalrous conflict governed by a win-lose metric story, and all of our major decisions are being made there. That's kind of shocking. I mean, when CS Lewis, in a book called *The Abolition of Man*, talks about the fear of *the conditioners*, generating new scientific methods in an omni-competent state. Lewis got a lot of it right, and he was talking about Skinner, particularly, but of course, **the issue is *not* the omni-competent state. The issue is the omni-competent, private set of tech plex leaders**, which Zak and I are calling *TechnoFeudalism*. It's our name for it. It's the name of one of our new books.

Essentially, this is a group of a couple of hundred people, max, who are actually running the major structures of the tech plex, as an omni-competent, private corporation, that is making all of the decisions that affect us. I'll just give you one example. Remember Google Glass back in 2014? It didn't go well. There was a very interesting story to track that. Essentially, high tech is coming for your face in the next two-three years. That's where it is going to try to go back, and try five or six different ways to re-extend ubiquitous computing and the internet of things. To come back to the face, because of course, the ostensible problem—from a purely pragmatic, limited perspective—is, well, you want your hands free, and you want easy access to everything. Let us solve that, economically, by creating some new version of Google Glass.

Okay, so let's take that as a given. Who is considering the implications of that—socially, existentially, spiritually, morally? It cannot be *no one*. I mean, it's actually shocking. In other words, there is something called the network effect, which means that when you impose something like Facebook on the system, essentially *everyone* has to participate. It's an effective monopoly, which operates in a different way than the classical rules of monopoly. Therefore, it's unprecedented, and therefore, it is not legislated.

High tech is coming for your face. No one is in the conversation. It's going to have massive ruptures in the social space and implications that are almost beyond imagination. When Mark Zuckerberg says two weeks ago that he is putting all his energy into VR, the *Metaverse*. What's his intention? His intension is quite clear. Immersive experiences are enormously important on multiple levels, and they can be used in enormously important and positive ways, but actually, he is looking at the Metaverse in a completely different way, which is going to change our entire experience of what it means to be human being, and **there's no discussion, not even to mention voting. There's no conversation.**

It is been completely hijacked by an omni-competent (Lewis's phrase)—but not state, but very small group of TechnoFeudalists, most of whom believe in a kind of *cyber-totalitarianism*, who are making decisions based

282

on the work of data scientists—who they have essentially hijacked. At that moment of existential risk there are about ten thousand leading data scientists in the world who all work for the techno-feudalism, because those data scientists have been essentially ensnared by $600 000, $700 000, $800,000 salaries, and great houses, and good status in the rivalrous conflict win-lose metrics.

In the time when we *need* those data scientists, desperately, in key domains—we have actually *drained* them. The amount of energy that went into operationalizing the Facebook newsfeed in 2006—imagine it went into responding to catastrophic and existential risk!

That's a sense of the second issue. Who voted for this? No one.

3. WE ARE VOTING LOCALLY ON GLOBAL ISSUES

Layman: The third one, if I'm remembering correctly, is: we are voting inside nation states, and the issues that are bedeviling us are international. I had a couple of discussions with John Bansal, the founder of Simple, trying to bring pressure to the international context, and that has helped me take this issue really seriously.

I guess the question is, how should we—or could we—respond to planetary level situations,

(a) without imposing excessive global governance, and

(b) taking decisions down to the lowest level at which they can be solved, so that top-level decision making is left to handle issues that are specifically international because people have a really strong gut reaction against the possibility of global governance?

We want to be able to say to them, hey, it's not going to be for things you can decide in your local city council. There are some things that have to be held at that level. How do we do that?

Marc: That's really, Layman, that's really important. I might make up a Hebrew name for you along the way, but that's a good one. I've got to think about it, but that's a good one. So, let's think about this for a second.

We already said in the beginning, that **all the core forms of catastrophic and existential risk require global coordination and global coherence**. We have already established in our opening conversation that you can only create global coherence by creating a new emergent order that responds to global intimacy disorder, and, in the structure that we laid out, that would be a new Story of Value, inherent value, rooted in First Values and First Principles.

Let's put that back on the table and from that place, look at this issue.

Take an issue like *data*, and take an issue like *sexual slavery*. Those are two really good issues. Sexual slavery and labor slavery. **We have five-six times more slaves in the world today than we did when Lincoln emancipated the slaves.** We grew up on this—I remember being in fourth grade, fifth grade history, and the excitement of Lincoln's emancipation and *Amazing Grace* (that happened earlier; Wilber Force, that gorgeous story in England)—and we think we got that one handled, but we don't.

I mean, the level of slavery in the world today is shocking. Slavery cannot be dealt with in any intelligent form. In 2006, after I went through a personal tragedy, I actually thought maybe I would spend the rest of my life working on this issue, and I failed. I failed to be able to muster sufficient influence to directly affect policy, and so I realized that's not the right way to go. I spent a lot of time on the issue, and I've remained on the issue. It's *beyond* important. One of the issues is that *you can't solve it*. That's when I first started thinking about this: you cannot solve it without parties on board from everywhere. You need a global solution to fight sexual and labor slavery, because it's a complete, interconnected hyperobject that cannot be dealt with without going all the way up, and all the way down.

And, clearly, the issue of *data*. Because of multiple traps, and the tragedy of the commons, and the race to the bottom, you cannot deal with data unless you deal with it in an international form of global coherence. Can't be done. In order to do that, we've got to turn to emergence theory. Emergence theory, remember, where should we go, my friend? We should go to 1954. Turing's about to pass away, a tragic story. Turing, the great code cracker, has been arrested for homosexuality in Great Britain. He's sentenced to hormone therapy, terrible story. It is unclear what happened (in one of the stories, he committed suicide), but he died then. And Turing is one of my great heroes. Turing is just an incredible figure, just a beautiful man. He created so much in the modern world.

Right before then, Turing writes an essay called *Morphogenesis*. In *Morphogenesis* he, essentially, give or take, lays down the tracks for understanding *the self-organizing universe*. What does it mean that reality *self-organizes*? Later on, Evelyn Fox, and what's his name, the second researcher at Columbia? They get together, and they challenge the general understanding of slime molds. They realize that slime molds are not run by a general pacer cell, and slime molds come apart and come back together, but, actually, slime molds are self-organizing.

How does the slime mold self-organize? That's very interesting. How does that happen? It turns out that Evelyn Keller Fox goes back to *morphogenesis*. She realizes, oh, how are they self-organizing? There are elemental, simple principles that keep getting repeated, repeated, repeated exponentially, and create complexity. That's really interesting. When I talk about First Principles and First Values, I am coming out of that dimension of complexity theory. That simple First Principles generate complexity, which goes to one of the things we talked about later in this article, which is: **in order for democracy to work, we need to universal grammar of value, rooted in simple First Values and First Principles.**

If you don't have those at play, you can't create global coherence. We need to have those at play—and they are not at play. You remember our friend Richard Nixon, 1960? So, here's something—you may know this, Layman, it's really interesting. Richard Nixon and John Kennedy were very good friends. Doesn't that make you happy? It's a good world. They met in 1947 on a train ride. They bumped together, became good friends. They were friends during all the years in the Senate. Richard Nixon wrote a very beautiful letter to Jackie when Kennedy was killed. They ran that fierce campaign against each other in 1960, but nonetheless, they had a deep friendship.

They had a deep common set of values. They didn't care about post-modernism; they experienced those as intrinsic values, and *that* allowed for an intimacy. **In order to have a world in which democracy works, we need democracies to be functioning *with* each other, emergent out of a universal grammar of value, and then functioning also in *collectives*—which is not precisely global governance, but at least global confederation.** Maybe I'll bring one last thing to the table. Bostrom has made huge contributions to this field. I think Bostrom is uneven, meaning (and Nick, if you are listening, I apologize—sweetly, but insincerely) he said unbelievably idiotic things about Spirit.

He said uneven and unbelievably brilliant things about your field, in your set of fields. Bostrom writes this brilliant essay in 2019 on *The Vulnerability Hypothesis*, and he talks about what happens if you take a black ball out of an urn, essentially meaning existential risk. It's not a gray ball or a white ball, it's a black ball. A black ball would mean a relatively easy to construct mass destruction weapon that didn't require enriched uranium and a nation state to generate it, etc. We shouldn't even talk too much about it. Bostrom says, how do we solve that? He says, well, get rid of the bad people that won't work, stop technology—all that's not going to work. Well, that's one option. Option two would be global governance. Three is worldwide surveillance.

This is something that Shoshana Zuboff doesn't understand in *Surveillance Capitalism* (and it's a very important book, but there are lots of problems with it.) Actually, we may *need* worldwide surveillance to respond to the black ball out of the urn. **The problem is not worldwide surveillance, the problem is worldwide surveillance without First Values and First Principles.** We may need *not quite* global governance. We understand the fear of that, but some kind of global confederation of shared value—not just shared *interest*, shared *value*—which then generates an ability to deal with sexual slavery, and with who owns the data. For example, obviously, climate—and the list go on and on—you cannot even begin to *touch* without global governance.

4. THE WIN/LOSE STRUCTURE OF DEMOCRACY UNDERMINES DEMOCRACY ITSELF

Layman: Well done! Good rant.

I got a couple the next two together, because the next two are **the preposterous nature of voting** and **the win-lose structure of democracy**. These are key issues for me, because I am always looking at the structural factors, and how we come together to make collective decisions, which lead those decisions to be of a fairly low quality.

We've got a ridiculous situation set up, where, for some reason, the most money usually wins elections because our brains are easy to hack by businesses, and algorithms, and tactical politicians. We are sort of inside a general civilization sphere of black magic, or something like that. It seems implausible that we could quickly educate people up to a level of social sophistication in which they are not falling for simple neuro-social hacking.

Then, beyond that, there are real questions about the capacity of our voting. We have secret ballot, which is nice, but winning a plurality, or even a simple majority, can still leave half the country disagreeing with the so called "will of the people." We always seem to be recapitulating a team sport dualism on every social issue that comes up. From your point of view, Marc, **why isn't voting working, and what openings do you see that could bring about a transformation in how we go about making collective decisions?**

Marc: Fantastic. Those are brilliant inquiries, and thank you. Let's see if we can tease them apart a little bit, if we can, for a second. Let's bracket the preposterous nature of voting, which is kind of its own issue, and we'll talk about that in a second. We have actually alluded to it before, when we talked about Eric Schmidt and micro-targeting, and Jim Wiley, Schmidt's Lieutenant who then went to Cambridge Analytical, but we will return to that.

Let us look at where you started the second issue, which is **the win-lose structure of voting.** Here, I just want to invoke my dear, dear friend, and beloved evolutionary partner and colleague, Barbara Marx Hubbard, who passed. We miss her dearly, and she was a very close friend of mine, also of my dear friend, Daniel Schmachtenberger.

We spent a lot of time talking about what Barbara called, it's her term (she may have borrowed it, but I heard it from her), *synergistic democracy*. I am going to credit her with that term. I think one of the things that we forget to do a little bit in the millennial world is people forget to *credit* people, so I want to credit and honor Barbara with that. It is very good term. Let's unpack the problem first. When we did the 2014 conference on Success 3.0, we basically said that **this win-lose, this rivalrous conflict governed by win-lose metrics is a form of what we call** *pseudo-Eros*.

There is a field of Eros. Eros is a much bigger conversation than everything we are talking about. When we get to the solutions, we start talking about what we call **a politics of Eros**. We'd have to create an *equation* for Eros, and what *Eros* means, and how does it relate to *intimacy*, and we'll get to all that. Maybe not today, but for now, let us just say that **when you don't have Eros, you have pseudo-Eros.** Reality doesn't tolerate a vacuum. In the emptiness, you cannot hold the emptiness, you don't have a genuine Story of Value, so you create a pseudo-story. You don't have genuine value; you create pseudo-value.

For example, you don't have a genuine sexual narrative that meets our experience of sexuality. Then you create pseudo-sexual narratives, what Anne Applebaum just called this week in *The Atlantic*, "*The New Puritans*." That was her article, and it was in the liberal *Atlantic*, interestingly enough.

When you don't have genuine Eros, you always have pseudo-Eros. Pseudo-Eros looks like Eros, but it's not. That's really important. What happens is, **when you don't have a genuine shared Story of Value, you are not going to be *without* a story. Another story is going to step in.** What stepped in is, basically:

- a success story
- a romantic story and
- a hero's journey

Those are the three stories, and how each one of those works is a different conversation, but let's just say, for now, **the success story is a form of pseudo-Eros, and therefore it is very powerful**.

Now, given that, what does that mean?

The win-lose metrics forms your very identity, so if you are not successful in a particular way, if you have not succeeded in a certain kind of *commodification in production*, which allows you to succeed in the rivalrous conflict, which is governed by the win-lose metrics—**you don't exist**.

That's identity. That's a failure of your very identity. We kill for identity.

What happens then? You create *polarization*. **Polarization means you are out of the *Tao*.** You are out of the field of value. When you are *in* the Tao, when you are in the field of value, then *opposing* values become *paradoxical*—because those values are expressions of the Tao. They are expressions of the field. When you have stepped out of the field, or you think you've stepped out of the field—you actually cannot step out of the field, but when you have an *experience* that you've stepped out of the field— what happens is you gravitate towards a value, but **that value becomes your pseudo-Eros**.

You are pro-life, or you are pro-choice. Really? All the pro-life people are against choice? Have they actually thrown out choice as a value? That's absurd. All the pro-choice people against life? It's a completely absurd framing of the situation. When you have stepped out of the field of value, then you take the value, and you make it not your *Eros*, but your *pseudo-Eros*, you *decontextualize* the value from the larger field and from its natural dialectical tension with other values, you transform that value into a pseudo-erotic absolute—and then you have polarization.

So, polarization always emerges from stepping out of the field of value, or at least having the experience of stepping out of the field of value. *That* is what creates the win-lose structure. In other words, **the way voting operates today is essentially a win-lose game**. What you try and do is: you want something to pass, you marshal all of your energy, all of your lobbying, all of your support, all of your money, you try and destroy the other side and pass your bill, which means you've got now 50% of the country, let's say in America, furious.

Now, as long as you were in a shared field of value, you could be okay with that. We are all watching Walter Cronkite, we have a shared experience, we have a shared field of value, we are going to still kind of hold you in our minds, because we don't want to create a too intense polarization, and we have shared sense of the world. But now we are in this new kind of digital hyper-mode, in which **we don't see the same things in the newsfeed**. We have no common experiences. **We, therefore, interpret reality completely differently**. We are not in a shared field of value, there are no Nixon and Kennedy who are meeting behind the scenes.

So, now we've got just a win-lose metrics voting game. Voting becomes a weapon. **We have weaponized voting as an expression of the win-lose metrics.** We moved to radical polarization, which in the end will break us apart. Ben Shapiro actually said a few days ago (and Ben is a kind of slick version of certain expressions of the right, and an intelligent version). He has a lot of intelligent things to say, but Ben said, quite shockingly, *let us just start talking about secession.* That's a wow! Can you imagine, Layman, someone would say that 20 years ago? What's this, talking about secession? It barely raised an eyebrow. That's the level of polarization. We need to deal with that.

5. THE PREPOSTEROUS NATURE OF VOTING

If we have time, let's just do the second thing you raised very briefly. The preposterous nature of voting. Just very briefly. This is a much bigger topic. Let's just look at it briefly because it is really important. We have really covered this already, but let's just apply it here.

In 2010, Facebook does a split test that for whatever reason they release, and the split test was with 61 million voters: *let us see, can we influence whether they're going to vote or not?* Now interestingly, people like Alex Pentland, in his book, *Social Physics*, 2014, MIT Media Lab, he reports on this exultantly. Isn't this interesting how this worked? He is a classical naive structured backbone of techno-feudalism (and how the MIT Media Lab functions in that way is a whole other conversation), but let us back up for a second.

They reported that study, and Facebook released it. What that study tells you is something which is shocking, which is that actually Facebook can swing an election easily because what they did is: they saw that showing people text encouraging them to vote didn't work, but showing people faces of their Facebook friends who *did* vote, did have a statistically significant impact on who voted in particular districts.

Now, we have to understand that when people say to me, *Oh, this stuff doesn't affect me*—no, no, the way you create digital dictatorship is not about whether it causes you to buy something or not. You create the digital dictatorship by creating peer groups that create statistically significant shifts in how many people vote or don't vote in micro-targeted areas. That changes elections. That makes elections actually irrelevant because if Obama had all the profiles and all the wavering voters in America, he could micro-target those people—and let's say he gets some of them to vote, and then, in another area, he gets people not to vote, and you get just enough—1%, 2% or 3%. Game over. This is not based on conspiracy theorists, but on the best academic research that's reported on by multiple serious scholars.

We are no longer talking about democracy, not democracy as we understand it in anyway. Voting, the classical notion of voting, becomes absurd—the notion that voting is a fair game in which you find your internal feeling and you go with it. That's not a game anymore. Your feelings are being completely manipulated, one, but two, through statistically significant movements and micro-targeting by split testing, we change the results of an election with *no one ever knowing*. Who is checking this information? No one. We have no access to it. So that's pretty significant. And again—Facebook released that study; this is not Cambridge Analytica.

Maybe the last sentence in this, about the big Cambridge Analytica scandal. I guess I am assuming that listeners know what I'm talking about, which I shouldn't, but the Trump campaign had hired Cambridge Analytica, which was using data from Facebook to micro-target voters in favor of Trump in the 2016 election, which everyone was furious about and castigated Trump. Now there's a lot of things to castigate Trump for, but this was not one of them. It wasn't a uniquely *Trump* issue. This was Obama's move. This was a straight Obama micro-targeting move, engineered personally by Eric Schmidt in 2008 and in 2012—which barely got reported. That's a big deal. That's in the very structure of voting. So that's number five.

Layman: These big structures, these information systems and analysis systems that are going on everywhere, it is very strange because one of the reasons it doesn't get reported is simply because people have a hard time making meaning out of it. It is such an abstract strange thing that they don't know how to feel about it, and I think a lot of the people who indulge in the less well-informed version of conspiracy theory are accurately sensing what's going on. They just don't have the ideation and the articulation to describe what the problem is, but they are aware there is a big problem, and it's roughly in a certain area.

Marc: You are absolutely right, Layman, and Zak and I, hopefully, will be putting out a paper on conspiracy theories. That's a separate dialogue by itself, but you hit something, as you have in everything you've said, each time you hit something on the nail (I think maybe it's a nail on the head or hit something somewhere). But you are correct. In other words, the conspiracy-theory people sense that there is something missing driving the narrative here. That actually not all the cards are on the table. There are too many false flags. That I am missing information. That I cannot trust the classical sources of information.

We are told by every major media news outlet today, just a good example, that it's been decided that Jeffrey Epstein committed suicide in prison. Now, who actually thinks that Jeffrey Epstein committed suicide in prison? Almost no one because there are so many facts available, and yet all the classical major media outlets keep repeating that Jeffrey Epstein committed suicide in prison. What happens is, there's this old phrase, *cognitive dissonance*, and so we stop trusting, we stop believing, and the conspiracy theorists have this general sense that there is a thread in the plotline here that we are missing. The old noble lie of propaganda doesn't work anymore, because we have a new information system.

There are enough anomalies flooding to the system, and then what conspiracy theorists often do is put them together in an inappropriate way. A good example is voting. Was this election stolen? Well, let's take a look. Well, I don't think so, but you could ask yourself two questions.

If you thought that Trump was an existential threat to the future of the world and you had the opportunity to steal the election, what should you do? Don't answer that question. Okay, that's one. That's an interesting thought experiment.

Here's the second thing, and I don't think the election was stolen, just to be clear. When you've got newscaster after newscaster saying there are no real issues with election irregularities, this is not true.

There's an entire set of data, which are shocking—and I don't want to take up our time, it's not our agreed upon topic, but we could spend a separate conversation on fraudulent elections, and it's shocking. What happens is, we have to actually, in our mainstream legacy media, say, yeah, there *are* real problems with elections. There *are* real problems with tallies of votes, and those things are real. But when the mainstream legacy liberal media says, no, *those aren't problems at all,* then you've got an enormous amount of information to go to. Even a mainstream right-wing outlet, like Prager University, which put out five-minute videos.

My old colleague, I haven't spoken to him in many years, Dennis Prager, accredited Prager University, Jordan Peterson, the whole gang are all doing quite good work within their realm, expressing that position. And just look at their videos, just do the simplest piece of research on fraudulent elections by the most credible people around—then compare that to what Rachel Maddow says. The gap is so shocking, that conspiracy theorist person says, *why are they lying to me?* We need to realize we cannot do the noble lie anymore. *There are too many anomalies.*

We actually have to be more honest in our communication, and educate the general public, and demand a higher level of citizenry, and create mechanisms to make that possible—which we can. **We've got to make it an absolute priority to engage citizens in the science of government.** That's a huge deal. We cannot rely on the noble lie. We cannot use propaganda. So that's a really good example. I think we have one more, right?

6. SYNERGISTIC DEMOCRACY ONLY WORKS WITH A SHARED GRAMMAR OF EVOLVING VALUES

Layman: Yeah, let's come back around to the sixth and final point of these broken democracy issues. **Synergistic democracy only works with a shared grammar of evolving values.** We've touched this a little bit already. What do these mean?

What the heck is synergistic democracy?

What is a shared grammar and what are these evolving values?

Marc: That's another six-seven hours, but let's just do it very, very briefly. **Synergistic democracy means *synergy*. It means there is a whole that's greater than the sum of the parts.** What we actually begin to do is, we begin, as a democracy, to inhabit each other's values. Take an issue like vaccines.

- How do we inhabit each other's values around vaccines?
- How do we disambiguate the propaganda and actually feel into what's actually happening here?
- What are the different values of play?
- How do we not demonize each side?

Bracket vaccines for a second. Just take any issue at play.

- What are the best values on each side?
- What are the most important validated insights in each side?
- And how do we inhabit each other's values?

I'll give you an example. We used it before, but it's applicable. Take something like abortion. If you look at the Talmudic tradition on this particular issue (from the 3rd Century till the 21st Century, there's a 1700-year beautiful scholarly tradition, which I've spent a lot of time in), you will see that **you don't have a pro-life versus pro-choice dichotomy.** The legal theorists, who are also *value* theorists, inhabit both values—the value of choice, the autonomy of a woman over her body *and* the value of life—and create gorgeous synergistic positions. That's obviously a much, much bigger topic, but the point is, there is no pro-life vs. pro-choice split, because the legal theorist are *value* theorists. They are in the field of value, and they are inhabiting *both* values.

Basically, we have this kind of left-right polarity.

- What are the values of the left that the right can inhabit?
- What are the values of the right that the left can inhabit?
- How do we then create a shared field of value, where we actually *synergize*, so that we were creating solutions that are

synergistic?

It's absurd not to, because the result is Ben Shapiro suggesting friendly secession. The level at which things are exponentially changing—this thing, which sounds completely absurd today, *couldn't have been said* ten years ago, which means that in ten years from now, it's going to be a real possibility.

Synergistic democracy is about how we create a shared field of value, based on a universal grammar of evolving value.

Now, what does that mean? Okay, your second question.

This is a bigger conversation, but let me just say it in a word. Star Wars, Episode 4, which is, I think, the first movie. We are at the end of the movie. Luke Skywalker, Mark Hamill is young, Princess Leia, we got Harrison Ford that decides to join the battle, and we are really upset. They are going for the Death Star, but a few aircrafts cannot take down the Death Star, that's clear. The Death Star is *culture*, and so we understand that you've got to score a direct hit, and direct hit is there, which cascades there, which moves there, and blows up the Death Star. **We need to score a direct hit in terms of value. How do we actually reclaim intrinsic value?**

I am not going to go into that conversation now. Zak and I are spending an enormous amount of time on it now, to re-emerge a new theory of value that is not so complex that you can't follow. It's actually *second simplicity*. That is a different conversation. Let's do a whole conversation on that, but the core is that **value is real and evolving**. That both of those are true.

When we say "eternal values", we don't mean *unchanging* values, we mean *eternal* in the sense that they are *grounded in eternity*, they are beneath time and beneath space—and yet they are evolving. That's a big conversation on evolving value, but we need a Universal Grammar of Value—which is not, like in Aquinas, *natural law*, which CS Lewis adopted, which is why CS Lewis got rejected. He was using an old natural law theory that's been correctly critiqued. Just like primal philosophy has been correctly critiqued. Jorge Farinha launched some legitimate and important critiques of primal philosophy that were important—that can be responded to. They have to be responded to through a new theory of value. You cannot have any of these conversations without understanding value. That's a completely separate conversation, which I'm delighted to have, I just want to honor the structure of our covenant and the time.

Let's just say if we don't have a universal grammar of value, we don't solve the value problem. **Solving the value problem is a "direct hit". It allows you to blow up the Death Star.** If we can actually reclaim a notion of value that works, that's a very big deal. Value that works all the way up and all the way down the evolutionary chain. The *intrinsic* value that is not just a human creation, but is *intrinsic to Cosmos*.

I believe the answer is that there *is* intrinsic value, unquestionably, but none of the old ways of doing that work. Natural law theory has gotten decimated. Amy Barrett is operating in that natural law theory world, as is Bill Barr. *That's* actually what they're championing. They are not a bunch of crazies. They are operating within a natural law theory, but that they haven't taken into account the post-modern critiques of natural law, which we need to take into account. There are seven or eight critiques. They're all true, but partial. When you take those into account and reconstruct value, that's a different conversation. That's what I'm referring to here.

Wow, we did a lot.

RESPONDING TO EXISTENTIAL RISK WITH FIRST PRINCIPLES AND FIRST VALUES EMBEDDED IN A STORY OF VALUE

Layman: Yes. We've covered a lot of ground here, which I appreciate.

I am thinking about the role that value plays in generating systems. Something comes to my mind which is ridiculous, but I think of it all the time: *what protects the mayor of my city from being killed by me?* The basic thing is, *I don't want to. If I really wanted to, I could.* The first line of immediate defense is that people generally don't want to do certain things and want to do some other things. That's absolutely essential, getting to this place where we have the right values and share these values.

Marc: You just hit the ball out of the park again, and let's just take your mayor example. That's so important. You are absolutely right. In other words, the only way to transform—and this is the major subject of this book that Zak and I are working on right now—**the only way to transform a complicated system into a complex system and to guide exponential emergence is not to** *regulate* **it (although sometimes regulation has as value, as it were), but to actually** *self-organize* **it**. Now, again, let's go back to the complexity theory, let's go back to morphogenesis, and Turing, and the research done on slime molds.

The way this works is that **simple First Values and First Principles guide the emergence of the system**. What does that mean? Let's say you've got lots of non-state rogue actors who have access to all sorts of technologies, and you cannot monitor all of them—even with a global surveillance system, it's going to be hard. **You need them to be part of a grammar of value**, in the same way that Layman is not going to assassinate the mayor of Detroit (or wherever he happens to live, somewhere in Michigan), because he is held in an inherent structure of value, which self-organizes, repeats itself exponentially, and includes the citizenry. Once you deconstruct that, you are in pretty big trouble, and this is the checkout point.

If you have a gun in the first scene, it's going to go off in the third scene.

If you deconstruct value, the gun is going to be fired in the third act, one way or the other.

Value was deconstructed not even in *post-modernity*—as Habermas pointed out, post-modernity is basically modernity on steroids. Hypermodernity. Zak pointed out to me that passage, and it's very important. **Deconstruction of value already took place in modernity, it's not a post-modern deconstruction, post-modernity is just amplifying it**. It goes from Hume all the way to Neo-Darwinism, all the way to Auguste Compton, through positivism, through existentialism, and through post-modernism. There's a thread there that's very clear. (There's another modernity that's an alternative modernity, but that's a different conversation.) *That* modernity has deconstructed value, and this is going to now come home to roost. That gun in the first act is going to be fired in the third act, it's going to be fired at the mayor—because we have deconstructed value. There weren't school shootings fifty years ago.

The reconstruction of value, what we would call at the Center for Integral Wisdom *the reconstructive project* **is the overwhelming moral imperative of our time.**

Ken Wilber has done a gorgeous job in creating the integral framework, which is one of the critical scaffoldings for that conversation, and Ken has deployed Habermas in a brilliant way, and played with complexity theory and chaos theory. He has done a great job. That's a key piece of the story. We are now going the next step.

Let us articulate now an entire new field of value.

Let us take it as our scaffolding—among other meta-theories, but integral distinctions are critical and brilliant and beautiful. I am always in debt to that gorgeous work that Ken did.

What we need to do now is create intellectual, spiritual, existential, moral, political, economic movement that generates a new field of value. *That* is the reconstruction of value. *That* is the conversation we are deeply in right now—and that is, literally, the burning.

This is why sometimes it's frustrating. In other words, sometimes you look at certain communities and you're saying, wow, what's going on here? *The house is burning*. Everyone should give their unique contribution—but we've got to pour all of our energy, and all of our love, and all of our Eros into doing what needs to be done at this moment in time because the house is on fire. That's real, and so we've got to be on fire in the best and the most beautiful way.

Layman: When you look forward, or *feel* forward, to the middle of the 21st century, given that the house is on fire right now, how does it look to you?

What do you think we can change?

What do you think is inevitable at this point?

What's your sense of the next couple of decades on this planet?

Marc: You know, that's a great question. Any attempts to be Nostradamus in any form always winds up leaving people quite embarrassed. It is generally not a good idea. I don't want to fall into that kind of hubris of Nostradamus. On the one hand, I've got no fucking clue. That's the best answer to that question. Having said that, the question is, very simply:

Will the vectors that are in play now continue, exponentialize and degrade?

If yes, we are going to face catastrophic risk on multiple levels within an X amount of time. The amount of time is unclear. Toby Ord, in his book, *Existential Risk*, did the math. He kind of crunched the hard numbers and he came up with a bunch of results. His result was:

In the next 100 years, there is one in six chance we could face existential risk.

One in six is a high number—and over the next several 100 years it was more like 50/50. Bostrom crunched other numbers and had slightly different numbers.

The question *is how you crunch those numbers?* That's a good question. **There is a pretty universal consensus that the danger is very, very real.** We have to actually understand, and we got to get very soft and very open— and we've got to be filled with fire, and filled with humility, and filled with audacity, all at the same time. We have to understand, Layman, that there is a covenant between the generations. In other words, **the past generations pass the baton to us.** All of their successes, and all that meaning, depend on us. At the same time, **the future has no voice other than us.** We are the voice of the future. **If we dropped the ball in this moment, the past would collapse in some way, and the future remains unborn.**

It is a shocking idea. The notion of a covenant between generations doesn't make sense, my friend, without First Principles and First Values. Without a sense of First Principles, and we can barely be responsible for someone who is across the ocean. But if you see the spatial distance as not only geographic, but temporal, we have to move out of our myopic temporality, and feel into the future, and feel the voice of the future, and the baby's whispering, the trillions of lives unlived, the love unloved, the creativity undone, the moral acts undone, the nobility unborn—all of this literally depends on us.

How can you *not* be on fire with both the trepidation, but also with the enormous privilege? Enormous, insane privilege to be able to have a seat at the table of history, and pour your life into engaging—and this is one of the places where, I think, our friends who are post-doomers (there's a whole post-doomer community) are making a tragic mistake: we cannot be looking down. In other words, **the very energy of evolution that moved us from single cell to multicellular organisms lives in us.** We need to be aware of that evolution alive *in us*, and we need to claim it, and we need to be madly humble, and madly audacious, and we need to be on fire.

We need to be on fire!

It's so often, Layman, that it just breaks your heart when you see, wow, people are just doing business as usual. Commodifying Spirit, selling it, competing.

Whoa, let us stop, friends. Let us find each other. This is our moment. These next ten years, twenty years are so important.

Layman: A call to madness from Marc Gafni.

Marc: Mad love and mad creativity is the madness that Rumi talked about—where you realize that **the only sanity is madness.** You are mad in the best and most beautiful sense of the word.

Layman: While you are saying these things, I'm thinking about First Principles and First Values, and it seems to me, there's a couple of different strategies to go about getting some agreement around these things in the world.

- It seems like some people would advocate that we sort of sell each other a shared advanced narrative of some kind, that by agreeing on that **we would sort of be plugged into a shared story that evokes these values.**
- Some people would say, maybe we don't need a shared story, but if we could **just acknowledge and agree upon what these principles and what these values are,** then we would all be acknowledging the same toolkit. We would have that in common.
- Other people might say that all of that stuff is too cognitive, too verbal, and what we really need to do is **engage in certain kinds of shared practices that produce these agreements about value and clarity about principles** as a kind of side effect of what we're doing together.

What do you think about those three? Where do you lean there—or is it something else entirely?

Marc: This is a very big conversation, and as we said before, the value conversation is a separate conversation. My inclination is, if you are up for it, maybe we'll do a separate conversation just on value because we need to unpack it. It is such a critical conversation, that we can't afford to get it wrong. I hope that, together with Zack, we'll put out a paper on this fairly shortly. We are going to try and unpack this in some, at least initial, depth, and then take it the next step.

Let us just say two things for now:

1. We need First Principles and First Values that are **inherent to Cosmos**, that's one.
2. Those First Principles and First Values need to be **coupled with a Story of Value.**

Very, very important. In other words, a "Habermas-ian" attempt by any other name, to articulate First Principles *by itself* won't work. I'll give you just a simple example, perhaps, maybe two examples. Let's say we do a broadcast on the eight ethical principles that demand that we engage slavery in Burma. We ask people for donations, no response. Then we put the picture of a nine-year-old girl, and we tell her story, and we say she's a slave in Burma. Huge outpouring. Why?

I'll give you just a second image. I know this might not be true for you, Layman, but for other people, it's probably true. It's late at night, you are exhausted, you got to relax, you permitted yourself to turn on Netflix on, and you got a choice. There is this great movie, or there is a really informative documentary. Just feel it in your body. You've got an embodied sense of those two. The reason I turn to embodied senses—we need a yoga, not just the Dharma here. A story *does* something, because **a story is not just a social construction of reality**.

The way the Hebrew lineage masters said, *God loves stories.* What they meant by that is that story itself is a First Principle and First Value. That's a big idea. I talk about that a lot. There is a narrative arc to Cosmos. **That story itself is part of the structure of reality, and therefore, it *organizes* reality.**

It is not enough to have First Principles and First Values, and it's not enough to have a story. You need a Story of Value, inherent value, that elicits and evokes *allurement* and *will*—and you need First Principles and

First Values, which your story is rooted in, that evokes will and allurement. **If you put those two together, you actually have a possibility of changing the vector of Cosmos.** That's a really big deal. Oh my God, that's madly exciting.

Neither will work by themselves. And they have to be intrinsic.

The other book I was looking at today, *Global Revolt*, written by a very nice young man. You know, I assume he's a nice young man. Nadav Eval, who's about 40, an Israeli columnist, friend of Harari's. Clinton writes a little blurb on it. He is talking about globalism and the underlying liberal values. One of my partners in the think tank sent it to me and said, *Marc, take a look.* So, I took a look because someone I trust recommended it. I took a look at it quite seriously. It was a heartrending book.

He didn't intend it to be heartrending in that way, but actually, Nadav is desperately searching for value. He wants there to be a theory of value that works—and again, Nadav is a very intelligent reporter, like Yuval, who's got a series of great lectures he gave at the Hebrew University and he put them together. He is a great lecturer; he is provocative, and entertaining, and insightful. Yuval is not a good thinker, with all due respect and love. Love to have Yuval and Nadav over for dinner, but he is not thinking, he is actually parroting the post-modern consensus, which means he is an important source—not for his thought, but for his uncontaminated reflection of what the post-modern consensus is.

Nadav is the same way. Nadav says, in a passing sentence, with this kind of sigh, he says, *but we all know that there are no preordained eternal values that we share, therefore, we are making them up. That's the only realm we can operate in.* It's very shocking. Nadav is expressing what he heard from his professors at Hebrew University—that's why it's important. It's an uncontaminated expression of where the kind of postmodern mind is (without even knowing the word *postmodern*). It is just a given. That's the hit on the Death Star. That's where we need to play, and that's where we are putting an enormous amount of energy and time. Again, if you are up for it, I'd be delighted, perhaps together with Zak, to have that conversation. It is a really important conversation, I just hugely appreciate you raising it.

Layman: Yeah, that would be great to do a three-way conversation around value because in that position you just clarified someone expressing, there is a strange performative contradiction. I think Nietzsche was already pointing this out 200 years ago, which is to say "We all understand there's no value" is an embodiment of the value of truth and the importance of communicating truth. So that person can't be outside of the value discussion. There's no position outside of it.

Marc: There's always a performative contradiction of playing. Post-modernity itself is one big performative contradiction.

One of the things that Jordan Peterson, I haven't tracked him, but I listened to about maybe 90 minutes of him over the last couple of years, just to get a sense of it, and it was a good rant. I mean, rant in the best sense of the word, but he just misunderstood post-modernity. He understood its weaknesses, didn't understand its strengths. Post-modernity is not all wrong. Post-modernity is an evolution of value and as it deconstructs value. It's at the very heart of it is a performative contradiction. Let's you and I, with Zak, have a deep conversation around that and perhaps when we actually come out with that document, maybe that'll be a good time to do that. That'd be great.

REVISITING THE INTIMACY FORMULA

Layman: Let's come back around to the notion of intimacy that we discussed at the beginning. You have a complex formulation of what intimacy consists of, and I think probably a lot of people are not immediately clear on **how the notion of human intimacy relates to the possibility of global intimacy, whether it's thriving or disordered**.

Marc: Let's just make it really simple. What we are always interested in our work at the Center is what we call **second simplicity**. With my friend and colleague, and Zak's friend and colleague, Clint Fuchs, we gave a course a bunch of years ago called *Second Simplicity*. It was a mini course. I think it must have been 2012, or something like that—back when we were all young. What I mean by second simplicity is **the simplicity that comes *after* complexity**, when you can actually formulate something *clearly*. It embraces an enormous amount of complexity, but you can state it clearly. The intimacy formula is a form of second simplicity. It should be the topic of its own dialogue, a different conversation, but let's just look at it now for a second.

> *Intimacy = shared identity in the context of relative otherness x mutuality of recognition x mutuality of pathos x mutuality of value x mutuality of purpose.*

Intimacy = **shared identity**. Here we are—Layman and Marc. We are both humans. We both have a passionate interest in making the world better. We have *otherness*: there is Layman and there is Marc. We are not in fusion, but it's **relative otherness**.

We realize that we are part of a *shared-ness*, therefore we **recognize** each other.

I've never met you before; we've passed by each other inadvertently here and there. And hopefully, in this first real meeting we have for the first time, we have **pathos**. We actually *feel each other* for the first time.

We have *shared values*.

And to be able to have this conversation, we have to have a *shared purpose*.

So, we have actually created a dimension of *human intimacy* here, a dimension of shared identity between us. We are not getting married—that's not what intimacy means. Intimacy means there is a dimension of shared identity, with these four mutualities—recognition, pathos, value, and purpose—and these mutualities, each one of them, can dial up and dial down, depending on the form of intimacy.

Let me say it differently. Let's just take one piece of it, *mutuality of pathos*, which is one of the four mutualities. Let's just double click on that for a second, because it's an easy way in. So, intimacy would mean: *I feel you, and you feel me.* The second loop of intimacy would mean, *I feel you feeling me, and you feel me feeling you.* Then a third look of intimacy would be, *I feel you, feeling me, feeling you.* It is very beautiful. Each one of the four mutualities is, in some sense, the place I most love to be in. I am speaking, articulating meta-theories these days, because I think there is an overwhelming moral imperative to do so. What I would really like to do is be in nature, and meditate, and pray, and talk about intimacy.

At this moment in time, *the house is burning.* We need to articulate meta-theories, but not in some geeky, weird way—but in a way that we are filled with mad love, we are filled with outrageous love, and **outrageous love generates our meta-theories.** This sense of intimacy means that we really recognize each other, we can really *feel* it. We can really feel each other, we can really feel the shared value, and we can create shared purpose from that. That's very beautiful. It's very beautiful—and **that's how intimacy works, paradoxically, all the way down and all the way up the evolutionary chain.**

Then, Layman, *for the first time,* **I can locate myself in Cosmos.** My intimacy is not dissociated or ruptured from Cosmos. **My intimacy is an expression of the intimate universe.** I begin to understand evolution as the evolution of intimacies. Wow! **Evolution actually becomes the progressive deepening of intimacy.** I had a beautiful conversation—back in 2014, Barbara suggested I go visit Urban Laszlo. We sat in Tuscany. We've done it again a couple years back, and we talked about evolution. The classical way to describe evolution is the evolution from *simplicity to complexity*, but of course, who wants more complexity? Really? Let's make your life more complex?

What we mean by complexity is not quite that. We use words in meta-theory and in science euphemistically, inappropriately. We want to use not euphemism, but *metaphor*. Euphemism is a form of lying; metaphor is a form of evoking a reality that we cannot fully formulate in a short phrase. So, complexity refers to a *radical deepening of nodes of interconnectivity*, but interconnectivity by itself is an exterior. **The *interior* of interconnectivity is intimacy.** More complexity is actually more intimacy. That we can understand evolution as the progressive deepening of intimacy is *wow*.

Then I realized, okay, who am I? I am a Unique Self.

What does that mean? That's a term I tried to create to describe something—but we are going to be putting out, with God's help, a new version of the Unique Self book because so much has changed in the last nine years.

I am a unique configuration of intimacy, consciousness and desire.

So there is a quality of intimacy that is Layman-ness, and a quality of intimacy named Marc-ness. The god you don't believe in doesn't exist. Let's say **we understand divinity as the *infinity* of intimacy,** and we are *unique qualities* of intimacy. Then between us, there is a new quality of intimacy; between Layman-ness and Marc-ness, in the space *in between*, **there is a new quality of intimacy that has never existed before.**

The space in between is when there is a new quality of intimacy. Wow! Then when I meet Layman, I'm like, wow, he's a unique quality of intimacy with a unique perspective—and so I get to be excited about you, Wow, every single question he asked was crazy intelligent. His formulations were all right on the money. One of the best interviews I've ever seen. Super well-informed, and relaxed, and calm, and delightful. I get to be excited about you. We are in a world where—like, *why* would I be excited about you? That must be manipulative. No, I *get* to be excited about you. I *get* to be delighted. Now we are talking about a world we live in.

Layman: It is a very interesting relationship between the way people perceive manipulation and the experience of excitement, like it is a kind of, you know, seduction; it shades back and forth between these things. I think it's absolutely fascinating, because it is so difficult for a lot of people to tease those things apart, but maybe we will get to things like that.

Marc: That's a great conversation because in mysticism, they distinguish between *holy seduction* and *unholy seduction.* Unholy seduction is when you seduce someone to break their appropriate boundary, for the sake of your greed. However you do it, that is inappropriate. It is a violation of boundaries and we all know how important boundaries are.

When mystics talk about what they call *pituy*, which is the Hebrew word for seduction, they are not talking about sexual seduction. We've exiled seduction to sexuality. Seduction is a much broader category, as you were implying. A holy seduction means we invite ourselves or someone to transcend the boundary of their contraction for the sake of their own highest expression, their own highest need and of course, those distinctions always need to be made.

So beautiful. Thank you.

THE NATION STATE, PLANETARY POLITICS AND COSMOCENTRIC INTIMACY

Layman: So maybe one final question on this planetary politics? That's **the role of the nation state**—because there are different ways of thinking about what *social holons* are.

It seems pretty obvious that *a family* or *a tribe* or *a community*—these makes sense to us, but when it comes to *the nation state*, it is very ambiguous. **Is this an actual legitimate natural chunk of human self-organization or is it a kind of interference between the levels?** Can we get to *planetary* much better if we overcame *countries* and just went at it as *cities* or as *geo-ethnographic regions*?

What's your take on where the nation state is situated? Is it a helper, or is it a hindrance?

Marc: That's a great question. I'm a big fan of the nation state. Yoram Hazony at the Schiller Institute, in Israel, wrote a great book on the nation state. Let us just talk about the classical relationship, which Kook talks about, Abraham Kook, in a passage in the book called *Lights of Holiness*, where he talks about what he calls *the fourfold song.*

> *There's the one who sings the song of the individual.*
>
> *There's one who sings the song of the nation.*
>
> *There's one who sings the song of the world,*
>
> *and there's one who sings the song of the Cosmos.*

By the *individual* he means *you and your family.*

It's a beautiful passage in Lights of Holiness—we could actually study it together at some point. Abraham Kook, who died in 1938, was one of the most important philosophers, mystics, evolutionary mystics. He talks extensively about evolution and he's talking essentially about what we would call egocentric consciousness—but I wouldn't call it egocentric consciousness, I would call it egocentric *intimacy*, ethnocentric intimacy, worldcentric intimacy and Cosmocentric intimacy. By intimacy, we now mean that there is a felt sense of shared identity and our four mutualities within that circle; this expanding sense of intimacy. **If you don't have a kind of nation state which coalesces around a shared sense of value and mutuality of recognition, then you don't have that experience of ethnocentric intimacy, which is a core human need**; that's number one.

Number two, from a geopolitical perspective, **the ability to have strong nation states that are democracies, bound together by a universal grammar of value, is actually the bulwark against global governance in its shadow forms.** It allows for a confederation on major issues, it disperses power, but creates balances of power and maybe the most important idea of the United States Constitution, which is genius beyond imagination, is *checks and balances.*

Checks and balances are unbelievably important. We've never seen, as Lewis points out in a number of books, we've never seen people who have stepped out of what we are calling a universal grammar of value, and Lewis calls the *Tao*—we have never seen people who have stepped out of the *Tao*, who've had access to power in history and used it benevolently. It's never happened. **Checks and balances in the world stage are critical.** When a nation state allows for—and this is a short answer, this is a two-hour conversation—but the short answer is it allows us to address the ethnocentric need of the human being (which is, by the way, why people root for their sports games).

I happened to be in Germany, back in 2010, I was on a tour with Diane, and we were there when Germany was in the World Cup. Germany has not been (for very good reasons) allowed to express national sentiment since World War II—and in every corner, people are listening to the game because here is this way of being German and *being excited about Germany.* I'm a child of Holocaust survivors, so I don't take this lightly, but you kind of felt like, wow, *this is a new generation.* When we destroy ethnocentric solidarity and passion and Eros, we are bypassing something essential in the developmental spectrum. We are dissociating, and we create pathology. That's on the developmental level, but on the geopolitical level, it also creates a checks and balances on the world stage. That's a short take on that.

Layman: This has been great. I think we are coming to the end now. There are so many openings and tangent pathways for us to have future conversations, which I look forward to. In particular, I mean, we talked a little bit beforehand about maybe doing something around meta-theory, specifically. I think this idea of doing a conversation with you, and me, and Zak around *values* would be fantastic.

Marc: When that paper is ready, we'll do that.

Layman: Yeah, when you guys are ready. I think the possibility of you and I sitting down and having a discussion specifically around roles for spiritual teachers and communities—and I think a lot about *perception*. There's obviously an issue with how a lot of people perceive you, and there are different explanations about how that perception goes down. It's not something that can quickly be gotten into, but I think it touches on a whole range of things, which is like, how teachers transform, how we trust each other, how we tell stories about each other, and community, things like that. If you are interested in having a discussion around that it would be fantastic.

Marc: I'd be delighted to have that conversation. It's a great conversation. I actually heard a rumor that I was a bit controversial, I was so surprised. You got to laugh about serious things, but I'd be delighted to have that conversation. It's actually an important conversation and there's a lot of depth and a lot of love in it and a lot of nuances in it. Anytime, I'm up for that anytime with delight.

Layman: Well, fantastic. Thanks for talking with me tonight, Marc.

Marc: Thank you, Layman. It was a pleasure. You were wonderful.

APPENDIX: SONGS

THE BATTLE HYMN OF THE REPUBLIC—
JULIA WARD HOWE[1]

Mine eyes have seen the glory of the coming
  of the Lord.

He has trampled down the vintage
  where the grapes of wrath are stored.

He has loosed the fateful lightning
  of his terrible swift sword.

His truth is marching on.

HOW COULD ANYONE—LIBBY RODERICK[2]

How could anyone ever tell you
  you were anything less than beautiful?

How could anyone ever tell you
  you were less than whole?

How could anyone fail to notice
  that your loving is a miracle—
  how deeply you're connected to my soul?

---

1 Julia Ward Howe, "The Battle Hymn of the Republic," 1862.
2 Libby Roderick, "How Could Anyone," on *If You See a Dream* (Turtle Island Records, 1990), CD.

I WANT TO KNOW WHAT LOVE IS—FOREIGNER[3]

I've gotta take a little time,
a little time to think things over.
I better read between the lines,
in case I need it when I'm older.
(Whoa, ooh-ooh, ooh-ooh)

And this mountain, I must climb
feels like the world upon my shoulders,
and through the clouds, I see love shine,
it keeps me warm as life grows colder.

[Pre-Chorus]
In my life, there's been heartache and pain.
I don't know if I can face it again.
Can't stop now, I've travelled so far
to change this lonely life.

[Chorus]
I wanna know what love is.
I want you to show me.
I wanna feel what love is.
I know you can show me.
Oh, oh-oh, oh (ooh)

I'm gonna take a little time,
a little time to look around me.
I've got nowhere left to hide,
it looks like love has finally found me.

[Pre-Chorus]

[Chorus]

[Outro]

(And I wanna feel) I wanna feel what love is

---

3   Foreigner, "I Want to Know What Love Is," recorded November 1984, on *Agent Provocateur*, Atlantic Records, vinyl LP.

(And I know) I know you can show me.
Let's talk about love.
(I wanna know what love is) The love that you feel inside.
(I want you to show me) And I'm feelin' so much love.
(I wanna feel what love is) No, you just cannot hide.
(I know you can show me) Yeah.
I wanna know what love is (Let's talk about love).
I want you to show me, I wanna feel.
(I wanna feel what love is) And I know, and I know.
I know you can show me (Yeah).
(I wanna know what love is) (I wanna know)
(I want you to show me) I wanna know, I wanna know, wanna know.
(I wanna feel what love is) (I wanna feel)
(I know you can show me).

HALLELUJAH—LEONARD COHEN[4]

Now, I've heard there was a secret chord
that David played, and it pleased the Lord.
But you don't really care for music, do you?
It goes like this, the fourth, the fifth,
the minor fall, the major lift.
The baffled king composing Hallelujah.

[Chorus]

Hallelujah, Hallelujah,
Hallelujah, Hallelujah.

Your faith was strong, but you needed proof.
You saw her bathing on the roof.
Her beauty and the moonlight overthrew you.
She tied you to a kitchen chair,
she broke your throne, and she cut your hair,
and from your lips she drew the Hallelujah.

---

4 Leonard Cohen, "Hallelujah", *Various Positions*, Columbia Records, 1984, LP.

[Chorus]

You say I took the name in vain,
I don't even know the name,
but if I did, well, really, what's it to you?
There's a blaze of light in every word,
it doesn't matter which you heard,
the holy or the broken Hallelujah.

[Chorus]

I did my best, it wasn't much.
I couldn't feel, so I tried to touch.
I've told the truth, I didn't come to fool you.
And even though it all went wrong,
I'll stand before the Lord of Song
With nothing on my tongue but Hallelujah.

OM NAMAH SHIVAAYA

Om Namah Shivaaya
Shivaaya namaha,
Shivaaya namah om
Shivaaya namaha, namaha Shivaaya
Shambhu Shankara namah Shivaaya,
Girijaa Shankara namah Shivaaya
Arunaachala Shiva namah Shivaaya

*I bow to the soul of all. I bow to my Self. I don't know who I am,
so I bow to you, Shiva, my own true Self. I bow to my teachers
who loved me with love. Who took care of me when I couldn't
take care of myself. I owe everything to them. How can I repay
them? They have everything in the world. Only my love is mine
to give, but in giving I find that it is their love flowing through
me back to the world...I have nothing. I have everything. I want
nothing. Only let it flow to you, my love... sing!*

INDEX

have to, 3, 15, 18, 24, 28, 34, 37, 43, 53, 62, 73, 74, 79, 80, 85, 88, 89, 93, 94, 100, 101, 102, 104, 108, 112, 115, 123, 125, 126, 129, 130, 131, 133, 141, 142, 143, 145, 146, 149, 163, 165, 166, 168, 169, 177, 180, 183, 197, 201, 208, 217, 220, 222, 223, 225, 239, 241, 243, 256, 257, 261, 262, 267, 269, 270, 273, 274, 277, 280, 281, 283, 284, 287, 290, 292, 293, 294, 296, 298, 299, 300, 303, 304, 311

heart, 1, 8, 13, 14, 15, 17, 27, 38, 39, 40, 45, 67, 73, 82, 84, 92, 96, 104, 109, 113, 116, 135, 173, 191, 195, 208, 209, 211, 267, 301, 305

heartbreak, 36, 74

heaven, 23, 35, 39, 61, 91, 207

Hebrew, 25, 28, 61, 62, 141, 205, 209, 211, 258, 281, 283, 303, 304, 308

   wisdom, 141, 209, 258

hero, 104, 289

hierarchy, 61, 71

holelut, 5, 28

holy and broken Hallelujah, 121

Holy of Holies, 261

Holy Trinity, 173

Homo amor, 116

Homo Deus, 66

Homo sapiens, 174

honor, 61, 79, 84, 103, 134, 135, 146, 163, 194, 210, 269, 288, 297

Hubbard, Barbara Marx, 34, 38, 79, 172, 186, 211, 288

human, 1, 4, 19, 31, 33, 38, 42, 43, 46, 47, 52, 55, 57, 61, 62, 66, 74, 79, 81, 91, 93, 94, 97, 102, 104, 107, 108, 112, 123, 124, 125, 133, 142, 143, 146, 149, 151, 155, 161, 169, 172, 184, 188, 199, 212, 231, 240, 246, 247, 250, 258, 270, 271, 272, 274, 277, 279, 282, 297, 305, 306, 309, 310

humanism, 111

humanity, 127, 132, 143, 187, 272

humans, 59, 65, 187, 306

Hume, David, 150

I

identified, 201, 205

identify, 201, 205, 210, 225

identity, 83, 84, 133, 134, 143, 159, 160, 161, 162, 164, 165, 169, 172, 204, 205, 216, 257, 273, 274, 276, 289, 306, 310

imagination, 63, 105, 222, 275, 282, 310

imagine, 11, 72, 139, 160, 188, 214, 222, 283, 290

immortality, 66

individual, 19, 28, 29, 30, 32, 35, 41, 52, 59, 108, 109, 110, 111, 128, 143, 153, 155, 161, 182, 186, 187, 189, 198, 199, 203, 224, 268, 272, 309, 310

individuals, 32, 61, 199, 200, 236

infinite, 4, 5, 8, 44, 64, 74, 110, 120, 126, 177, 179

Infinity of Intimacy, 4, 26, 28, 43, 44, 64, 126, 177, 178, 259

Infinity of Power, 26, 44, 177, 258, 259

ABOUT THE AUTHORS

Dr. Marc Gafni is a visionary world philosopher and futurist, one of the leading formulators of world spirituality and religion of our time, and a beloved teacher and public intellectual. He holds his doctorate in philosophy from Oxford University, as well as Orthodox rabbinic ordination. He co-founded the activist think tank, now called the Center for World Philosophy and Religion, where he serves as the co-president with Dr. Zachary Stein. He also served with Barbara Marx Hubbard as co-president of the Foundation for Conscious Evolution, which he consented to lead at Barbara's request after her passing.

He is known for his "source code teachings"—including Unique Self theory and the Five Selves, the Amorous Cosmos, a Politics of Evolutionary Love, a Return to Eros, and Digital Intimacy—and has more than twenty books to his name, including the award-winning Your Unique Self, A Return to Eros, and three volumes of Radical Kabbalah.

He teaches on the cutting edge of philosophy in the West, helping to evolve a new *dharma* or meta-theory of Integral meaning that is helping to re-shape key pivoting points in global consciousness and culture, with the aim of participating in the articulation of what Dr. Gafni and Dr. Stein, along with other colleagues, are calling CosmoErotic Humanism.

At the core of CosmoErotic Humanism is what Dr. Gafni and Dr. Stein are calling First Principles and First Values, Anthro-Ontology, and a Universal Grammar of Value. This is the ground of a new shared Universe Story and a new narrative of identity for the new human and the new humanity. This is what they are calling the emergence from *Homo sapiens* to *Homo amor*. This shared story rooted in First Principles and First Values can then serve as the matrix for a global ethos for a global civilization.

Together with Dr. Stein and Ken Wilber, Gafni is writing a series of seminal books under the collective pseudonym of David J. Temple, which intend to evolve the source code of consciousness and culture in response to the meta-crisis. The first of those books is *First Principles and First Values: Forty-Two Propositions on CosmoErotic Humanism, the Meta-Crisis, and the World to Come.*

Barbara Marx Hubbard (born Barbara Marx; December 22, 1929–April 10, 2019) was an American futurist, author, and public speaker. She is credited with the Wheel of Co-Creation, and together with Dr. Gafni, the Wheel of Co-Creation 2.0, as well as the concepts of the Synergy Engine and the "birthing" of humanity.

As co-founder and president of the Foundation for Conscious Evolution and the chair, for the last five years of her life, of the Center for World Philosophy and Religion, she posited that humanity was on the threshold of a quantum leap if newly emergent scientific, social, and spiritual capacities were integrated to address global crises.

She was the author of seven books on social and planetary evolution. In conjunction with the Shift Network, she co-produced the worldwide "Birth 2012" multimedia event. She was also the subject of a biography by author Neale Donald Walsch, *The Mother of Invention: The Legacy of Barbara Marx Hubbard.* Deepak Chopra called her "the voice for conscious evolution."

In 1984, she was symbolically nominated for the vice presidency of the United States. She also co-chaired a number of Soviet-American Citizen Summits, introducing a new concept called SYNCON, to foster synergistic convergence with opposing groups. In addition, she co-founded the World Future Society and the Association for Global New Thought.

VOLUME 35 — The Evolution of Democracy

LIST OF EPISODES

www.ingramcontent.com/pod-product-compliance
Lightning Source LLC
Chambersburg PA
CBHW031144270326
41931CB00006B/132